"Of all his critics, Erica Jong is most open to [Miller's] two sides. She herself obviously sees the value of sexual writing, but is also aware of its drive toward transcendence, and is appreciative of Miller's spiritual side as well. . . . [She] has seized on the key to all of Miller's work. . . . [*The Devil at Large*] enriches our view of Miller. It doesn't dodge difficult questions. Above all—the ultimate test for any such work—it makes us want to go out and read Henry Miller again. I'm glad Jong didn't write a more official book. It is all the better for being personal and vulnerable. I can't help thinking it is the kind of book Henry Miller himself might have written. It is also a book he would have read with great enjoyment, and have been proud to be a part of."—David Guy, *The New England Review*

"A wonderful new genre—far more interesting and revealing than straight biography."—Noel Riley Fitch, biographer of Anaïs Nin

"Probably the most perceptive and heartfelt portrayal of Henry Miller ever written."—Noel Young, *Santa Barbara News-Press*

"Wonderful . . . the best book that I have read on writers and the creative crisis at our tag-end of the century."—Ian MacNiven, editor of *The Durrell-Miller Letters* and the *Lawrence Durrell Journal*

The Devil
at Large

The Devil at Large

E R I C A   J O N G

o n

H E N R Y

M I L L E R

Grove Press

New York

Grateful acknowledgment is made to the following for permission to reprint previously published material:

CAPRA PRESS: Excerpts from *Book of Friends* by Henry Miller. Copyright © 1987 by The Estate of Henry Miller. Excerpts from *The World of Lawrence* by Henry Miller. Copyright © 1980 by The Estate of Henry Miller. Reprinted by permission of Capra Press, Santa Barbara.

GROVE PRESS: Excerpts from *Tropic of Cancer* by Henry Miller. Copyright © 1961 by Grove Press. Excerpts from *Sexus* by Henry Miller. Copyright © 1962 by The Olympia Press. Copyright © 1965 by Grove Press. Excerpts from *Tropic of Capricorn* by Henry Miller. Copyright © 1961 by Grove Press. Excerpts from *Black Spring* by Henry Miller. Copyright © 1963 by Grove Press. Reprinted by permission of Grove Press.

GUNTHER STUHLMANN: Excerpts from *Letters to Anaïs Nin* by Henry Miller, edited and introduced by Gunther Stuhlmann. Copyright © 1965 by Anaïs Nin. Copyright © 1988 by The Anaïs Nin Trust. Excerpts from "A Boost for *Black Spring*" Copyright 1937 by Anaïs Nin. Reprinted in *Anaïs: An International Journal*, Volume 5, 1987. Copyright © 1987 by Gunther Stuhlmann. Reprinted by permission of the Author's Representative, Gunther Stuhlmann. All rights reserved.

HARCOURT BRACE JOVANOVICH, INC.: Excerpts from *Henry and June: From the Unexpurgated Diary of Anais Nin.* Copyright © 1986 by Rupert Polo as Trustee under the last will and testament of Anaïs Nin. Reprinted by permission of Harcourt Brace Jovanovich, Inc.

NEW DIRECTIONS PUBLISHING CORPORATION, INC.: Excerpts from *The Colossus of Maroussi* by Henry Miller. Copyright 1941 by Henry Miller. Excerpts from *Big Sur and the Oranges of Hieronymus Bosch* by Henry Miller. Copyright © 1957 by New Directions Publishing Corporation. Excerpts from *Letters to Emil* by Henry Miller. Copyright © 1968 by Henry Miller. Reprinted by permission of New Directions Publishing Corporation.

Originally published in 1993 by Turtle Bay Books, a division of Random House

Grove Press paperback edition published in 1994

Printed in the United States of America

ISBN 0-8021-3391-6

Design by Beth Tondreau Design

Grove Press
841 Broadway
New York, NY 10003

10 9 8 7 6 5 4 3 2 1

*For Georges Belmont
and to the memory of
Hortense Chabrier*

*Henry's gifts,
dear friends*

Because when you get down to the basic Henry
Miller I think you'll find not that you're dealing
with a sex addict or an adventurer, you're dealing
with a metaphysician, a juggler . . . not a juggler
but a magician, I think . . . I like all that's very
serious . . . always looking for the secret of life . . .

—HENRY MILLER TO ERICA JONG, 1974

These novels will give way, by and by, to diaries
or autobiographies—captivating books, if only a
man knew how to choose among what he calls his
experiences, that which is really his experience,
and how to record truth truly.

—RALPH WALDO EMERSON

CONTENTS

The Devil
at Large

Why Henry Miller?

Why should we care about Henry Miller today and why should there be another book about him? Because we are no freer today than we were in 1934, when he published *Tropic of Cancer*; in many ways we are more enslaved. Because his message has *still* not been heard—and if he were to be alive today, we would probably be equally oblivious to what he is trying to tell us. (Perhaps we would be even more resistant, because we falsely believe we have dealt with our sexual fears and phobias.)

Miller remains among the most misunderstood of writers—seen either as a pornographer or a guru, a sexual enslaver or a sexual liberator, a prophet or a pervert. All the questions his life and oeuvre raise about the role of the writer in society, the impact of books on sexual politics, the impact of sexual politics on books, the threat of censorship to free speech and written expression are, unfortunately, as fresh today as they ever were.

What is the function of art in a society that has little use for anything but the most simple-minded entertainment or insidious propaganda? How does free speech survive? How does literacy keep a society free? How is our sexuality related to our intellectual honesty, our politics, our art? Miller's work addresses these questions. And they are questions that desperately need answering in our time.

We do not see our society as one that is squashing freedom of expression on all sides because the very nature of expression has changed, hence the nature of censorship has changed. Our dominant forms of communication are visual, not verbal, and we seldom wish to analyze how the information that appears before our eyes as "news," as "entertainment," as "politics," as "public affairs," shapes our world and everything we think about it.

Our access to information and entertainment (*infotainment* is a telling word) is so skillfully manipulated that we do not even see it as such. We flatter ourselves that we have free choice. We flatter ourselves that we are free. The truth is that we are already in a sort of *Brave New World* in which we are drugged by our distractions and by those who select them for us.

The fact that we are as oblivious to this manipulation as our puppetmasters wish us to be will anger some of us and provoke hearty denial in others. The most skillful manipulation looks like choice to those who are targeted. We may like to think we have free choice, but the truth is we can only choose between A and B. If, as Marshall McLuhan said, the medium is the message, then our addiction to visual images has already paved the way for our enslavement. It only remains for some unborn Hitler to learn how to use our pleasures to enslave us totally. As yet we use our media only for selling things—including, of course, political candidates. What will happen when someone masters the art of selling souls?

Henry Miller foresaw our world of restricted opportunity and widespread mediocrity and railed against it before it arrived. He understood that we would rather relegate sex to a commodity—alternately condemned and slavered over—than try to understand its deep and pervasive power in our lives. He became, like so many prophets—from Jesus to Savonarola—the victim of his own predictions. He railed against America's sexual schizophrenia and he was rewarded by being banned, burned, pirated, deprived both of his livelihood and his power to reach his potential audience. He railed against the conformity and ugliness of America's treatment of the nonconformist, the poet, the artist, and he became the victim of that treatment. Ironically, he was silenced first by close-minded puritans and then by open-minded feminists pursuing sexual honesty and gender-fairness. It fell to him to both express and to exemplify the role of the creative artist in a world that has increasingly little use for dissent, for art (except as a saleable item), for honesty, for any kind of entertainment or information but that which lulls the senses or sells a product—from a president to a war to a pair of jeans.

The worst of all this is that the lulling and the selling are often indistinguishable from each other. The airconditioned nightmare has come to be our waking reality—and we are all semisleepwalking to the flickering of our TV and computer screens.

Henry Miller predicted all this. Henry Miller never stopped fighting against our somnolence. Henry Miller still matters because he still has the power to wake us up.

There is a rumor abroad in literary America today that sex isn't sexy anymore. We have done it all—and now with the tragedy of AIDS and a recalcitrant recession, the human hormones are exhausted.

I find this wishful thinking on the part of those who hoped sex would solve all their problems and, finding that it wouldn't, decided to rejoin the religion of their ancestors: puritanism.

The sexual revolution was deeply superficial: it never eradicated either guilt or anhedonia. Given the excuse of a tragic epidemic, dyed-in-the-wool puritans masquerading as pagans decided that sex was boring and that writers like Henry Miller were therefore irrelevant. These trimmers—a lovely eighteenth-century term meaning those who cut their consciences to the times—never understood Eros at all. Eros is life force and if you pronounce it boring, you inadvertently announce your own death. Perhaps we don't believe that sexual freedom will turn the universe from war to peace—but only the very young ever believed that, *anyway*. As we grew older, we realized that life is far more complex. Sex is not dead in the human psyche, it is only looking for new forms. The devastation of AIDS has given the zealots and vigilantes the excuse they needed to call again for censorship. But their motives are political, not sexual. The new slavery takes many forms: political correctness in the case of anti–First Amendment, pro-censorship feminists, supposed "family values" in the case of right-wing zealots. The message is the same: they want to tell us what to do and feel.

If Eros is life force, then censoring Eros is death. Henry Miller matters because he understood this; he demanded life more abundant above all. He did not use Eros promiscuously—even in his books. And he was not demanding that we do. What he *was* demanding was that we understand the connection between Eros and life. And we have still not understood. That is why I wrote this book.

I always knew it was to be an unconventional book—part memoir, part critical study, part biography, part exploration of sexual politics in our time. But I did not anticipate how difficult the task was to become or how much of my own bag as a writer I would have to unpack before I could begin to unpack Henry's bag.

Henry once said to me, "When you write about me, make it all up!" Thereafter he proceeded to tape-record hours and hours of recollections, regale me with anecdotes, and inundate me with letters about writing, mysticism, art, his life and times.

Here was the paradox: Miller, supposedly the most autobiographical writer who ever lived, remained maddeningly elusive and could only be approached through the creation of a fiction. And I, too, so often accused of literal autobiography, found it nearly impossible to write in a voice of historical truth. What Miller said about D.H. Lawrence as he struggled with his book *The World of Lawrence* also seemed true of my struggles with Miller:

> The only way to do justice to a man like [Lawrence] who gave so much, is to give another creation. Not explain him, but prove by writing about him that one has caught the flame he tried to pass on.

The more I thought about all I knew about Henry, Henry's work, Henry's life, the more impossible it became to find one voice in which to tell the story. I felt as I often did when beginning one of my own novels—lost in mist, looking for a voice . . . and a trail of breadcrumbs.

If Henry's books were such obvious autobiographies, why was it so difficult to evoke the essence of the man? And if Henry's life and books were one, why did I feel the uneasy sense that I was fudging the truth when I sat down to describe the man I knew?

I think it is because Henry Miller's genius lay not in his subject matter, its often-cited explicitness about the body in particular, but rather in his invention of a new kind of fictive voice.

"I have no money, no resources, no hope, I am the happiest man alive," he exults on the first page of *Tropic of Cancer*. It is his exuberance, his freedom, his bumptiousness that is infectious, not his chronicles of copulation. That sensuous terrain Henry Miller called *the land of fuck* is seductive because of its radical innocence, not because of its repetitive frictions. Rubbing, after all, is just rubbing. But ecstasy partakes of freedom, a glimpse of the divine. Henry Miller used the body to transcend the body, and something in his impish, mischievous voice implied that he could extend this freedom to us, his readers. That was his primal seduction—freedom, not fornication.

Art is always an energy exchange. The book, once opened, interacts with the mind of the reader to create an alchemical reaction. Again and again, people have said to me, in various ways: *I was dying in the prison of myself and Henry Miller freed me, gave me new life.* Henry Miller was a life-giver, a spiritual teacher, as much as he was a writer, and people turned to him and to his books, to be reminded in the prison of their days (as Auden would say) how to be free men and how to praise.

His freedom still terrifies. That is why he is critically dismissed, not taught in most universities, relegated to the remainder table. He is a seer. And what he sees is not pleasant. Yet we need his vision more than ever. Our freedoms are being taken away while we look at a flickering light show. More than ever we need to be enlightened. Our very survival depends upon it.

Perhaps enlightenment *is* the ancient function of the poet/prophet/seer. "The divine literatus" was Whitman's term for this being. And Henry Miller had deep ties to Whitman, as he did to Hesse and Thoreau. He wanted to be more than just a writer; he wanted to be a prophet for his readers, and he became one—for good or for ill. We turn our backs on his prophecies at our peril.

As one of his "disciples"—I use the term ironically—I tell this tale of our connection. I have let Henry dictate the voice from wherever he hangs out nowadays.

CHAPTER 1

Born Hungry: Henry and Me

When obscenity crops out in art, in literature more particularly, it usually functions as a technical device . . . its purpose is to awaken, to usher in a sense of reality. In a sense, its use by the artist may be compared to the use of the miraculous by the Masters . . . the real nature of the obscene lies in the lust to convert.

—HENRY MILLER, *REMEMBER TO REMEMBER*

henry Miller and I met in a way that was most Millerish: by letter. A few days after Easter 1974, this letter appeared in a stack at my door:

Easter—April 14, 1974

Dear Erica Jong,

I have just written your publishers congratulating them for having published your Fear of Flying. *. . .*

I don't know when I've read a book by a woman which has made such an impact upon me. I started it against the grain, then found it impossible to put down until I had read about a hundred pages.

Though I enjoyed the gay, witty, thoroughly uninhibited way in which the book was written, I was also very much taken by its serious side. So much suffering! Jewish suffering. It reminded me of certain passages in Céline's works in which the saddest events call forth laughter. But men have so much to learn from your book, as well as women. It is a text book as well as a novel or autobiography.

I could not help but feel drawn to Adrian, hypocritical bastard though he was—because for all his foul play he did the most for Zelda of all her lovers. He put her face to face with reality and herself.

I hope you will give us more books!

Sincerely
Henry Miller

Enclosed was another wildly effusive letter, which Henry, with characteristic openhandedness, had already sent to my publisher.

April 14, 1974

To Editor
Holt, Rinehart & Winston
Dear Sir:—

Allow me to congratulate you on publishing Erica Jong's most delightful book, Fear of Flying. *I notice that you call it a novel, but is it? Isn't it more of an autobiographical piece of writing? At any rate, it is rare these days to come upon a book written by a woman which is so refreshing, so gay and sad at the same time, and so full of wisdom about the eternal man-woman problem. One can learn more on the subject from this "novel" than from the huge, dull tomes authored by analysts, psychologists, medical authorities and such like. The book strikes one as utterly true and sincere. In spite of the wit and humor which the author narrates, one realizes that she is in dead earnest and aware that she is making a major contribution.*

Could you tell me, please, if you or any other publisher are contemplating publishing another book of hers? Also, who published the two volumes of poetry she has written: You are at liberty to quote any part of this letter, if it will serve your purpose.

Sincerely,
Henry Miller

What did I know about Henry Miller at the time these two missives, scrawled in black felt pen on yellow legal sheets, appeared on my doorstep? Not much. My image of Miller was probably almost as distorted as the banal image of the dirty-old-man writer that haunts Miller's name in the public prints. Though I'd read bits of *Tropic of Cancer, Remember to Remember, The Henry Miller Reader,* and *Henry Miller on Writing,* I did not have a clear picture of Henry Miller either as a writer or a person. I vaguely remembered seeing pictures in news magazines of an old Miller and his young Japanese wife. And I remembered reading about a notorious obscenity case involving Miller. But I had no idea that the awesome sea change that occurred in publishing in the sixties was to be traced almost directly to Miller.

I myself had experienced this metamorphosis of publishing in my most vulnerable years. I was a high school student at Music & Art in New York City when suddenly *Lady Chatterley's Lover, Fanny Hill, or Memoirs of a Woman of Pleasure,* and *Lolita* were published by "mainstream" New York houses and each caused a sensation. As a junior in high school, I ran out to buy *Lady Chatterley's Lover* in paperback, and read it with the excitement which comes only from the conjunction of eros and revolution (which are anyway the main themes of adolescence). It was not until my junior year in college that *Tropic of Cancer* finally appeared in the United States. I realize now that I did not know even a fraction of the Miller canon when he first wrote me and in this I was probably typical of most readers. The last thing I remembered about Miller was the feminist fracas Kate Millett had created in 1970 when she published *Sexual Politics.*

It was Millett's thesis—as everyone remembers—that Miller's entire apprehension of sex was misogynistic. In this she was not wrong, but her attack had the effect of proscribing once again a writer who had been largely unobtainable in his own country for almost four decades.

It is not without irony that Miller was first unread because of official puritanical censorship and later unread because of unofficial feminist censorship. And it is also not without irony that certain recent American feminists (forgetting the genesis of our movement with such free spirits as Emma Goldman, Margaret Sanger, and Victoria Woodhull) seem to have joined the anti-sex league. Still, *Sexual Politics* set the terms of the debate about Miller all through the latter part of his life. Was he or was he not a "sexist pig"? Everyone today has to deal with that question in addressing Henry Miller—irrelevant as it is to the books he most wanted to be known by: *The Colossus of Maroussi* and *The Smile at the Foot of the Ladder.*

Miller was faintly disreputable—that much I knew. He was associated with Paris in the thirties, Big Sur in the

fifties, banned books, young Oriental women, sex. But I
also remembered that when I was searching for the freedom to write *Fear of Flying*, I picked up *Tropic of Cancer*
and the sheer exuberance of the prose unlocked something
in me. And I also remembered reading an essay of Miller's
which had hit me right between the eyes. The modern
writer uses obscenity as the ancient writer used the sacred,
Miller alleged, in "Obscenity and the Law of Reflection."
The modern writer, in using obscenity, is trying to rekin-
dle the awe, the shock, the wonder that the ancients found
at Delphi or Eleusis. Something about that perception
struck me as absolutely right.

Interestingly enough, Tennessee Williams (as quoted
by Gore Vidal in *Two Sisters*), said something quite similar about the uses of sex in literature. He used sex, Williams told Vidal, to "raise the temperature of the audience.
You key them up. Then you can tell them anything."

I had not studied Miller in Modern American Literature class at Barnard. Or in the Ph.D. program at Columbia. He was not taught. Bookworm and passionate
scribbler that I was, Miller had largely eluded me. In part,
this was because his most famous books were banned, and
the others were poorly distributed or out of print.

If I could have obtained Miller's books easily, I would
have gobbled them up. Friends who are five or ten years
older report the tonic effect on their literary lives of smuggled copies of *Tropic of Cancer* brought home from Paris.

Discovering literature at a time when publishing was
undergoing a revolution led to abrupt changes in my freedom to read. I have a recollection of having had to track
down *Fanny Hill, or Memoirs of a Woman of Pleasure*
from a locked case in the rare-book room at Butler Library, but this recollection must go back to high school
days because, by the time I was in graduate school, she was
available in paperback almost everywhere.

In the sixties, after the freeing of *Tropic of Cancer*,
younger American writers began to respond to this new
freedom with books that could never have been written, let
alone published, before. After John Updike's *Couples* in

1968 and Philip Roth's *Portnoy's Complaint* in 1969, American fiction dared to open the bedroom door. I think we conveniently tend to forget how recently all this occurred. And Miller was at the root of this change though he was never given official credit.

Fear of Flying was a dare to myself to write from the female point of view with as much verve (and nerve) as Roth and Updike had written from the male. *Fear of Flying* traveled a road less rocky than *Tropic of Cancer*'s, but rocky nonetheless. The first printer refused to set type. TV networks would not take ads. And I remember my own astonishment at the sheer violence of some of the critical responses to the book. Cloistered in the Ph.D. program at Columbia, I had imagined that everyone knew Chaucer, Rabelais, Lawrence, and Joyce were full of sex—so why all the fuss? I had not bargained on book-chat sexophobia—of both the feminist and male chauvinist variety. It was as if I were advocating the barbecuing of infants!

Nor was the book calculated to win easy acceptance in the hotly politicized climate of 1973. Separatist feminists attacked it as "soft on men" (because my heroine was heterosexual—something considered counterrevolutionary by some politically correct feminists of that era), and certain literary male chauvinists pronounced the liberated female voice trash. Had John Updike not rescued the book in *The New Yorker*, it might not have stayed in print long enough for Henry Miller to read it. So Miller's first letter came as a *planche de salut*—a life raft—to a young author who had been hurled into a political maelstrom by the experience of publishing a book. I had been called a "mammoth pudenda" in *The New Statesman* by none other than Paul Theroux, so I had every reason to be grateful to Miller and Updike.

I remember sending my two books of poems (*Fruits & Vegetables* and *Half-Lives*) to Miller in a hurry, but agonizing over what I termed "a *real* letter." As I was mulling and brooding about how to respond to a living legend (and reading more of his books to make myself worthy) still another Miller letter arrived.

April 30, 1974

Dear Erica Jong—

*I'm not very strong on poetry and so I didn't expect to care
for yours. (I do like some poets!) But I was surprised—I
like your poems very much indeed. You are like a fire-
cracker going off continually and interesting even when
sputtering. You are so bright, so intelligent, so perceptive.
You must have had straight A's all through school, non?*

*It was good of you to send me these two books of
poems, with your charming dédicaces. I just finished reading the first one. I liked especially "If a woman wants to
be a poet." You mention several times Sylvia Plath. I
ought to look up her work—unknown to me. I notice all
the good writers you quote or recommend—excellent
taste. The French poet "Ponge" was a surprise. I see you
are going to write me a letter. I look forward to it eagerly.*

*Jong is Chinese, isn't it? At first I thought it was a
variation of the Swiss "Jung."*

*Somehow somewhere I got the impression that Her-
mann Hesse was a writer who belonged to your youth—
and not to be taken too seriously. I am probably wrong.
But I hope (why, I don't know) that you regard him as
first-rate writer. For me, in some ways, he is a master. I
would love to be able to write a book like "Siddhartha"
or "Narcissus and Goldmund."*

Enough! I wait to hear from you.

Cheers!
Henry Miller

This missive was written on Henry Miller's black-and-
white printed stationery, which bore the address 444
Ocampo Drive, Pacific Palisades, California. At the very
bottom of the page, in tiny type, was the Portugese motto
cuando merda tiver valor pobre nasce sem cu (*"when shit
becomes valuable, the poor will be born without ass-
holes"*)." Enclosed was a tattered fortune out of a fortune
cookie that said: "Your name will be famous in the future."

Imagine a young writer receiving this fortune one day and attacks the next. It was dizzying and disorienting.

Eventually, I summoned the courage to write back, making it appear that I had read more of his writing than I had:

May 4, 1974

Dear Henry Miller,

Thanks so much for your delightful and generous letters to me and my publisher. I was absolutely knocked out by them. I love your writing—love its wonderful energy and life and I've always felt a deep kinship with it. Also, some of your observations on writing, sexuality, obscenity and literature have taken me through very dark times and have given me courage. All your books attest to the fact that a writer needs great courage as well as great talent and they give courage to readers, too. I thank you for your letters to me and for all your splendid books.

At one time, Fear of Flying *was to have an epigraph from you—about the impossibility of ever telling the truth about one's life, the impossibility of literal autobiography—but, ultimately, I didn't want to tip my hand that way. The book is spiritual—if not literal—autobiography. Events and characters are sometimes invented, sometimes not. Everyone takes it for literal memoir—and in a way I find that a compliment. The book is coming out in paperback in the U.S. in November—and it is just now being published in England where some of the reviews read as if they were written by Mrs. Grundy herself. The* New Statesman *says I am "a mammoth pudenda" and my book "crappy," "loathsome," "horrible and embarrassing." Fortunately your first two letters arrived with the British reviews and softened them considerably. All those little well-bred boys who think sex is "horrible and embarrassing!" Amazing to find the world* still *so full of them.*

I mailed the two books of poems to you in a post box that frequently disappears from the corner, so I was really

*delighted that you received them and that you responded
so generously. Some characters in this neighborhood are
running an ingenious hustle in which they remove the
mailbox from the sidewalk, take it to a nearby basement
where they break it open and remove any checks. I never
know when I'm going to find the corner bereft of mailbox
(with those four tell-tale holes in the street where the
bolts were). Somehow it seemed more exciting to mail the
books in that mailbox!*

*I was delighted with your most recent letter and the
enclosed fortune. Yes, my name is Chinese and so is my
husband—who is not nearly as inscrutable as he was a
few years ago when I used him as a model for Bennett
Wing. The book has changed him much for the better.
Life follows literature, doesn't it? Have you often found
that people you've written about are much improved by
the experience—humanized, so to speak? I'd really be
curious to know!*

*I haven't read Hermann Hesse since I was 15 and
mooning over* Siddhartha. *I must read him again, now
that I know a little more about writing and people. He
will probably seem like a totally different writer.*

*I wonder whether you would like Sylvia Plath's po-
etry. She is a splendid poet (much less good as a novelist), but her work is so life-denying and obsessed with
suicide that I think you would be put off. She learned a
great deal from Theodore Roethke and has the same
kinds of very condensed, laconic and intense images, but
all her brilliance is in the service of her death obsession—
she did finally take her own life at the age of 31. A
terrible waste, really. I know many of the details of her
life and know that she was always a rather disturbed
woman—but I persist in believing that her suicide was
hastened by the fact that she had to live in England with
all those goddamned Englishmen! Her husband, Ted
Hughes, is a hulking Yorkshireman who always seemed
like a warlock to me, and the literary gents in London
never seemed to have much use for women themselves.
They mostly like each other, and thrive on literary in-*

fighting. Healthy sexuality is so unknown to them that when they come upon it, they shriek with horror. My character Adrian was something of a secret pervert himself. His trip was not sex, but mind-manipulation. Nevertheless, it was true that the intensity of that experience brought Isadora to her senses. . . .

I wish I could convey to you how much joy and courage I have gotten from your writing in the past. Just last week I was reading and rereading your remarks on obscenity and literature in Remember to Remember. *They seem brilliant to me. I think it's true that the modern artist uses "obscenity" as the ancient artist used the miraculous—to jolt the reader and create an epiphany. I could go on and on about your work and the things it's done for me at different times in my life, but I'll stop in the interest of getting this letter to California (via my floating mailbox).*

Love and thanks,
Erica Jong

Henry responded almost instantaneously.

From bed—May 6, 1974
(Can't always see clearly, lost one eye during recent operation.)
Dear Erica Jong—I hope you don't think I'm a nut! *I am only your devoted fan, and more than ever "just a Brooklyn boy." I write you with a smile on my lips because everyone is Talking about you. You are the sensation of the year! I am going to order copies of your books so I can give them to those who can't afford to buy them. It seems to me my best readers—in the beginning—could not afford to buy my books. What a struggle I had to sell Tropic of Cancer to the public. If it had not been for the hundreds of letters I wrote (praising the shit out of my work) together with the enthusiasm and devotion of a poor Jewish lesbian who peddled my books from café to café, the book might never have been known. Your triumph seems so easy—and natural. You are admired by high*

and low. Even that filthy sheet "Screw" gave you a serious write-up a couple of weeks ago.

(Incidentally, I wonder what Germaine Greer and Anaïs Nin think of it! or Kate Millet.)

I lent the novel to my daughter, Val, and she was thrilled—found a resemblance, in some ways, between herself and you (which I don't see). She may write you too.

I am going to send copies to Lawrence Durrell and my boon companion of Paris days, Alfred Perlès, who now lives in Cyprus. (I know his bloody Scottish wife will hate it.)

I am always delighted to run across names of poets and other writers you mention in all your books. What excellent taste, as I remarked before. A bit omnivorous, dare I say—or, as the French say, "boulimique" (what a word!) (How about our English word—aboulia?) One poet whose name I expected to encounter but did not is St. John Perse. Who haven't you read? (You don't mention Céline or Blaise Cendrars either but I suspect you have read them.) They are my two favorites as you probably know.

My daughter-in-law, Diane Miller, who tries to write poetry, says she found it hard to understand you sometimes. (The poems.) I tried to explain to her that we don't have to understand everything. Are we stirred, tickled, delighted, angry? Quite enough, don't you think? I don't understand everything—or even want to. (Though it's not quite à propos I must say I love St. Thomas Aquinas' last words, on his death bed—"All that have written now seems to me like so much straw." (Compared with his illumination)

I shall be very curious to see and read your second novel. The second book is usually very different from the first one—like a "revolt in the desert." I imagine your first book left you feeling sick of yourself, if I dare say it. Everything you say about writing (as a refuge, a support, etc.) is so trenchant. Like Céline, curiously enough, you

*make me laugh when you tell of your suffering. And you,
very fortunately, most fortunately, can laugh at yourself.
Hurrah! So damned few women who can do that! I don't
know anything more frustrating and depressing than a
sorrowful looking woman!*

Enough! Good luck and cheers!

Henry Miller

By then, my first novel was gathering steam. Letters
were pouring in, and many of them were the most vulnerable letters I'd ever received. My correspondents were seeking salvation and appointing me their guru. This was my
first taste of public life in America and I was amazed. I
wrote a piece for *New York* magazine called "The Writer
as Sexual Guru." In it I wondered why writers were seen
as gurus when all they were advertising was their own
confusion. It elicited a passionate response from my new
pen pal:

6/21/74

Dear Erica—

*Bradley [Bradley Smith, publisher and author] gave me
your piece in the* New York *magazine about the Writer as
sexual guru. I have often wanted to write about my correspondents. You said it all—except maybe for one group
I find most interesting—the nuts. The really crazy ones.
They usually write fantastic letters, and as you know,
can draw and paint most interestingly. When I married
my third wife I asked her to help me read & file my c/s.
To my dismay, she took it upon herself to destroy all the
nutty letters! I was furious. She thought the letters from
professors and serious high-brows were the ones to preserve. I told her it was just the contrary.*

*I am enclosing a postscript in red ink from a recent
fan. . . . She sent this after reading that line in Time mag.
not long ago wherein I praise Oriental women. (She knew
I was married to a Japanese and now in love with a
Chinese.) Don't you think she's off her trolley? And how*

come these statistics? I never found the "vaginal pas-
sages" too short in any woman. As for the business of a
big prick, it's all a myth, don't you think?

Last night I made Irene Tsu, the Chinese actress (I'm
not in love with her) promise to read your book. Every day
I make new converts to it. You have started a new reli-
gion, it seems.

How is the second book coming? More difficult to
write, I suppose, than the first. But don't let that bother
you.

Incidentally, does the New York mag. pay for arti-
cles?

I look forward to seeing you here soon. Cheers! And
love and kisses.

Henry

The correspondence with Miller galloped on into the
summer of 1974. Sometimes Henry would write two or
three letters a day and I would struggle to keep up with
him.

Meanwhile I was undergoing a public metamorphosis
from graduate student and "younger poet" to somebody
whose name—and even face—at times brought knowing
nods. Buffeted by the contradictory reviews of my first
novel, I looked forward to the balm of Henry's letters. My
book had struck a nerve, and people detested or adored it.
It became an event in their lives and they tended to hold
the author responsible for the consequences. Henry Miller
understood, perhaps better than anyone, what I was living
through. His understanding kept me going.

Henry knew that however much one may be grateful
for sudden recognition, it is also a cataclysm. When *Fear
of Flying* was published I still half-expected to go back to
graduate school at Columbia, to finish my Ph.D., publish
poetry and criticism, and teach at a university. Serious
writers, I believed, could not reach a wide audience. (I had
all the academic prejudices and snobbery typical of my
epoch at Columbia.) The scholar in me—which Henry

always twitted me about—was quite horrified by the idea
of popular success, however much the narcissist in me may
have welcomed it.

Fear of Flying was not a predictable bestseller. For the
first year of its life, its hardcover publisher never quite
believed in its commercial potential. There were never
enough copies printed and whenever it hit the bestseller
list, it would promptly go out of stock. Foreign publishers
were initially also wary.

"Frenchwomen don't need psychoanalysis," I was told
by one French editor. *"I'll publish it if I can edit out all
the anti-German parts,"* I was told by a German editor.
Male editors, who were threatened by the female boister-
ousness of the book, found all sorts of other reasons to
reject it. Henry, ever the defender of the underdog, took
up *Fear of Flying*'s cause, sending it around the world to
publishers and editors he trusted. Many of the friends he
made for me as a writer have lasted to this day.

Irritated by the stupidity and male chauvinism of the
responses to *Fear of Flying*, Henry wrote an essay for the
op-ed page of *The New York Times* (see p. 259). In it he
shows more charity toward women's writing than some
feminist zealots, who judge every book against an imaginary yardstick of political correctness and care for neither
irony nor imagination. Henry was neither a zealot nor an
ideologue, and he proved more open to a woman's writing
than many women. He called *Fear of Flying* the female
counterpart to his own *Tropic of Cancer*—a description
that delighted me. In his assessment of the book, there was
no trace of the spite and competitiveness one usually finds
lurking in reviews. I had every reason to be grateful to
Henry Miller when in October I finally went to Los Angeles
with his private phone number in my pocket.

I drove my rented Buick down Sunset Boulevard—the
only road I knew—to the Palisades. With some difficulty,
I found Henry's house, an unremarkable white raised
ranch house at 444 Ocampo Drive, which seemed awfully
bourgeois to be the home of an old bohemian.

On the door, which was unlocked, was a quote from Meng-tse, an ancient sage invented by Herman Hesse as a pseudonym:

> When a man has reached old age and has fulfilled his mission, he has a right to confront the idea of death in peace. He has no need of other men, he knows them already and has seen enough of them. What he needs is peace. It is not seemly to seek out such a man, plague him with chatter, and make him suffer banalities. One should pass by the door of his house as if no one lived there.

This was obviously placed to deter unwelcome literary groupies. But Henry was charmingly ambivalent about groupies. He was one of the most gregarious people on earth and was apt to blast his own concentration by inviting in the very visitors the sign on the door seemed meant to discourage.

I opened the unlocked door. Twinka Thiebaud, a beautiful redhead who was Henry's cook and caretaker in those days, came out to greet me.

I was invited into a hallway with a staircase, and followed Twinka into a room dominated by a Ping-Pong table, a piano, and Miller's watercolors. In the small patio outside, a pool glimmered in the golden October sunlight. Pleased to have found the house without mishap, I was tingly with anticipation at meeting my literary benefactor.

A thud of rubber in the adjacent hallway. Henry arrived, hunched over an aluminum walker, which he wielded like a shield.

"Hello!" he said in his gravelly voice, redolent of Brooklyn. He wore pajamas and carpet slippers, an old bathrobe, and a hearing aid. He was an old man but his eyes were young.

We sat at the dining table and our talk ignited. Twinka served tea and chimed in from time to time. I have not the faintest recollection of what we talked about, except that it was an extension of our letters—and that Henry was warm and free. Henry's conversational vitality made him seem my contemporary. In the pictures taken at that time, he was clearly an old man. But my distinct sense was that he was spiritually younger than me. His exuberance was like a shot of the life force.

Proust said in his essay "Contre St. Beuve," "A book is a product of a different self than we manifest in our habits, our social life and our vices." This is true. The inner self of a writer, the self destined to live beyond the flesh, is not always visible in the writer's daily life. But the writer's true voice, once discovered, *is* congruent with the writer's soul. This voice is what all writers seek, and a very few find—to raise a cry that is integral with one's soul.

Here is the paradox of writing. You can't hide behind words. What and who you are shines forth on every page—whether you pretend objectivity or not. You strip down to the essential self. That is why the misunderstanding of one's writing is so painful. It is the misunderstanding of the essence of one's self.

What Henry had that others so resented was wholeness. Though his daily life and his writing life were not necessarily one and the same, his exuberance, the happiness that comes across in his work, was visible in him even when he was old and ill. The voice he found expressed the abundance of the man. It was not the sex the puritans hated and feared. It was the abundance. It was not the four-letter words; it was the five-star soul.

We talked and talked all that afternoon and our talks went on intermittently until he died. They were concentrated in the years I lived in Malibu (1974–76). Sometimes Twinka was present, sometimes Val and Tony Miller, Henry's daughter and son, sometimes Jonathan Fast, my lover, later my husband, sometimes Tom Schiller, a young comedy writer, sometimes Mike Wallace, the interviewer who recorded our conversations for *60 Minutes* in 1974.

We ranged over dozens of subjects: Paris in the thirties, literature, mysticism, food, life. Henry's rasping voice, punctuated with a very Brooklynese *doncha know?*, his habit of saying *hmmm hmmm* like a meditative mantra, rings in my ears as I write. I wish every reader could *hear*

Henry as well as read him. Henry was a mixed-media person and printed words alone don't do him justice.

I always promised Henry I would write a book about him—but for years I resisted the notion. Too hard, I felt, to write in my own persona. Masked by characters of my own invention, I can be free. But history is a death mask. Writing about factual events is daunting because one knows that objectivity does not, in truth, exist, and that "the facts" are really just another fiction.

"Make it all up!" Henry often told his would-be chroniclers—including me. "That's the only way to get it right—make it all up!" But the former graduate student in me could not allow that, though the novelist wanted to tell a rattling good yarn even if "facts"—whatever they are— were ignored. So this is the story of my search for Henry after his death, the story of a young writer trying to recon- struct an old writer, of a person of one generation trying to understand someone old enough to be her grandfa- ther—with the manners, mores, and prejudices of her grandfather's generation.

Henry's story and my story have one thing above all in common: the search for the courage to be a writer. The courage to be a writer is, in a sense, the courage to be an individual, no matter what the consequences.

Doris Lessing points out in her introduction to a reis- sue of *The Golden Notebook* that the "artist as exemplar" is a relatively new protagonist for the novel, and wasn't the rule one hundred years ago when heroes—there being few heroines—were more often explorers, clergymen, soldiers, empire builders. This may well be because the artist is seen as the only true individual left in an increasingly chained society. Both Henry's persona "Henry Miller" and the real historical Henry Miller spoke to this longing for freedom. He freed himself—and then he passed the gift along to us.

So now you know: I am in his debt. Debts are uncom- fortable. Perhaps this accounts for the fact that between the first page of the first chapter of this book and the last, a year mysteriously disappeared. Normally a fluent writer, I couldn't write. I was furious at Henry. I didn't want to pay the debt. I did research, reread Henry and books about Henry. I also debriefed various elderly Millerian disciples before they died. But I was fighting this book in my head and heart. I could not let it go. It would not ride, as Robert Frost says somewhere, on its own melting.

"Writing problems are always psychological problems," I used to tell my writing students. "They're obstructions which you haven't yet recognized and named. Once you find the obstruction, you discover that the problem disappears." But I couldn't take my own advice. I was enraged at Henry and I didn't want to write about him. Once I knew this, I was already halfway there.

"What's the secret about Henry that you don't want anyone to know?" a friend asked.

"I don't know," I said.

"What's the first thing that comes to your mind?" she asked.

"That I don't really *like* Henry Miller," I blurted out.

"Why?"

"Because of his sexism, his narcissism, his jibes at Jews. And because he's so free," I said. "I work so hard at my writing and he's such a slob. I rewrite and rewrite and he lets it all hang out. He's such a *blagueur* and I try so hard to be honest. Everything is cake to him. He treats women horribly and doesn't seem to care. He turns on the people who help him. Even his suffering seems like fun."

So I had unwittingly discovered the source of the Miller animosity, discovered it in myself (where one always discovers everything, as Freud knew). *Miller is having too much fun.* He seems unashamed of his failings. He lets all his warts show, and for this I envy him and hate him. For this I want to attack him, even though I am in his debt. Is my jealousy of his freedom poisoning my affection? Does my reaction show why the happy man—that rarity—is not beloved by the general unhappy lot of manunkind (and womanunkind)?

This perception should have opened the floodgates, but it didn't. The ice froze around my heart. I read, interviewed, began a novel, edited a volume of my poems, worked on adapting a novel for the musical stage. In short, I ran away. The deadline came; it passed. I told my agent I was giving back the advance. Then I changed my mind. Then I changed it back.

"I *hate* Miller," I told my friend. "I don't want to be his flame keeper. I don't want to serve the patriarch. I have books of my own to write. Fuck Henry Miller's memory! So what if he's misunderstood—we're *all* misunderstood."

"So why don't you begin by writing why you hate Henry Miller?" my friend asked. "Maybe you'll discover something that way."

Literary grandfathers. It has something to do with that. Henry Miller and my grandfather were nearly contemporaries. Both were Victorians who sought to liberate themselves. Miller wrote the things he feared the most—and became notorious. My grandfather painted proper portraits and kept his dark imaginings in secret sketchbooks, which he bequeathed to me. He never became famous—though he was a better artist than many who did—and, in a sense, my lust for fame was conditioned by his having embraced obscurity. I was famous *for* him, I felt. In his place. And Henry, who did so much to propel that fame, was both grandfather and literary alter ego. On one hand, I had fantasies of devoting my life to rescuing my grandfather's work from obscurity; on the other, I fiercely wanted to press on with my own career. Knowing as I did that the path was always clearer for women to be flame keepers than to be creators in their own right, I was torn. Some part of me craved the sanctified good-girl role of flame keeper. But I also wanted the damnable and dangerous bad-girl role of making my own books. The Miller book clicked into the conflict in my head: my life or Papa's? Which was it to be? The tigress or the lady? That old battle between self and soul had come back to haunt me and here it was again wearing Henry's face!

So I hated Henry for putting me back in my old stew.

And I also hated him for not really being my grandfather. And I hated him for being famous when my own grandfather was not. And I hated him for claiming the filial fealty I never gave to my own grandfather's memory. And I hated him for liberating himself publicly as my own grandfather could not.

Complicated stuff. Writing problems are always psychological problems. And the choice of subjects is always overdetermined. Simone de Beauvoir writes *The Second Sex* and then "repents" with *Must We Burn Sade?* I validate women's fantasies in six novels and seven books of poetry and then "atone" with a book on Miller.

Am I loving the fascist, the brute, the boot in the face? Kate Millett would probably say so. She accuses Miller of adhering to "the doctrine of the cave" in which women who are not sexually compliant are properly beaten for it (and women who *are* sexually compliant are also beaten for it). Women, as Millett knows, are always seen to be in the wrong. Women, as Millett knows, are always beaten. And yes, there *is* blatant sexism in Miller's depictions of sexual seduction. He *does* hold up the mirror to patriarchy and tells it true. He *does* show the violence of intercourse no less than Andrea Dworkin shows it. He shows it from a man's point of view as she shows it from a woman's. The question is: is he *advocating* this violence? Or is he showing it because it *exists*?

This is a primal question with Miller—and with all literature. This question has come up repeatedly lately because, I think, we have lost the sense of what literature is. Was Bret Easton Ellis advocating murder in *American Psycho*, or was he mirroring the violence of our culture? Was Salman Rushdie blaspheming Mohammed in *The Satanic Verses*, or was he creating an antimythology for our antimythological age?

We seem less and less able to tell the difference between myth and fact, between wisdom and factoids. In a television culture, we no longer seem to know the social function of literature. And so we lynch those very sages who have the doubleness of vision our age requires, while we follow the fools and sycophants, the sloganeers and politicians who tell us what we want, for the moment, to hear.

Henry has fallen into this abyss of sexual politics. He is attacked for a simplicity he would never have embraced, let alone recognized. He was neither pure pig (who is?) nor pure humanist. He was complicated, a mass of contradictions—like all human beings, like all great writers.

Nature *is* red in tooth and claw, and men and women need each other so badly that they also hate each other when sex is at its hottest. Only the woman who utterly renounces her need for the penis, only the woman who shuns penetration and embraces exclusively her own sex, can find violence purely a phallic attribute. Cruelty is built into the dance of life, the longing of one sex for the other, the fear of rejection, the hatred for the lover who may leave, who may exercise the ultimate betrayal, abandonment. Women, if they are honest, also see their own potential for cruelty in love. For we are also capable of using others as objects, and we also experience the fusion between love and hate.

Can we admit that basic psychological fact and yet mass our solidarity against rape, against sexual and intellectual harassment, against the battering of women? I hope so. It would be tragic if the feminist dialectic became as rigid and unforgiving as the male chauvinist has often been.

Vulnerability in love is at the root of each sex's fear and hatred of the other. Naked need is at the bottom of all our rage. Which is not to say that Miller is *not* a chauvinist. He is. He was. My grandfather was. Most men of that generation (and the next, and the next) were. But the charge of chauvinism does not invalidate everything he has to say. It does not wash away the perfection of *Maroussi* or the energy Miller's best prose has injected into American literature.

But I was busy hating Miller—have I forgotten? Hating him for going to Paris, for being a man, for living off women: June, Anaïs, Lepska, Eve, countless others. The life open to him was never open to me. The happy vagabond on his "racing wheel," the *clochard* sleeping under the bridges of Paris; the psychopath of love fucking the wives of his hosts; the guiltless fucker, the schnorrer, the artist of the easy touch, the free meal, the man who comes to dinner and eats the hostess.

Who am I to identify with this bounder, this braggart, this blowhard? I, the A student, the Ph.D. candidate, the scribbler of sonnets who then rebelled against academe and wrote impolite novels. I should have identified with Virginia Woolf or Emily Dickinson or Simone de Beauvoir. And, of course, I did. But there was something in the lives of literary women (except Colette, except George Sand) that smelled of the lamp. Our heroines had all been forced to choose between life and work and those who chose work were strange as women. And those who chose womanhood sometimes were forced to submerge the work. Or else they died in childbirth.

So I hated Henry for not having to choose, for having a cock (and the freedom that goes with it), for having the vagabondage no woman ever knows, for having the freedom to be a fool, and the freedom to indulge his follies, and to die at a ripe old age, surrounded by young women.

So here are the things I hate him for thus far: my debt; his happiness; his cock; his being my grandfather; his *not* being my grandfather; his writing with freedom; his being honest about sex and rage; his being a male chauvinist; his being enough of a feminist to validate me.

In short, I hate him because I love him. In short, I hate him because he's great enough to encompass the contradictions of life.

What great writer do we *not* hate? The nature of greatness is that it irritates. It irritates by being new, by being honest, by baring bone.

"I celebrate myself, and sing myself," Whitman brags, "and what I assume you shall assume." And the college practitioner of sonnets (myself at nineteen) hates him for being so free. At thirty, that same young writer, having grown old enough to praise, loves him. And for the very same exultant spirit she once hated.

"A great writer modifies everything," Anthony Burgess says in *Re: Joyce*. And it is natural that at first we hate those writers for modifying everything and changing our precious point of view. T. S. Eliot, Ezra Pound, Gertrude Stein, Virginia Woolf, James Joyce, Henry Miller, D. H. Lawrence are great in proportion to their power to irritate. We know that Emily Dickinson is a great writer because she irritates us so on first reading: because she must mold us as an audience to read her, because she changes the conditions of verse, of language itself. She melts down the language as in a crucible and makes it into quite a new thing. She modifies everything.

So it is not unusual to hate great writers before we learn to love them. Because they have created something that did not yet exist, they must also create their audience. Sometimes the audience is not yet ready. Sometimes it has yet to be born.

I write all this balanced on a ledge of time before the end of the century. I believe I belong to the last literary generation, the last generation, that is, for whom books are a religion. Books require readers and readers are rapidly becoming passé. Books require solitude and the new world of virtual reality booths and roboreaders abhors solitude.

Mixed media will be the art of the future. Giant jukeboxes, with scanners or modems or faxes built in, will blaze at us from every wall and we will couple interactive "art" with electronic pencils or voice commands so as to eradicate solitude. CD ROM is the voice of the future. Cartoonovels are its eyes. Already the novels of Trollope, George Sand, not to mention Fielding or Smollett, are unreadable by most. Those fossils (like me) who worship the ghosts of Petronius and Rabelais are getting long in the tooth. And we tend, in truth, to worship more than read them.

The generation that replaces us will be bewitched by electronic images that collage the works of all past ages without knowing or crediting their sources. Perhaps copyright will also pass away. Solitude surely will. And when these go, so inevitably will the Bill of Rights and the freedom of expression it promises. The meditative calm of one book/one reader will become a heresy, as Aldous Huxley predicted in *Brave New World.*

We are more in danger of totalitarianism coming from appealing to the pleasure principle than from appealing to the death instinct—as Huxley also knew. And the world of the future will certainly be one in which people are controlled by omnipresent sensory input. All our battles of books will eventually seem quaint and inexplicable. Whether Henry Miller was a pornographer, a male chauvinist, or a Zen monk will seem utterly antique when the new mixed-media world arrives, since neither he nor anyone else will be read, there being no longer any real readers. If he is remembered it will be for his pop persona: the man who listed his free meals and rotated them through the nights of the week, the ultimate example of the man who came to dinner.

But we are not yet in the postliterate world. And I still write for a few dying librophiliacs like myself. The violence of my love/hate for Miller shows that he did indeed have the power to move the brain molecules around. And that's all the virtual reality machines and cartoonovels will be able to hope for: metamorphosing those molecules, rearranging by a nanometer the electrical charge of thoughts. The rest is silence. And radioactive dust.

I belong to a generation for whom reading and writing are sacraments. Perhaps that is one of my ties to Miller and his younger contemporary, Lawrence Durrell.

I went to see Lawrence Durrell in Sommières, in pagan Provence, shortly before he died. I needed to talk to him about Henry Miller, needed to hear about the flavor of their friendship at firsthand. Durrell had written enough about Miller for me to have it from texts, but now that Larry is gone (he died November 1990, in Sommières, at the age of seventy-eight) I'm glad I went. Though Durrell had expressed himself thoroughly on the subject of our mutual friend Henry, it was still a revelation to talk to him if only to know the impish humor behind the mellifluent prose.

The English publisher of *The Durrell-Miller Letters* had at first wanted to bowdlerize the photo on the jacket (a nude picture of Henry Miller and Lawrence Durrell on a Greek beach, circa 1940) by "cutting off Henry's cock," as Larry said.

"To think that at the end of my life I'd have to defend the *zizi* of a genius!"

He flung the witticism with perfect good humor and went on to explain that for him Miller had always been the *maître* and himself merely the acolyte.

"In order to find your own voice as a writer," Durrell said matter-of-factly, "you have to have a nervous break-down. Henry Miller and T.S. Eliot gave me myself. . . . And yet, I always considered myself a talented also-ran." He knew, he told me, that a real book is "a tentative chance one takes on the infinite." Miller wrote real books; he, Durrell, merely wrote literary ones. He had not, he felt, taken that chance on the infinite.

It was Durrell's modesty that was so beguiling. He was not going to make Miller's mistake "of accepting the Nobel Prize before it was offered." He was touched when I brought him some of his poetry books to autograph, but when I also turned up a first edition of his novel *Tunc*, he said: "Oh, forgive me."

Self-importance is endemic in literary circles. Larry had a lovely humility. *We are all just stumbling human beings*, his demeanor seemed to say, *doing the best we can.*

Durrell thought of himself—and I daresay the "liter-ary world" (whatever that is) thought of him—as "a minor poet," who happened to write novels. *The Alexandria*

Quartet (which my husband describes as "wading through halvah") seems to me to deserve better than that. I have a rather higher opinion of Durrell's poetry and of his wonderful last book about Provence (*Caesar's Vast Ghost,* 1990). But I liked him above all for understanding Henry's courage, for understanding that the difference between a small writer and a great writer is that rare commodity, *the courage to create.*

After he had shared his reminiscences about Henry on that gray January day in Provence, Durrell spoke of T.S. Eliot. What Larry said about Eliot seemed the absolute definition of the daring that makes a major writer: "He took full responsibility for being an artist in a maelstrom," Larry said. "In a world of Masefields, Eliot seemed even more shocking then than now." He was attacked for "The Wasteland," but it rolled off his back like water off a duck's. He knew, Durrell said, that one can only incarnate the unrealized pattern of the race by a "surgical operation on the self."

Who knows if Durrell was a *maître* or an "also-ran"? Only time knows. But he and his generation of writers had a kind of courage that seems lacking now. Whether it is the fault of conglomerate publishing controlled by accountants or a failure of inner-directedness on the part of writers, my generation seems focused upon crowd-pleasing and success to the detriment of being free to tell the truth. As much as their publishers and agents, my contemporaries seem to worry about grosses and sales figures. And often the deal is far more memorable than the book. A sort of literary Gresham's law has set in with the mass-marketing of hardbacks. The bestselling books of our time are rehashes of *Gone with the Wind,* gossipmongerings about "first" ladies, princesses, and movie stars, and ghostwritten *bubbe-mayses* by ephemeral celebrities. Miller didn't write that way, nor did Durrell. No one can write a real book looking back over his shoulder at the critics or at the publisher's number-crunchers.

"How is it to be old?" Larry asked, rhetorically. "Well,

your balls drop off—you don't know where to look. They cut your eyes out and don't necessarily put them back at the same angle. But thank God I can still drink."

"To Henry," I proposed.

"Yes, to Henry," he countered, emptying his glass.

And to Larry. And to a generation that knew what the calling of author meant. Authority. Being the place where the buck stops.

As we inch into the last decade of this century, the older generation of writers is disappearing day by day. Every week brings a new death crop: Alberto Moravia, Lawrence Durrell, Roald Dahl, Graham Greene, Isaac Bashevis Singer, Jerzy Kozinski. (The women writers are not dying as fast, but then the critics have already killed their reputations.) The idea that a writer can be a generalist, not a specialist, seems to die with this generation. The idea that poets can write prose and novelists poetry, that adults can write for children and that authors can maintain the radical innocence (if not the childishness) of children, seems to pass with them. I would like my generation of writers to catch some of their largeness of heart, some of their willingness to crack open genres and take a chance on the infinite.

A dreary censorship, and self-censorship, has been imposed on books by the centralization of the book industry. But what use is it to be a writer if one doesn't take chances? "Hating" Henry, after all, was about my own fear of self-exposure. But without taking chances one cannot tell the truth, and what use is it to be a writer if one doesn't tell the truth?

CHAPTER 2

Henry Hero

Rimbaud restored literature to life; I have endeavored to restore life to literature.

—HENRY MILLER, *THE TIME OF THE ASSASSINS*

For me, the book is the man that I am. . . . The confused man, the negligent man, the reckless man, the lusty, obscene, boisterous, thoughtful, scrupulous, lying, diabolically truthful man I am.

—HENRY MILLER, *BLACK SPRING*

most people are not free. Freedom, in fact, frightens them. They follow patterns set for them by their parents, enforced by society, by their fears of "they say" and "what will they think?" and a constant inner dialogue that weighs duty against desire and pronounces duty the winner.

"Lives of quiet desperation" Thoreau called such existence—though today's version is noisy desperation. Occasionally, a visionary comes along who seems to have conquered the fears in himself and seems to live with bravado and courage. People are at once terrified of such a creature—and admiring. They are also envious.

One who has conquered human fears is recognized as a hero—or heroine. But such a figure inspires mixed emotions. We are provoked by their example, but we are also inclined to blame ourselves for having lived too timidly. So the hero or heroine is often attacked, even killed, because of the envy of ordinary mortals. But if we could see the hero as embodying our own aspirations, we would not need to destroy but could rather emulate and learn.

Henry Miller was such a hero. He did not start out fearless but he learned to overcome his fears. And he wrote a book—*Tropic of Cancer*—that breathed fresh air into American—and world—literature. The fresh air he breathed was freedom. And it was like pure oxygen to those who would take it in. For the others, the fearful, the envious, those who refused to breathe, Miller had to be discredited as a pervert or a sex maniac because his message was too terrifying. Life is there for the taking, he said. And those who refused to live fully had to blame him for their own failure.

Like Byron, Pushkin, George Sand, and Colette, Miller became more than a writer. He became a protagonist and a prophet—the prophet of a new consciousness.

His writings and his life mingled to create a larger myth, a myth that embodies the human attraction toward freedom. Miller's writing is full of imperfection, bombast, humbug. Sometimes its very slovenliness makes it hard to defend. But the purity of his example, his heart, his openness, makes him unique among American writers. He will surely, however, draw new generations of readers to him. At present, Miller's reputation still hangs in the balance and even those who have written about him seem to disapprove of him.

Miller is in many ways a world unto himself. One searches in vain for a contemporary to compare him with. *Tropic of Cancer* burst forth into the world in the same year, 1934, that gave us F. Scott Fitzgerald's *Tender Is the Night*, Isak Dinesen's *Seven Gothic Tales*, Robert Graves's *I, Claudius*, Edna St. Vincent Millay's *Wine from These Grapes*, and Langston Hughes's *The Ways of White Folks*.

Not only is Miller's characteristic style comparable to none of his contemporaries, but his spirit harks back to Whitman or Rabelais. In an age of cynicism, Miller remains the romantic, exemplifying the possibility of optimism in a fallen world, of happy poverty in a world that worships Lucre, of the sort of gaiety Yeats meant when he wrote of the Chinese sages in "Lapis Lazuli," "their eyes,/ Their ancient, glittering eyes, are gay."

I only knew Henry Miller in the last decade of his life. In a number of ways, he became my mentor.

I was a very young writer, very green and suddenly famous; he was a very old writer, seasoned in both fame and rejection, when we met—by letter—and became pen pals, then pals. I feel lucky to have known him, but in some sense I only got to know him well after his death.

Miller was the most contradictory of characters: a mystic who was known for his sexual writings, a romantic who pretended to be a rake, an old-fashioned Victorian sexist who could nevertheless be enormously supportive and loving to women, an accused anti-Semite who loved and admired Jews and had no use at all for prejudice or political dogma. He was, above all, a writer of what the poet Karl Shapiro called "wisdom literature." If we have trouble categorizing Miller's "novels" and consequently underrate them, it is because we judge them according to some unspoken notion of "the well-wrought novel." And Miller's novels seem not wrought at all. In fact, they are rants—undisciplined and wild. But they are full of wisdom, and they have that "eternal and irrepressible freshness" Ezra Pound called the mark of the true classic.

In the profound shocks and upheavals of the twentieth century, from the trenches of World War I to Auschwitz to the holes in the ozone layer, we in the West have produced a great body of "wisdom literature," as if we needed all the wisdom we could garner to bear what may be the last century of humans on earth. Solzhenitsyen, Primo Levi, Günter Grass, Pablo Neruda, Idries Shah, Krishnamurti, Jean-Paul Sartre, and Simone de Beauvoir have all written predominantly wisdom literature. Even among some of our most interesting novelists—Saul Bellow, Natalia Ginzberg, Nadine Gordimer, Doris Lessing, Iris Murdoch, Isaac Bashevis Singer, Christina Stead, Gore Vidal, Kurt Vonnegut, Marguerite Yourcenar—the fictional form is often a cloak for philosophical truths about the human race and where it is heading. The popularity of writers like Margaret Mead, Joseph Campbell, M. Scott Peck, and Robert Bly in our time also serves to show the great hunger for wisdom. We are, as Ursula LeGuin says, "dancing at the edge of the world," and it takes all our philosophy to bear it.

Henry Miller remains the most disturbing and misunderstood of prophets. Because even the *style* of writing he discovered has become convention; it is hard today to grasp how electric his voice was in 1934. The feminist critique of the sixties came in to bury Henry under rhetoric—just as simplistic in its way as the simplistic rhetoric of male supremacy. But the feminist critique, valid as it is, neglects to address the main question Henry Miller poses: how does a writer raise a voice? How does a writer take the chaos of life and transform it into art? The raising of a voice is the red thread through chaos. The raising of a voice is the essence of freedom. It is where every writer, every person, must begin.

Can a woman writer learn anything from Henry Miller's voice? Doesn't his sexism invalidate his work? Shouldn't we boycott his work because of its underlying politics?

I don't think so. Just as Shakespeare's monarchism does not invalidate the beauty of his verse, Miller's sexism does not annihilate his contribution to literature. Besides, if we proscribe all literature whose sexual politics we do not agree with, we shall have nothing left to read—not even the Bible, Homer, or the novels of Jane Austen (whose heroines are often happy to make conventional marriages).

In fact, the freedom that Henry Miller discovered in finding his voice can inspire women writers as well as men.

It is the voice of the outsider, the renegade, the underground prophet—and isn't that, after all, what women still are?

The problem of finding a voice is essential for all writers. It may be more fraught with external difficulties for women writers, because no one agrees what the proper voice of woman is—unless it is to keep silent—but it is still basically the same process of self-discovery. To define the self in a world that is hostile to the very notion of your selfhood is still every woman writer's challenge. It was Henry Miller's challenge, too—for different reasons. In tracing his self-liberation, we can, by analogy, trace our own.

I do not mean to minimize the differences between the male writer's odyssey and the female writer's. The pen, as so many feminist critics have shown, has been treated as analogous to the penis in our literary culture. This accounts for the trouble that feminists, myself included, have with Henry Miller. Henry liberates himself, becomes the vagabond, clown, poet, but the open road he chooses has never really been open to women. Henry's picaresque sexual odyssey was, for centuries, a male prerogative. Still, it is useful for writers of both sexes to trace the steps of his liberation. The freedom of Paris plus first-person bravado equals the voice we have come to know as Henry Miller.

Listen:

> I have no money, no resources, no hopes. I am the happiest man alive. A year ago, six months ago, I thought that I was an artist. I no longer think about it, I *am*. Everything that was literature has fallen from me. There are no more books to be written, thank God.
>
> This then? This is not a book. This is libel, slander, defamation of character. This is not a book, in the ordinary sense of the word. No, this is a prolonged insult, a gob of spit in the face of Art, a kick in the pants to God, Man, Destiny, Time, Love, Beauty. . . . I am going to sing for you, a little off key perhaps, but I will sing. . . .

Henry is retracing his steps as an artist here, telling us exactly what happened between his early, unsuccessful efforts at writing fiction, and *Tropic of Cancer:* he let go of literature. It reminds me of Colette's advice to the young Georges Simenon: "Now go and take out the poetry."

Good advice. A writer is born at the moment when his true voice of authority merges at white heat with the subject he was born to chronicle. Literature falls away and what remains is life—raw, pulsating life: "A gob of spit in the face of Art."

For the truth is that every generation, every writer, must rediscover nature. Literary conventions tend to ossify over time, and what was once new becomes old. It takes a brave new voice to rediscover real life buried under decades of literary dust. In unburying himself, Henry unburied twentieth-century literature.

What was it about Paris in 1930 that enabled Henry Miller to find his voice? And what was it about New York that prevented it?

The New York Henry left when he settled in Paris in

March 1930 was nowhere as fraught as the New York of today, but it still bore certain similarities to it. In New York it was a dishonor to be an unknown writer; in Paris one could write *écrivain* on one's passport and hold one's head high. In Paris it was assumed (it still is) that an author had to have time, leisure, talk, solitude, stimulation. In New York it was, and still is, assumed that unless you fill up your time with appointments, you are a bum. More than that (and more important, particularly for Henry) was the American attitude toward the vagabond artist—an attitude that unfortunately persists to our day. "In Europe," as his friend the photographer Brassaï says in his book on Henry Miller, "poverty is only bad luck, a minor unhappiness; in the United States, it represents a moral fault, a dishonor that society cannot pardon."

To be a poor artist in America is thus doubly unforgivable. To be an artist in America is to be a criminal (its criminality only pardoned by writing bestsellers or selling one's paintings at outrageous prices to rich collectors and thus feeding the obsolete war machine with tax blood). But to be poor *and* an artist: this is un-American.

Which of us has not felt this disapproval, this American rejection of the dreamer? "Poets have to dream," says Saul Bellow, "and dreaming in America is no cinch."

In the last few years we have seen a dramatic replay of these attitudes in the debates over censorship and the National Endowment for the Arts. Our essential mistrust of dreamers leads us to cripple them with restrictions of all sorts. We seem not to understand that the basic riches of our country—wealth and emotional health—come from our creative spirit. Even with Japanese conglomerates buying our movie companies, even with statistics that prove our movies, music, television shows, and inventions are our biggest exports in real dollar terms, we still honor the money counters and money changers over the inventors and dreamers who give them something to count and change.

This is a deep-seated American obsession, and one whose historical genesis we must explore in retracing

Henry Miller's steps. It comes, of course, out of puritanism's assumption that the dream life and imagination are suspect. And it results in a love-hate relationship with sexuality—a violent alternation between fascination and disgust which I call sexomania/sexophobia. We must understand how Henry was buffeted by these powerful forces and how he fled to Europe to be reborn.

"It was the scorn which ultimately Miller could not stand," says Brassaï. "It was the scorn that he wanted to escape. Madness and suicide threatened him."

"Nowhere have I felt so degraded and humiliated as in America," Miller writes in *Tropic of Capricorn*.

Miller's life as a protagonist, as a mythic hero—or antihero—is intimately related to this struggle between puritanism and the life of the dreamer. Henry made a religion of art (as did his disciples). In doing this he was following in the footsteps of Whitman, his model of the American writer.

There are at least two Millers in the books and articles that have been written about Henry. One is the real, historical Henry Miller, born in 1891 in New York, died in 1980 in Los Angeles—a character full of contradictions. The other is Miller the mythic hero or antihero, whose hegira is emblematic of the hegira of the American artist.

Constrained by puritanism, provoked by a society in which dreaming is no cinch, Miller the antihero creates a way for an American—or anyone—to be an artist, and in doing so makes a path for all of us. One is continually struck by the interplay between these two Millers, but my interest is principally in the Miller who leads the way for a creator—particularly a creator who comes from a culture where creativity itself is suspect. Since I long ago gave up the Ph.D. program for the life of a professional author, I approach Miller with a writer's rather than a scholar's point of view. Like many storytellers, Henry was an outrageous self-mythifier and critics have pointed out the disparities between "the truth" of his life and the grandiosity of his fictions. He tells the same story differently on every occasion, they complain.

My point of view is necessarily different. In tracing the steps of another writer, I have empathy for the creative process itself and an understanding of its difficulties. I *expect* a writer to "lie" in order to get at a deeper truth. I take for granted that imaginative writing exaggerates and rearranges "facts" in the name of a higher fiction. I also understand how hard it is to survive one's own fame.

Henry's writing is often misunderstood precisely because of the ways it parallels—yet deviates from—his own life. Since he uses the name "Henry Miller" for his fictive protagonists, readers are thrown even more astray. This is a fate I know well because it has also been my own. Though I have called my heroines by different names, the parallels between my life and the mythic lives I lead in my novels have often had the effect of leading my self-appointed judges to attack me personally. Henry was one of the first to see this parallel between our fates, and as a result was enormously kind to me. Curiously enough, it fell in part to Henry to rescue my first novel from the obscurity that might otherwise have claimed it. And since I believe in the universal law by which circles get completed, I find it not at all odd that it falls in part to me to puzzle out the many contradictions of his posthumous reputation.

A large part of the problem Miller presents to the literary critic comes from his perception of the chaos of life and his passionate need to reflect that chaos in his books. Henry Miller is the poet of what Umberto Eco calls *the chaosmos.* When he writes, he is in touch with pure desire—the desire to be one with the primal flux of creation, the desire to be as creative as a god.

> I like desire. In desiring things no one is wounded, deranged nor exploited. Creation is pure desire. One possesses nothing, one creates, one lets go. One is beyond what he does. One is no longer a slave. It's an affair between oneself and God. When one is truly rendered naked everything is done without effort. There is no recompense—the effort, the deed itself suffices. Deed is desire and desire deed. A complete circle.

How to write a coherent book about such a primal force? It is not easy, as all Miller's biographers attest. Clearly Henry Miller did not *want* to be the subject of a biography and he spread confusion even as he scattered clues. He knew he had told many tales that were not true and he was nervous that someone might catch him in his lies. A good example of Henry's ambivalent relation to the truth is the way he hated his pal Brassaï's rather accurate portrait of him in *Grandeur Nature*, a book not yet translated into English, perhaps because Henry despised it so. He felt he had adequately chronicled his own life in his books, and wherever there was some fictionalization that did not correspond to the "facts" (in which, anyway, he did not believe), he was more than happy to provide chronologies, interviews, conversations that elucidated the truth, *his* truth, for his rapt listeners. (Some of these "documents" also contain plenty of fiction.) He was an artesian writer, so overflowing with stories and ideas that to this day he still defeats bibliographers and biographers. Whenever you think you have read all the essential Miller, another pamphlet, brochure, treasure trove of letters, watercolor or print turns up with more Henry, ever more Henry. He embodied in both his writing and his life the paradigm of the writer as the giver of gifts, the voyager into the underworld who comes back with a boon for humankind.

Ironically, Henry Miller is best known for his worst writing—the boastfully graphic sexual scenes in the *Tropics*, *Quiet Days in Clichy*, and *Sexus*. These finally interest me less than the transcendentalism of *The Colossus of Maroussi*, his spiritual travel book about Greece. For me *Maroussi* is his central work and it stands squarely in the American transcendental tradition. It has a kind of perfection and purity that you can find in books like *Walden*. And yet, paradoxically, without the scandal surrounding the "sexual" writings, Miller would perhaps not be known at all.

That Miller was a transcendentalist in the indigenous American tradition of Thoreau, Emerson, Dickinson, and

Whitman he himself apparently knew. He referred to Whitman as an ancestor and influence. (He also regarded *Maroussi* as his best book.) He was a mystic in the way of Thomas Merton and Lao-tzu, seeing in ordinary life the way into the extraordinary. Like many liberators who seek first to liberate themselves, he saw in sex one path of self-liberation—a way out of the body through the body. In this, he is not so different from Whitman or from Colette.

He was always seeking "life more abundant" as he says at the end of *The Colossus of Maroussi*. Sex was one path toward abundance. Travel, another. Conversation, letter-writing, and painting were still others. He saw the world in terms of abundance rather than scarcity, and it often seems that this distinction is the most critical one of all where writers are concerned. Writers tend toward either free flow or toward agonized laconicism—Henry Miller being at one extreme and Samuel Beckett at the other.

Henry Miller was as great a conversationalist as he was a writer. He was the primeval author, in the primeval cave, telling stories to keep the tribe awake and alive, safe from the saber-toothed tigers outside. Like any shaman, he worked in a variety of forms: voice, watercolor, the photographs he posed for, the documentaries he conspired in. In many ways, he anticipates Cindy Sherman, Art Spiegelman, and other postmodernist artists, using his own photographic or painted persona to create his own oeuvre. In other ways he is like Picasso, inventing and reinventing himself in different media and inventing and reinventing his wives and his muses in many of the different characters that appear in his books. All of them are Woman or Muse, just as Henry himself, the autobiographical protagonist who bears his name, is Everyman. To speak of him as the real historical Henry Miller is a mistake, for had he not elevated his life above mere autobiography and made it emblematic nobody would be interested in it but himself and perhaps a few enemies, relatives, friends.

Because Henry Miller became his own protagonist, the appreciation of his work is further confused. Always, when a writer is transformed this way, it makes the assessment of the work more problematic, for some will inevitably see him as a villain and in reaction others will plump for him as hero. We have seen both these responses to Miller in recent years and it is doubtful that either view has been accurate.

This transformation is what all artists seek: to become like mythic heroes—Prometheus, Achilles, Odysseus, Alcestis, Athena—so that we mortals can see our fates reflected in their journeys as we do in the journeys described in ancient myths.

But Henry is not a hero to all. Many see him as a villain. His fate has not been so different from de Sade's: either canonized by cultists or burned at the stake by puritans, either hailed by hippies seeking a hip father figure or dismissed by literary Anglophiles who would prefer that American literature consisted only of Henry James.

Things are not so simple. Our apprehension of Miller, as of de Sade, implicates our entire apprehension of sexuality, our notions of sexual politics, as well as our notions of what constitutes literature. That is why he is such a pivotal and important figure.

"Life is that which flows . . ." said one of Miller's Paris roommates, Michael Fraenkel, in an essay about the composition of *The Tropic of Cancer*. The paradox for every creative artist is that life flows and art must stand still. But it must stand still like the hummingbird, as Miller would say. It must move and yet have form, because without form it is not graspable; without form it cannot be art.

Miller's art is always bursting the boundaries of form as we know it. It strains beyond the frame of the picture. This is partly its subject, and it also accounts for the difficulty a form-ridden commentator has with it.

Postmodernists have already discovered Miller as the artist of the future. But the artist who is ahead of his time never has an easy job making a living *in* his time. Witness Vincent van Gogh. And Emily Dickinson. And Walt Whitman. Miller is an artist of similar protean and prophetic gifts. If he has to date received little serious literary consideration, it is because he cannot be formally categorized. But rather than seeing this as a fault—as many of his detractors do—I see it as his very subject matter. Henry's "message" was the message of all the Zen masters and mystics: that there is no stability, only flux. "The angel is my watermark!" he writes in *Black Spring*.

Henry Miller's recent biographers try, willy-nilly, to fit him into preexisting patterns; and when they fail, they blame *him*. But Henry's very message is that life is formless, and that creativity partakes of the divine chaos. He struggles with this paradox in every book.

Ironically, we live in an age when literary biography is more read than literature. Writers' lives tend to have more commercial viability than their own books. In his most fertile time, Henry Miller could never have been published by a mainstream New York publisher, yet in his centennial year several vied to bring out books *about* him. I suspect that if *Tropic of Cancer* came upon us today, it would still have trouble finding a publisher despite our much vaunted (but essentially fake) "sexual revolution." Yet Miller the protagonist continues to inspire books and films.

What is it that we find in the lives of writers—particularly nonconformist writers—that thrills us, makes us identify? The story of a person inventing himself? The story of a person finding personal freedom in an age of corporate and totalitarian conformity? Has the myth of the nonconformist writer hitting the open road become a substitute for the initiatory ritual Robert Bly and others claim our society lacks? Why else do so many novels and movies about writers strike a resonant chord in readers who are not writers?

Surely there is no more toilsome, self-flagellating profession than that of author. Ingrown toenails, Henry called us. Voltaire said, "The only reward to be expected for the cultivation of literature is contempt if one fails and hatred if one succeeds." But the average nonwriter seems to see in authorship a relaxing, hedonistic profession, affording ample time for travel, dalliance, and debauchery, an aristocratic profession carried out in dreamily scenic places, with lovely members of the opposite sex in attendance. The average nonwriter sees the writer as someone who has made ordinary life heroic.

Contrary to popular myth, authors lead "a sort of life" (the phrase is Graham Greene's), imprisoned behind a desk. Painful solitude is required for the cultivation of literature, and even a bad book requires that one be good at cutting oneself off from other human beings in order to write it. A writer's most ecstatic hours occur alone, yet the myth of hedonism persists. And the fact is that many writers ruin themselves trying to live up to it. Or maybe it is true that in a world where busy-ness and business drown out every spiritual pursuit, the writer's solitude is the most envied pleasure of all. "A sort of life" it may be, but vastly preferable to the kind of empty busy-ness that characterizes most people's lives.

Miller was a happy man (for this he was and is also hated). He was generous and free of envy. Though he sometimes boasts of idleness in his books (as he boasts of lechery), he was, in truth, never idle. He was such a scribomaniac that even when he lived in the same house as Lawrence Durrell they often exchanged letters. For most of his life, Henry wrote literally dozens of letters a day to people he could have easily engaged in conversation—and did. The writing process, in short, was essential. As it is to all real writers, writing was life and breath to him. He put out words as a tree puts out leaves.

So we come to the paradox of biography—especially the biography of a writer who amply chronicled his own life in many forms. ("Biography is one of the new terrors of death," said Dr. John Arbuthnot, the poet Alexander Pope's friend. And in 1891, in his *The Critic as Artist*, Oscar Wilde wrote, "Every great man nowadays has his disciples, and it is always Judas who writes the autobiography.") Who can chart the events in a person's life with accuracy and without distortion? No one. Not even the person himself. That is why biographies must be rewritten for every age, for every new wrinkle in the zeitgeist. That is why biography is essentially a collaborative art, the latest biographer collaborating with all those who wrote earlier.

With a writer who has already mined his own life in letters, in novels, in paintings, and in films, the biographical problem becomes even more vexing. Even the most seemingly autobiographical writer changes, heightens, and rearranges "fact" to make his fictions. It is naïve to read his stories literally, but it is equally unsatisfactory to read them as if they had no connection whatsoever to his life.

I hope I can make peace with all these paradoxes by writing about Henry Miller in the same spirit that he first wrote to me in 1974—with complete candor and no hidden agenda. It will not be the last word on Henry Miller, but the only people worth writing about are those about whom the last word cannot be said.

CHAPTER 3

Just a Brooklyn Boy

I was meant to be the sort of individual that . . . [is] born on the 25th day of December . . . and so was Jesus Christ. . . . But due to the fact that my mother had a clutching womb, that she held me in her grip like an octopus, I came out under another configuration. . . . Even my mother, with her caustic tongue, seemed to understand it somewhat. "Always dragging behind like a cow's tail"—that's how she characterized me. But is it my fault that she held me inside her until the hour had passed?

—HENRY MILLER, *TROPIC OF CAPRICORN*

assuming that you know as little about Henry Miller as I did when I first heard from him in 1974, I am going to give you the crash course in Miller that I wish someone had given me. This will not be a true biography, for several voluminous biographies of Miller have appeared in the last few years (and new information is constantly emerging as Anaïs Nin's unexpurgated diaries are released), but a writer's take on another writer, with just enough detail to prepare you to read (or reread) Miller with greater understanding.

Perhaps you are like me when I first heard from Henry: you've read only *Tropic of Cancer,* and maybe not even the whole book. It's possible you only flipped through for the "good parts." In Henry's case, this can be totally misleading. I want to give you an overview of Henry's life so that you can read his books with pleasure and grapple with the issues they raise.

Notwithstanding Henry's protestations about not wanting a biography or a biographer, he seems always to have been documenting his own life, leaving the most minutely detailed histories in letters. This antlike attention to detail belies his feigned *sprezzatura.* Even as Henry protests *No biographies, please!* he leaves careful (and misleading) recitals of his life. Indeed Henry seemed always to be looking backward from the future, accounting for himself to twenty-first–century biographers.

How did Henry Miller find the courage to be a writer? A large part of the answer can be found in the bitterness of his mother's milk. Born in the Yorkville section of Manhattan at 12:17 P.M. on December 26, 1891, Henry was the son of Louise Nieting Miller and Heinrich Miller, both first generation German-Americans. It was one day after Christmas, a fact Henry always regretted, since he would have liked the distinction of sharing Christ's birthday.

Such coincidences meant much to him, as did astrology, so it is important to add that he was a Capricorn, and that Pluto and Neptune were the planets that influenced his nativity.

Capricorns are said to be tenacious ("I was born with a cussed streak in me," Henry says) and true to form, "they had a hell of a time bringing me out of the womb." Elsewhere, he blames his mother's "clutching womb" as the reason for his missing, by one day, the Messiah's birthday. But clearly there was something in his Capricorn tenacity that made him very happy to stay there. Happiness in the womb is a state he refers to often, from his earliest writing to his latest. One feels that he almost *remembers* the womb, so lovingly does he refer to it:

> The ninth year of my life is approaching and with it the end of my first Paradise on earth. No, the second Paradise. My first was in my mother's womb, where I fought to remain forever, but the forceps finally prevailed. It was a marvelous period in the womb and I shall never forget it. I had *almost* everything one could ask for—*except friends.*
>
> And a life without friends is no life, however, snug and secure it may be.

Marvelous period or not, Henry also attacks his mother for holding him "in her grip like an octopus." This is typical of Henry Miller both as writer and man: he always tells the same story from at least two opposite points of view.

In the first year of his life, Henry moved to Brooklyn from Yorkville and ever after referred to himself as "just a Brooklyn boy." The family lived at 662 Driggs Avenue in Williamsburg, at a time when Brooklyn was still a separate city from New York, as it had been in Whitman's time.

The family spoke German at home, and as a baby, Heinrich was the darling of his parents and his maternal grandfather, Valentin Nieting, who lived with them. Valentin Nieting was a tailor who was then working at home, often assisting Henry's father. He had trained in Savile Row and spoke sonorous English, which Henry admired. His grandson also admired him for being a socialist and trade unionist while his own father, Heinrich senior, was a "Boss Tailor." Such were the myths of Henry's childhood. Henry's maternal grandmother had been confined to an insane asylum when his mother was a child. The family story was that she was "taken away." Louise's strong sense of order, the iron hand with which she ruled her men, may have been a reaction to the chaos of her early life.

Henry's only sister, Lauretta Anna, came into the world on July 11, 1895, so Henry was a pampered only child for four years. Even when competition came in the form of a sibling, the sibling was a girl—and retarded. Henry's mother must have been devastated.

By all Henry's accounts, Louise was a harridan, and Heinrich *père* a dreamy alcoholic. In today's psychobabble, we would call Henry Miller's family "dysfunctional." His mother goaded him into achievement, and his father, a wonderful raconteur and hopeless drunk, set the example of spinning webs with words that Henry was to emulate all his life.

But it was Henry's mother who spurred both the writer and the rebel in him.

"My mother was a first-class bitch," Henry said to Twinka Thiebaud.

> She tried to scold and shame me into respectability. . . . What she didn't realize was she was creating a very restless, angry person. When finally I found the courage to write about what I'd been storing up for years, it came pouring out into one long relentless tirade. Beginning with the earliest memories of my mother, I had saved up enough hatred, enough anger, to fill a hundred books.

Henry's recollections of his mother—Louise Nieting Miller—are almost always about her Prussianness: her oppression of him, of his father, and of his retarded younger sister. According to Henry, his mother beat Lauretta for the "crime" of being retarded; she screamed at his father for being drunk; she hid Henry's typewriter in a closet because she was so embarrassed to have a son who wanted to be anything as shiftless as a writer. She was a woman given to random rages who must have been frustrated by the difficulties of her marriage. It's not hard to empathize with Louise and take, with many grains of salt, her son's violent depictions of her. But to the boy Henry she must have been terrifying, larger than life. How many writers escape into the world of words to find a haven from the uncontrollable world of childhood? The pattern is so common as to seem to be a general rule.

Miller's idealization of women as love objects and his simultaneous need to strip them brutally naked in his novels is usually traced to his troubled relationship with his mother. But if we look at the dynamics more carefully we see that he was also a very good little boy, who must have worshiped his very strong and domineering mother and who was whiplashed between the opposing poles of her personality.

He even seemed to know this about himself, for in his book on Rimbaud, *The Time of the Assassins*, this astonishing passage appears:

> . . . [O]ne is still bound to the mother. All one's rebellion was but dust in the eye, the frantic attempt to conceal this bondage. Men of this stamp are always against their native land—impossible to be otherwise. Enslavement is the great bugaboo, whether it be to country, church or society. Their lives are spent in breaking fetters, but the secret bondage gnaws at their vitals and gives them no rest. They must come to terms with the mother before they can rid themselves of the obsession of fetters. "Outside! Forever outside! Sitting on the doorstep of the mother's womb." . . . It is a perpetual dance on the edge of the crater. One may be acclaimed as a great rebel, but one will never be loved . . .

Henry's longing for the sweetness of his mother's womb followed him all the days of his life. So did his anger at being cast out. In his letters to the critic and professor Wallace Fowlie in the 1940s, he says that Rimbaud was most important to him for helping him recognize his mother-fixation. So we know he came to accept this truth about himself. Still, he could not control his alternation between dependency and rage.

Always, Henry required a muse-mother-lover figure in order to write. First it was his second wife, June, then Anaïs Nin, whom he often credited with the greatest flowering of his creativity. Nin's recent book, *Incest* (1992), shows how extraordinarily close their connection was and how much each became the other's double, lover, and muse. The violence of his depiction of women, which Kate Millett so meticulously analyzes, is a secret tribute to the immense power women had over him. His essay "The Enormous Womb" could have been the title of the book of his life. Henry saw in Rimbaud what he saw in himself:

> And what is the nature of this secret? I can only say that it has to do with the mothers. I feel that it was the same with Lawrence and with Rimbaud.

Men with domineering mothers (Miller, Mailer, Lawrence) are likely to become prisoners of sex who seek to break their chains with violent words. Under these violent words is often a quivering romanticism. "He has the German sentimentality and romanticism about women," Anaïs Nin said of Miller in *Henry and June*. "Sex is *love* to him." How can we reconcile this observation with the pop image of Miller the fuckabout misogynist?

The feminist attack on Miller sees in his anger toward women a disregard of them. I think, on the contrary, he grants them too much power and thus must then expose and destroy them. Miller's depictions of ravenous cunts are akin to the horned hunter's quarry depicted on the walls of the caves of Lascaux: the painter-shaman fixes the image of the fearsome creature as a magical way of containing its mystery and capturing its power forever.

Miller's example shows us the dark heart of sexism: a man trying to demolish the power he knows is greater than his own—the power to give life, the seemingly self-sufficient womb.

Henry was so enthralled by women that he sought to demystify their mysterious parts through the violent verbal magic of his books. The violence is rooted in a sense of self-abnegation and humiliation before them. He is, as the Freudians would say, counterphobic. Terrified of women, he reduces them to sex objects, cunts if you will, which he subdues with his penis and his pen.

He had to kill his mother to become a writer. He had to skewer her on his pen even as the "Henry Miller" of *The Tropics* and *Clichy* and *The Rosy Crucifixion* skewers cunts on his cock. His enchantment in later years by Oriental women (his Japanese fifth wife, Hoki, his last beloved, the Chinese actress Lisa Liu), his adoration of exotic Anaïs, of the femme fatale June, all betray an unacknowledged longing for another mother: the sweet caring Madonna of his early childhood whom for most of his life he cannot even remember.

At the end of Henry's life he told Twinka Thiebaud of a dream that inspired him to rewrite his mother as a Madonna:

> Suddenly my mother appears and she's completely different from my memories of her. She is wonderful, radiant, sensitive, even intelligent! After writing that piece ["Mother, China, and the World Beyond" in *Sextet*], my view of her softened. I had created a mother of my own making, one I could relate to, one I could love even. It occurred to me that if my mother had been like the mother I had dreamed about, perhaps I wouldn't have become a writer after all. I might have become a tailor like my father. I might have been an upstanding pillar of society like she wanted me to be.

So the courage to create is fueled by rage. (*Courage,* after all, could be imagined as *heart* plus *rage.*) Perhaps this accounts for the problem critics have with women creators: women are not allowed rage. But only through rage can we separate from our parents and become autonomous creators. Every artist has to make this transition, and for women it is a forbidden one.

Look at how hard it was for Henry—even as a man! He had to renounce his parents, expatriate himself, find a new mother-muse in Anaïs Nin. (June, his second wife, had been the taunting, torturing mother who, despite the pain she caused him, was the first person to believe in him as a writer.) We can never reconstruct the "real" Madonna-mother of Henry's early childhood. She left no physical traces. But we can posit her existence by tracing Henry's psychological history.

With a raging mother, a retarded sister, a drunken father, Henry's childhood cannot have been easy, yet he remembers it as having been "glorious"—and the streets of Brooklyn were, according to him, his preparation for the writer's life.

> Summer nights in New York, or Brooklyn, as it happened to be, can be wonderful when you're a kid and can roam the streets at will . . .

Henry says in the *Book of Friends,* written in his eighties. Looking back eight decades from Pacific Palisades to Brooklyn, Brooklyn—specifically Driggs Avenue in the fourteenth ward, later on Decatur Street in the Bushwick section—seemed like the second Eden of his life.

When Henry recounted his childhood memories of Brooklyn, he invariably stressed the positive: "Born with a silver spoon in my mouth. Got everything I craved, except a real pony."

He seems to have had a pervasive sense of entitlement, a sense that he would always be cared for. When the kids in his kindergarten class were given Christmas gifts, he refused to accept them, knowing that he would do better at home. "I know Santa is going to bring me better things," he told his mother. His mother's reaction to this was to slap him, grab him by the earlobe, and drag him back to school to apologize to the teacher.

"I couldn't understand what I had done wrong," Henry said years later. "This . . . left in my childish mind the feeling that my mother was stupid and cruel."

His friends were other immigrant kids—Polish-American, Italian-American, and Irish-American. In his many autobiographical writings, he mentions Stanley Borowski, Lester Reardon, Johnny Paul, Eddie Carney, and Johnny Dunne. The whole microcosm of the American melting pot was found in Henry's Brooklyn. He was not to find another world as varied and congenial till he went to Paris in 1930. "There in Paris, in its shabby squalid streets teeming with life, I relived the sparkling scenes of my childhood."

What kind of marriage did Henry's parents have? This incident, recounted in Henry's *Book of Friends*, evokes it, seen through Henry's child-eyes:

> After dinner in the evening my father would dry the dishes which my mother washed at the sink. One evening he must have said something to offend her for suddenly she gave him a ringing slap in the face with her wet hands. Then I remember distinctly hearing him say to her: "If you ever do that again I'll leave you." I was impressed by the quiet, firm way in which he said it. His son, I must confess, never had the courage to talk that way to a woman.

Sensitive, creative, inclined to drown his sorrows in drink, Henry's father obliged Louise to be the tyrannical disciplinarian. But this incident, which Henry relates with such approbation, shows the way Henry's father nevertheless shaped his son's ideals of manhood. Henry exhibited the same sensitivity and dreaminess as his father, but in his most notorious novels he invents a fast-fucking, fast-talking, hypermanly antihero—just the man to subdue the otherwise overbearing Louise.

Henry was a great reader as a child, and loved to read aloud. He adored Old Testament stories, and he was reading long before he began elementary school. In school he was both pushed to achieve by the fierce disappointment his mother experienced with Lauretta, and pushed to make mischief in rebellion against his mother's tyranny.

He experienced his first taste of the forbiddenness of sex with Joey and Tony Imhof, his "country" friends in Glendale, Long Island, whose father, John Imhof, was "the first artist to appear in my life." (Imhof was a friend of Henry's father and was a watercolorist who also made stained-glass windows for churches.) Henry's father revered Imhof for being an artist, and so, of course did Henry. We can trace Henry's reverence for artists directly to this childhood mentor.

Henry and the Imhof boys played together sexually between the ages of seven and twelve—a fact one of Miller's biographers points to with horror, as if homosexual experimentation were not the rule rather than the exception in childhood.

Henry seems to have been both fascinated and terrified by sex. In *Book of Friends*, he reports being invited by a girl named Weesie, a friend of his Yorkville cousin, Henry Baumann, to make love to her. Henry was afraid, and hesitated until the opportunity passed. He also hesitated for three years with his great high school love, Cora Seward, a blonde angel whom he idealized too much to fuck. Henry writes about her in *Book of Friends:* "Strange that I never thought of fucking her," he says. But Cora was love to him, not sex. And at this time in his life he kept them very separate. "I never mixed the two—love and sex, which shows what an imbecile I must have been."

How wonderful to be sitting beside her in the open trolley, on our way to Rockaway or Sheepshead Bay, and singing

at the top of our lungs—"shine on, Harvest Moon, for me
and My Gal" or "I don't want to set the world on fire."

Cora was the girl he obsessively fantasized about even
when he had his first real sexual relationship. Initiated
crudely into sex in a brothel, Henry had to wait to meet
Pauline Chouteau, his "first mistress," to begin to explore
his sexuality. After he began his affair with Pauline, he
seems to have ruminated constantly on his inability to fuck
the idyllic Cora—a failure of nerve he apparently regretted
all his life. The man who was destined to liberate American
literature first had to liberate himself.

Henry graduated second in his class from Eastern Dis-
trict High School in Brooklyn, a school in his old childhood neighborhood he had insisted on going to over the
protestations of his parents. He was attached to the old
neighborhood, but the old neighborhood had changed a lot
since he was little. It was now dominated by newly emi-
grated Eastern European Jews, and Henry was one of the
few gentiles.

To the end of his life he referred to himself as "a goy,"
as if he really *were* a Jew viewing himself as the outsider.
This is remarkable, because Henry always had an ambigu-
ous relationship with Jews, envying their culture and
bookishness, repeatedly falling in love with Jewish women,
having many Jewish boon companions, and eventually
even introducing the Star of David into his watercolors as
a sort of talisman. According to Anaïs Nin's report in
Henry and June, Henry claimed to be Jewish on their first
meeting. If this is true, and not some misunderstanding of
Nin's, then it shows the deep nature of Henry's ambivalence.

In Henry's high school world Jews were objects of both
resentment and envy, and Henry was never to lose his
complicated feelings toward them. He regarded them as
outcasts like himself, eternal wanderers—but wanderers
who at least belonged to a community. He envied them. He
wanted to be one. "I too would become a Jew," he says in
Tropic of Cancer. "Why not? I already speak like a Jew.

And I am as ugly as a Jew. Besides, who hates the Jews more than the Jews?"

Passages like these have led to a persistent charge of anti-Semitism, which I find understandable but basically simplistic. The Henry I knew was not an anti-Semite, nor was he a misanthrope, though he railed against the ugliness and pettiness of humanity in all his books and letters. It is Henry's lifelong habit of letting it all hang out that often makes him appear bigoted, if his words and phrases are taken out of context. One can find just as much criticism of Germans (*idiots*, he calls them), of Swedes (*bores*, to Henry), of Viennese (*treacherous*), of Italians (*two-faced*), and any other ethnic group you can name. Henry is not a bigot so much as he is an acid satirist of all human hypocrisies. Hear him on his own people:

> My people were entirely Nordic, which is to say *idiots*. Every wrong idea which has ever been expounded was theirs. Among them was the doctrine of cleanliness, to say nothing of righteousness. They were painfully clean. But inwardly they stank. Never once had they opened the door which leads to the soul; never once did they dream of taking a blind leap into the dark. After dinner the dishes were promptly washed and put in the closet; after the paper was read it was neatly folded and laid away on a shelf; after the clothes were washed they were ironed and folded and then tucked away in the drawers. Everything was for tomorrow, but tomorrow never came.

And yet, for all his acid satire, he remains a cockeyed optimist, always sure there's a pony in the shit pile, always merry and bright and the happiest man alive. This curious paradox in Henry's character makes him as enigmatic to his biographers as he often was to his friends and lovers.

Henry began City College at eighteen, but dropped out after two months. He claimed he didn't like the absurd reading list he was given. Apparently the culprit was Spenser's *Faerie Queene*, about which he said, "If I have to read stuff like that, I give up." He then worked briefly at a series of jobs for which he proved entirely unsuited. Eventually he moved out of his parents' house, only to move in with Pauline Chouteau, the woman he described as "old enough to be my mother." She was, in fact, thirty-two to his eighteen, and Henry had met her while teaching piano to one of her friend's little girls.

Pauline Chouteau, whom Henry called "the widow," was the mother of a consumptive son, George, who was a bit younger than Henry. In moving out of his parents' home and briefly into Pauline's, Henry had recreated a weird and dysfunctional family to rival his own weird and dysfunctional family. But Pauline was kind where his mother was harsh, and this made Henry feel even more obligated to her. He needed her sexually, but felt her age made her unsuitable. In an attempt to shake Pauline's hold on him, in 1913 he fled out West for six months. Like many of his generation he dreamed of becoming a cowboy, or striking it rich in the goldfields of Alaska.

He always claimed to have had a life-changing experience on this trip—listening to Emma Goldman speak in San Diego. But the historical record belies his recollection, for it seems that Emma Goldman was prevented from lecturing by vigilantes on the dates he would have been there. It is probable that Henry's Emma Goldman story was another example of his chronic mythmaking.

He told the story so many times that eventually he seemed really to believe he *had* heard her speak. And surely it is true that she was one of his heroines. Emma Goldman's autobiography, *Living My Life* (1931), mentions a "Henry Miller" only once and that is in connection with the little theater on Third Street, where the Orleneff troupe performed for what Goldman calls "the whole Radical east side." It is quite unlikely that Goldman is referring to the same Henry Miller, since in 1905 he would have been only sixteen and "a Brooklyn boy." Still, Goldman's depictions of radical New York give us a sense of Miller's era and the things that shaped him: anarchism was in the air, the Russian Revolution was in progress, and the world was changing drastically. As an intellectual boy in Brooklyn who worshipped the likes of Emma Goldman, Henry Miller must have realized that he lived (as the Chinese curse says) "in interesting times." Coming to intellectual consciousness in the era of Emma Goldman and the theosophist Madame Elena Blavatsky, Henry retained a fascination with anarchism and transcendental wisdom throughout his entire life.

Henry's cowboy and gold-rush dreams did not materialize. He wound up picking fruit in Chula Vista. Eventually Henry returned to New York and announced to his mother that he was going to marry Pauline. His mother flew into an insane rage and threatened him with a knife. Henry tried to placate her by finally agreeing to help out in the family shop, though he had no interest in tailoring. It was there that he learned not to tailor, but to write.

> I wrote long literary and humorous letters to my friends, which were really disguised essays on everything. Wrote out of boredom, because I was not interested in my father's business. During this period the first thing I remember writing, as a piece of writing in itself, was a long essay on Nietzsche's "Anti-Christ."

Letters remained the chief literary product of Henry's life. His mind seemed most at ease in the epistolary form, where he could range over the wide assortment of things that mattered to him, without worrying about his nemesis—form—but only about content. Had Henry lived in another age, he might never have attempted novels.

During the period of Henry's literary apprenticeship in the tailor shop, America was preparing for war. The United States would not break its isolationism for some three years, but the world was in a state of tumultuous change as the Europeans fought "over there." Women would not get the vote until 1920, but they were already pressing for changes in their status. Feminism was much discussed in Henry's youth, though it was destined to ebb and flow for another half century before women really organized to give themselves direct access to the political process.

For Henry as a young man, the lack of reliable contraception was horrific and ever present. His passionate live-in relationship with Pauline Chouteau was already on the wane when she became pregnant with his child and aborted it. He came home to find a bloody five-month-old fetus in a drawer and Pauline collapsed on the bed. Torn between his moral obligation and an equally pressing desire to escape her, he chose escape—as he would many times in his life. Once again, his solution was to fall in love. He met a pretty young brunette who shared another of his lifelong passions, playing the piano. Pauline's days were numbered.

This newest excuse for escape was Beatrice Sylvas Wickens, a girl from Brooklyn whom, in 1917, Henry was to make his first (legal) wife:

> From about the age of ten I had been playing the piano. Soon after I joined my father I fell in love with a woman who was my piano teacher. I had been teaching the piano myself, to eke out a little spare money from about the age of 17 on. Now I became serious about it and thought I might possibly become a concert pianist. I married the woman and that finished it. From the day we hitched up it was a running battle. In a year or two I dropped the piano for good, which I have regretted ever since.

Henry adored the pursuit and conquest of Beatrice, a good girl of whom his mother could approve, but it was only the war that convinced him to marry. He had fled the tailor shop and Pauline's house to work briefly in Washington before the selective service claimed him. It was his draft notice that cemented his resolve to take Beatrice as his wife.

Once married, he found to his dismay that he was again living with his mother: Beatrice, critical and disapproving, sneered at his ambition to write as much as

Louise had, and like her, tried to get him into the "real world" of work.

But Henry seemed unable to hold a job. Once he married Beatrice he gamely tried an astonishing variety of gigs—from streetcar conductor to indexer to mail-order catalog compiler. Nothing held his interest; he was clearly not meant to be anyone's employee. He would invariably be fired for scribbling or reading philosophy on company time. Growing disillusioned with work and the ball-and-chain of marriage, Henry wrote (in *The Black Cat* magazine at a penny a word):

> the single truth about marriage is that it is a disillusion. . . . It only takes about three days of matrimony to open a man's eyes . . .

It was one of his first pieces to be published.

Since Henry always married as a quick fix, he was always quickly disillusioned. His marriage to Beatrice deteriorated sexually, romantically, musically, financially. The pressure of a baby (his first daughter, Barbara, born in 1919) didn't help, nor did Henry's dalliance with his mother-in-law the previous year.

On a belated and definitely odd honeymoon that Henry and Beatrice took at Beatrice's mother's house in Delaware the year after his marriage to Beatrice, Beatrice's mother supposedly seduced Henry in her bathtub. Mother-in-law and son-in-law made love all summer, practically under the noses of their mates.

Only after Barbara was born did Beatrice confront Henry with this incestuous infidelity. She'd apparently known about it all along. The marital war escalated. Beatrice was determined to make Henry into a proper bread-winning spouse and Henry was just as determined to resist.

The dalliance with Beatrice's mother is another example of Henry's mythmaking. He tells of this affair so vividly in *Sexus* and *The World of Sex* that it appears to be biographical truth. But what if it was only a might-have-been affair, born of Henry's rich imagination? What if it was intended to "explain" his growing estrangement from Beatrice?

People do lie to themselves and to the world in order to live, and writers are inclined to use their books to "explain" the failures of their lives. Beatrice's mother probably turned him on. *Ergo:* a love affair was born. But, like his meeting with Emma Goldman, it may have happened only in his imagination.

In 1920, the Miller family tailor shop finally failed and even though Henry no longer worked there, this was a liberation of sorts. Propelled by Beatrice and fatherhood, Henry took the job at Western Union that was to prove so fateful in his literary career. Even the way he got the job was to prove fateful. At first he couldn't even get hired as a messenger.

The story of his employment at the "Cosmodemonic Telegraphic Company," as Henry tells it in *Tropic of Capricorn,* is the literary analogue of Fritz Lang's *Metropolis* or Charlie Chaplin's *Modern Times*. Here is modern man on the speeded-up assembly line of life—frantic, maddened, moving at a thousand frames per minute.

Henry's account of the world of work in New York circa 1920 (he began at Western Union in 1920 and left in 1924) is truly hallucinogenic:

> The whole system was so rotten, so inhuman, so lousy, so hopelessly corrupt and complicated, that it would have taken a genius to put any sense or order into it, to say nothing of human kindness or consideration. I was up against the whole system of American labor, which is rotten at both ends. . . . I had a bird's eye view of the whole American society. It was like a page out of the telephone book. Alphabetically, numerically, statistically, it made sense. But when you looked at it up close, when you examined the pages separately, or the parts separately, when you examined one lone individual and what constituted him, examined the air he breathed, the life he led, the chances he risked, you saw something so foul and degrading, so low, so miserable, so utterly hopeless and

senseless, that it was worse than looking into a volcano. You could see the whole American life—economically, politically, morally, spiritually, artistically, statistically, pathologically. It looked like a grand chancre on a worn-out cock . . .

The facts were these: Henry had applied for a messenger job and been refused. That got his dander up. He didn't want to be a wage slave, but having been refused a job any slob would get, he was mightily pissed off. He took his pique, his rage, his rhetoric in hand and marched into the management headquarters of the company that would ever after be known as "the Cosmodemonic." It was a historic moment—like Byron arriving in Venice, or Colette following Willy to Paris: literature was about to be born of this encounter between place and person.

. . . [T]hey had rejected *me*, Henry V. Miller, a competent superior individual who has asked for the lowest job in the world. That burned me up. I couldn't get over it.

So, in the morning, he put on his best clothes and "hotfooted it to the main offices of the telegraph company" up to the empyrean aeries of management, high above the tip of Manhattan.

Of course the president was either out of town or too busy to see me, but wouldn't I care to see the vice-president, or his secretary rather. I saw the vice-president's secretary, an intelligent, considerate sort of chap, and I gave him an earful.

Henry had stumbled into shit—and, as the proverb predicts, into good luck. The "Cosmodemonic" happened to be worried about their hiring policies. They saw a weakness in their own system—and Henry's rhetoric convinced them that he was just the man to save them.

Refused as a messenger, he was hired at several times the salary as one of the employment managers and as a sort of company spy. This was his first taste of real power and his first taste of the pleasures of playing Robin Hood—a game that he would continue all the days of his life. For Henry had a Robin Hood–like concept of money. He was as generous as a guest at a potlatch and just as confusing to the average mercantile mind:

> In the beginning I was enthusiastic, despite the damper above and the clamps below. I had ideas and I executed them, whether it pleased the vice-president or not. Every ten days or so I was put on the carpet and lectured for having "too big a heart." I never had any money in my pocket but I used other people's money freely. As long as I was the boss I had credit. I gave money away right and left; I gave my clothes away and my linen, my books, everything that was superfluous. If I had had the power, I would have given the company away to the poor buggers . . .

In this passage from *Tropic of Capricorn*, Henry sounds like an early Christian or a nineteenth-century communal utopian:

> I never saw such an aggregation of misery in my life, and I hope I'll never see it again. Men are poor everywhere— they always have been and they always will be. And beneath the terrible poverty there is a flame, usually so low that it is almost invisible. But it is there and if one has the courage to blow on it it can become a conflagration. I was constantly urged not to be too lenient, not to be too senti- mental, not to be too charitable. Be firm! Be hard! they cautioned me. Fuck that! . . . If I had had real power, instead of being the fifth wheel on a wagon, God knows what I could have accomplished. I could have used the Cosmodemonic Telegraphic Company of North America as a base to bring all humanity to God . . .

Miller's tone is hyperbolic. But he is telling the abso- lute truth here. His truth. And he *would* find a way to use the Cosmodemonic to bring all humanity to God, though he would not find it yet. Still, he was on his way.

His brain boiled and his marriage deteriorated. He was *engaged* at the telegraph company if not entirely happy—and being engaged is the closest thing we mortals know to happiness. To have our energies used—this is the beginning of bliss.

Henry says he never slept during his years at the Cosmodemonic. And that he never stopped whirling like a dervish. Certainly when one reads his account in *Tropic of Capricorn,* one feels an almost Keystone Kops syncopation and a sense of Jazz-Age energy. What turmoil! What madness! Henry was soaking up experience like a sponge. He was "saturated with humanity." He was "waiting for a breathing space" when he could write it all down.

Until then he had been a writer without a subject. He knew he had plenty to say, but how to frame it in human experience? He had the drive to write, but no stories to tell. His life had yet to catch up with his ambitions.

It was at the Cosmodemonic that life presented Henry with his first real subject matter: the messengers themselves.

Every novelist must start with empathy and with a great curiosity about people. In many ways, those qualities are even more important than language—important as language is.

Henry was fascinated with people—with the nuts, the clowns, the destitute refuse of life. At the Cosmodemonic, he saw them all, the misery of humanity:

> . . . the army of men, women and children that had passed through my hands, saw them weeping, begging, beseeching, imploring, cursing, spitting, fuming, threatening.

What got Henry going on his first real attempt at a book, *Clipped Wings,* in 1922, was an offhand remark made by the vice president of the Cosmodemonic that somebody ought to write "a sort of Horatio Alger book about the messengers."

"I'll give you an Horatio Alger book," Henry thought, "just you wait!"

I entered the Western Union as personnel manager in 1920 and left towards the end of 1924. About 1922, I think it was, I wrote my first book, while on a three-week vacation. I forget the title I gave it, but it was about twelve messengers whom I had studied. The ms was over 75,000 words long and I did it in the three weeks and nearly killed myself doing it. (My second wife probably has the manuscript, but I don't know where she is and she probably wouldn't surrender it, or has destroyed it, along with a lot of other manuscripts I wrote while with her—and all the water colors I made then too—and my library of over a thousand books, and my wonderful unabridged dictionary, which I miss more than anything—more than my wife!)

Clipped Wings owes its inspiration to many factors and the Horatio Alger remark is only one of them. Henry had turned thirty in 1921—an age when most would-be writers start to feel the pressure of time at their backs. He had read Knut Hamsun's *Hunger*, which, above all, had inspired him to believe that he could transform his own autobiographical odyssey into fiction. And he was in that desperate shit-or-get-off-the-pot mood which turns a would-be into a writer.

In March 1922, Henry methodically set out to write the book that would prove once and for all he was a writer.

I wrote it straight off, five, seven, sometimes eight thousand words a day. I thought that a man, to be a writer, must do at least five thousand words a day. I thought he must say everything all at once—in one book—and collapse afterwards. I didn't know a thing about writing. I was scared shitless.

Henry's honesty about this first literary effort as he recounts it over a decade later is touching. Anyone who has ever attempted to write will recognize the ring of truth in it:

Perhaps one does it just because nobody believes; perhaps the real secret lies in making people believe. That the book was inadequate, faulty, bad, *terrible*, as they said, was only natural. I was attempting at the start what a man of genius would have undertaken only at the end. I wanted to say the last word at the beginning. It was absurd and pathetic. It was a crushing defeat, but it put iron in my backbone and sulphur in my blood.

Many people have found in Miller's writing just this honesty. He knew what it was to fail, to be desperate, to hit bottom. "Had I succeeded, I would have been a monster," Henry says. "You have to be wiped out as a human being in order to be born again an individual."

The way Henry worked on this first book is telling. It shows the drivenness of the writer in him. More perspiration than inspiration, more pastiche than poetry, but when it was done he knew once and for all that he could sit down and actually finish a book.

Tropic of Capricorn, though written in the thirties, is more understandable if it is seen against the background of 1920s New York. This was the Jazz Age, the age of bobbed hair and bobbed skirts, discarded corsets and the introduction of Trojans. Free love was in the air. Margaret Sanger was on the march. Speakeasies were serving drinks called "Between the Sheets" and modern women were learning to drink, smoke, and make love. Henry had married Beatrice before all hell broke loose and now he was getting restless.

Seven years with Pauline, seven years with Beatrice, and Henry was again ready to shed a skin. It was always a woman who took him to the next level in his life. And the woman was always a muse.

My career began with hitching up with my second wife. I wrote two novels while with her, and God knows how many short stories and articles and essays and crazy undefinable things which belong to my own private Dada

period. The first novel I called "Moloch", the second
"Crazy Cock." The first around 100,000 words; the second
longer still, but completely revised when I got to Paris,
and reduced ultimately to less than 300 pages, and ruined.

Henry's most enduring muse, June Mansfield (called
"Mona" or "Mara" in the novels), was a dark, beautiful
Jewish femme fatale—he called her Rebecca in some love
letters—with a great gift for theatricality and chaos. When
Henry met her in 1923, June was working as a taxi
dancer—a five-cents-a-dance girl—in a Broadway dance
palace, one of those places that proscribed, and yet clearly
invited, "dirty dancing." Henry promptly disregarded the
rules and fell madly in love. He fell as much for June's talk
as for her walk, for her mind as for her body; he was utterly
bewitched and besotted.

His marriage to Beatrice was doomed, but Henry had
found his first great heroine. June gave Henry the courage
to quit his job and start writing in earnest. In 1924 he
divorced Beatrice and married June. Again, Henry was
escaping from responsibility, and the guilt about leaving
his daughter and wife tortured him for years.

Henry's marriage to June was full of passion, madness,
and faithlessness, and perhaps that was why it nourished
Henry's fiction for the rest of his life. For much of the time
June openly carried on passionate affairs with women and
permitted a succession of rich married men to support her
(and therefore Henry). For his part, Henry eventually took
up with Anaïs Nin, who was also for a time madly infatuated with June. Nevertheless, the chaos of this marriage provided Henry with something he never found
again in a wife. What was it? June had the same mythmaking ability as Henry. Neither of them knew the difference between fact and fiction. Being with his psychological
double proved to be powerful magic.

With June, Henry wrote his first real novels, *Crazy
Cock* and *Moloch* (unpublished until 1991 and 1992), ran
a speakeasy in Greenwich Village, painted and exhibited

watercolors, and first toured Europe in 1928, whetting his appetite for the expatriate decade to come.

If Henry's relationship with his mother was the incubation of the writer, the marriage to June was the hatching of the egg. Henry could not make himself into an antihero without simultaneously making June his antiheroine. By the time June and Henry split in 1933, *Tropic of Cancer*, written in Paris, was ready to burst forth into the world.

What happened to Henry when he met June? He fell in love in a way he had never experienced before, and never expected to again. "The whole being was concentrated in the face," he writes of June in *Tropic of Capricorn*. "I could have put it beside me on a pillow at night and made love to it."

And June could *talk*. Crazy, dramatic, a reader, June spoke of characters in books as if they were alive; she identified with them as Henry did. She talked about Strindberg's heroines as she wove the facts and falsehoods of her life into one shimmering web. She was more than just a femme fatale. She was mythic—Venus, Lilith, earth goddess. Henry mentions his favorite word "womb" repeatedly in the hallucinatory last section of *Tropic of Capricorn* where he recounts meeting "Mara" (one of his first names for June).

"She's America on foot, winged and sexed," he says, identifying Mara/June with the continent he must conquer to become himself and an American writer. "Amurrica, fur or no fur, shoes or no shoes. Amurrica C.O.D." And Henry is quaking. "One can wait a whole lifetime for a moment like this," he says.

What is astounding about his introduction of this muse in *Tropic of Capricorn* is his understanding that through June he will find himself, that only through such transforming love can a man's soul, a writer's soul, be born. And whatever Henry's feminist detractors may have said, June is not merely an isolated organ to him. June is a weaver of fantasy and an artist like himself. She also believes in him as an artist. That, primarily is what attracts him.

That—and the craziness.

Has anyone ever written about the propensity writers have to fall in love with crazy people? My own first love was a brilliant schizophrenic. F. Scott Fitzgerald linked his life with Zelda, finding her more compelling than other, calmer, women. Henry married June knowing that she could not distinguish fiction from reality, reality from fiction. She had "no boundaries," we would say today. And, having no boundaries, she opened up his art.

The trancelike state the writer needs to tap the unconscious is one that borderline or psychotic people find comes easily to them. Such people are *like* artists in being able to invent fantasy worlds, but they are unlike artists in not knowing the difference between fantasy and reality. We are caught up in the web of living with their inventions—and disaster ensues.

This was the pattern with June. Her rhapsodic belief in Henry helped him become a writer, but her inability to live in the real world nearly drove him mad. "She put him through the tortures of hell, but he was masochistic enough to enjoy it," said Alfred Perlès in *My Friend, Henry Miller.*

Henry and June commenced a chaotic life that was to take him from Brooklyn to Paris, from would-be to published author. Madly in love with hypnotic June in Jazz-Age New York, Henry clearly believed he could do anything—open a bootleg joint and get rich, write the great American novel and get famous. Did Henry live to write about it, or did he write to survive his life? No writer ever knows for sure.

June and Henry first toured Europe in 1928 (the year that Amelia Earhart flew the Atlantic), making a kind of bohemian grand tour before the Wall Street crash changed the world. Their relationship was tumultuous always—and always she tortured him with other lovers, particularly women. In the Greenwich Village of the twenties it was suddenly chic to be gay—and June was nothing if not a modern woman of fashion.

In 1930, Henry traveled to Europe without June (she

remained in New York to support them with her various liaisons) and embarked upon what was to become the most fecund and joyous period of his life. The early months were desperate and threatened by starvation, but after a year or so of living by his wits, Henry's gift for friendship saved him and he found himself surrounded by "boon companions," lovers, and friends. By 1931 Miller was released (or released himself) to write *Tropic of Cancer*, the book that forever changed the way American literature would be written. The Brooklyn boy was about to be born again in Paris.

CHAPTER 4

Crazy Cock
in the
Land of Fuck

There is only one thing which interests me vitally now, and that is the recording of all that which is omitted in books. . . .

—HENRY MILLER, *TROPIC OF CANCER*

henry Miller went to Paris in March 1930, hoping to find the freedom to become a writer.

He had always felt constricted in New York, hemmed in because it was his native city and his relatives lived there, hemmed in because of his failed marriage and abandoned child, hemmed in because in New York not to produce money is to be a bum, since New York (the most yang city on earth) measures everyone and everything by the ability to generate money. The artist requires idleness—right-brain dream time. And while idleness is possible in New York, guilt-free idleness is not. Busyness and business are the gods of New York, and art needs other gods: ease, idleness, the ability to receive life as it flows.

Henry Miller's early novels *Moloch* and *Crazy Cock*, written in New York, show a man at war with his surroundings, trying to make the uncompromising asphalt bloom. In Paris he frees his unconscious to dream, his voice to sing, and his body to lead him in recording all the things previously left out of books.

The voice Henry Miller discovers in Paris is full of the exuberance of escape:

> It is no accident that propels people like us to Paris. Paris is simply an artificial stage, a revolving stage that permits the spectator to glimpse all phases of the conflict. Of itself Paris initiates no dramas. They are begun elsewhere. Paris is simply an obstetrical instrument that tears the living embryo from the womb and puts it in the incubator. Paris is the cradle of artificial births. Rocking here in the cradle each one slips back into his soil: one dreams back to Berlin, New York, Chicago, Vienna, Minsk. Vienna is never more Vienna than in Paris. Everything is raised to apotheosis. The cradle gives up its babes and new ones take their places. You can read here on the walls where

Zola lived and Balzac and Dante and Strindberg and everybody who ever was anything. Everyone has lived here
some time or other. Nobody *dies* here. . . .

Why does the American artist feel that nobody dies in
Europe when obviously this is not true? What the expatriate artist feels in Europe is a spiritual rebirth: the old self
dies; the new self feels immortal.

I have had this feeling myself, writing in Italy—*my*
chosen place—and I have argued with myself about it,
much as Miller did. Europe for the American writer means
the proximity of culture, a perpetual *wanderjahr*, a place
where one's family skeletons do not rattle in closets (only
other people's family skeletons do that). Even in the new
Europe, one does not have to justify being a writer or artist
with bestsellerdom or a prestigious gallery. The pursuit
itself is honored—and sex, not money, is in the air.

Exile is necessary to many writers who come from
puritanical cultures. Joyce is another example. One cannot
imagine him writing *Ulysses* in Dublin. He had to leave
Ireland to see it clearly. This is partly because of the
simple need to remove oneself from the X-ray eyes of
family in order to discover and utilize one's gifts. But for
the American writer it also means a necessary escape from
bourgeois values, from those people who assume that
"making a living" is the same as making a life. Henry
Miller had to go to Paris to escape the ghost of his father's
tailor shop and the hallucinatory Cosmodemonic Telegraph Company. It was that simple.

Why Paris? Because for Miller's generation and the
generation before his, Paris was midwife to the arts. Henry
Miller had to dream of Paris. Any would-be would.

What was Paris like when he arrived? If you were a
novelist trying to create the Paris of 1930, what details
would you pick to distinguish it from the Paris of today?
The life of a city, as anyone who has tried to recreate
another era knows, dwells in its plumbing and transport,
its food and drink, its cafés and theaters and the hours it
keeps.

I always think of it as the Paris of *petits bleus* or *pneumatiques*—those instant communiqués, the faxes of their time—that crisscrossed the city in vacuum tubes. It was a city of bicycles, of buses, of all-night cafés, of refugees from everywhere in the world. It was a city in which certain districts, Montparnasse, for example, resembled an endless carnival. People who lived in Paris in those years remember its extraordinary Rabelaisian gaiety. Far more than New York, it was a city that never slept, and a stroll on the night boulevard was always an adventure.

Paris in 1930 was utterly hospitable to the artist with no money.

Here is Georges Belmont (one of Henry's French translators and later mine) speaking about the Montparnasse of 1930:

> In Montparnasse, particularly, you had plenty of those people who had absolutely no money, like Henry, and you could sit at a table, have a café crème, and stay there for the whole evening. Nobody would throw you out. Even at five, they wouldn't expel you but people would go finally because they were exhausted. At La Coupole, for instance, there was dancing upstairs with jazz and downstairs there were different corners. There was the chess corner, the writers' and painters' corner. You could see Chagall, and Foujita with his famous lover, Kiki de Montparnasse—a remarkable woman. I met her later when she was Robert Desnos's mistress. She was very beautiful, small, and had a marvelous face, round with big eyes, a humorous face. From time to time I saw Picasso in La Coupole and plenty of others. . . . People met and spent hours together, discussing ideas.

It is easy to see why this Paris was so much more congenial to Henry than the New York he had fled—a New York dominated by the crash of 1929, and the decade of mad optimism about business that had preceded it. Here Henry's inability to keep a job, about which he always had guilt feelings, was the precursor of art. Henry was enough of his mother's son to wonder whether he was a genius or a ne'er-do-well. In Paris, at least, that question was settled.

Even Georges Belmont (known in those days as Pelorson), a good boy from the Ecole Normale Superiéure, fled both the Sorbonne and the intellectual life and went instead to Montparnasse.

> Montparnasse got particularly interesting late. It was after eleven that the *real* things began. You had the kind of people who didn't care if they got up at twelve—who had absolutely no positive reason to get up at six o'clock or seven o'clock to go to work. And it's very difficult to capture this—there was *life*, there was *movement*, all the time.

Despite the economic collapse, there were plenty of Americans in Paris "and the Americans were still jolly," according to Georges. They continued to act as if they were on holiday. "They were important because they still had money and they liked to spend it."

Paris was also the center of sin. Opposite La Coupole was the Sélect, a gathering place for homosexuals of both sexes. And there was a kind of tolerance there still unknown in New York. In fact it was the sort of place where one was embarrassed to be straight. Again, in Georges's description:

> It was a kind of zoo. Lots of people didn't *dare* enter the place because they didn't feel at ease. I had a very good homosexual friend whom I had known at school, so I was accepted. My friend lived with one of the queens of the lesbians in Paris—and they were in love. They never *made* love—but they were in love and they were both terribly jealous. Once I saw a marriage there. Two men got married. One was dressed in a long, white gown, a crown of orange flowers, a veil, everything. They exchanged rings, received a religious blessing from a pseudo-priest. That was the essence of Montparnasse in those days.

"Montparnasse in those days." A different sense of time. The contrast between the New York of *Crazy Cock* and *Moloch* and the Paris of *Tropic of Cancer* is just this. And it is this different sense of time that creates freedom. Paris breathes freedom into Henry and Henry responds by breathing it into his prose.

I think few of us in the world of the nineties are aware of how much we have lost now that such leisure has gone. Most of us are imprisoned in our own schedules, our days broken into half-hour fragments like the rulings in our Filofaxes. It is almost as if our notebooks rule us, rather than us ruling them. The life of the cafés, of talk, of walk, of leisure, of *dolce far niente* seems an indulgence to us, as does reading, dreaming, sleeping. There are "success-ful" people in our world who boast of how little sleep they get, who compete at being busy. But the truth is that all creativity takes idleness; when we lose it, we lose our ability to invent the next phase of problem-solving for the human race.

There was a vast difference between prewar and post-war days in Paris. World War I had turned Europe upside down and left an unparalleled despair in the writers and intellectuals who flocked to Paris in its wake. Inner and outer weather had changed—as had fashions. Bowler hats, celluloid collars, gas lamps, and horses had disappeared. Women had finally been liberated from whalebone and now wore comfortable clothes—what would later be called a unisex look. The Jazz Age had liberated both bodies and minds.

Now, suddenly, the boom atmosphere of twenties' Paris was gone, and with it the superfluity of parasites (designers, art dealers, courtesans) who live on the rever-berations of boom.

The change between 1928 and 1930 was abrupt—sud-denly hard times arrived. But, as the metamorphosis from the fat 1980s to the lean 1990s in our own era has shown us, this can happen breathlessly fast.

Paris in 1930 was a city on the edge of an abyss. There

would soon be thirty million unemployed in the world (four million in Germany alone) and by 1933 the planet would have a new would-be master in Adolf Hitler. But for Henry, who had been poor and dishonored in America, poverty with honor in Paris felt like release. Freedom breathes through the prose of *Tropic of Cancer*—the story of a man learning how to breathe. Or, as he describes it in one of his remarkable letters to his friend Emil Schnellock, "The Paris book: first person, uncensored, formless—fuck everything!"

Henry found his exuberant new voice, the voice of *Tropic of Cancer*, primarily in his letters to Emil Schnellock, his painter pal from his old Brooklyn neighborhood who lent him the ten dollars that was in his pocket when he sailed to Europe in 1930. Henry's *Letters to Emil* (collected and edited in 1989 by George Wickes) constitute an amazing record of how a writer discovers his sound. The transition from the tortured prose of the two fledgling books to the explosive simplicity of *Tropic of Cancer* is all there. We hear the explosion. We see the contrail streak across the sky.

Henry Miller's writing odyssey is an object lesson for anyone who wants to learn to be a writer. How do you go from self-consciousness to unself-consciousness? How do you come to sound on paper as natural as you sound in speech? *Crazy Cock* and *Moloch* will show you the first parts of a journey. *Tropic of Cancer* is the destination.

In between come *Letters to Emil*. These letters are crucial because they are written to someone who accepts Henry completely and with whom he can be wholly himself. In them, he tests the voice that will revolutionize the world in *Tropic of Cancer*. It is the voice of the New York writer revolting against New York. And it is the voice of the weary *pícaro*—weary of flopping from pillar to post:

> Two years of vagabondage has taken a lot out of me. Given me a lot, too, but I need a little peace now, a little security in which to work. In fact, I ought to stop living for a long while and just work. I'm sick of gathering experiences.

There'll be a lot to tell when I get back to New York. Enough for many a wintry night. But immediately I think of N.Y. I get frightened. I hate the thought of seeing that grim skyline, the crowds, the sad Jewish faces, the automats, the dollars so hard to get, the swell cars, the beautiful clothes, the efficient businessmen, the doll faces, the cheap movies, the hullabaloo, the grind, the noise, the dirt, the vacuity and sterility, the death of everything sensitive . . .

Emil gave Henry the strength to embrace his freedom:

I will explode in the Paris book. The hell with form, style, expression and all those pseudo-paramount things which beguile the critics. I want to get myself across this time— and direct as a knife-thrust.

Emil freed Henry by being the perfect audience:

You see, Emil, this book (which I call, tentatively, "The Last Book") is like that beautiful big valise of yours, of stout leather, that expands or collapses, that you throw things into pell-mell regardless of whether they are starched or pressed or stained or not stained. . . . I've gotten over the idea of writing literature, if you can understand what I mean by that. . . . Almost from the day I arrived I sensed something different in the air, in my air. . . . New York always gave me a sinking feeling when I came back. . . . Paris is smiling—she welcomes you without distinction of race, creed or color. Her vegetables look brighter, her women gayer, her workers more industrious, her cops more intelligent. She is aged but not careworn. The roofs are so wonderful—all those fucking chimney pots, the black of them, the slanting studio windows, the walls with their traces of rooms which no longer exist, the bridges, each one like a poem. . . . Well, it's like my home now, though I remain a foreigner and always will be. But whenever I make a journey, it will always be Paris that I want to think of coming back to—not New York. New

York belongs in a finished past, a past like some evil dream. . . .

Brassaï also records the transformation that came over Miller in Paris: "In France, his brow smoothed out, he became happy, smiling. An irrepressible optimism irradiated his whole being."

This optimism, among other things, creates the unique sound of *Tropic of Cancer:*

> To sing you must first open your mouth. You must have a pair of lungs, and a little knowledge of music. It is not necessary to have an accordion, or a guitar. The essential thing is to *want* to sing. This then is a song. I am singing.

Compare this open, direct song to the reader with the fustiness of *Crazy Cock,* which Miller began in New York in the late twenties as *Lovely Lesbians.* The voice of Miller in *Crazy Cock* is third person, stilted, dusty. Henry appears to be ventriloquising a Literary Voice—with a capital *L.*

The writer who invented first person, present tense exuberance for the twentieth century is writing in the third person! And it doesn't suit him. It makes him use words like "wondrous," "totteringly," "blabberingly," and "abashed." Here is Henry the Victorian, the reader of Marie Corelli, writing in a pastiche of Victorian romance and Dreiserian realism.

But *Crazy Cock* is fascinating for what it tells us about Henry's literary roots. Henry Miller was born heir to the Victorian age—even in the seventies, when I knew him, he used to rave to me about Marie Corelli—and *Crazy Cock* shows us what Henry had to overcome to find his writer's voice:

> More wondrous than ever was her beauty now. Like a mask long withheld. Mask or mask of a mask? mask or prism? Protective or deflective? Fragments of questions racing through his mind whilst he arranged harmoniously the disharmony of her being. . . .

Suddenly he saw that she was looking at him, peering at him from behind the mask. And all the riddles that had perplexed and tormented him fell away. A rapport such as the living establish with the dying. Like a queen advancing to her throne she approached. He rose totteringly, his limbs quaking. In his heart there was a tumult. A wave of gratitude, and abasement, engulfed him. A desire seized him to fling himself on his knees, to thank her blabberingly for deigning to notice him.

Blabberingly indeed.

That blabbering voice was the one Henry brought to Paris. What he came home with was the sound of his native speech rediscovered.

How did this transformation occur? Can we trace the steps?

When Henry first arrived in Europe in February 1930, on the *American Banker*, he debarked in London. By mutual consent, he had left June, who had promised to send him money, in New York. He endured a grim, dreary time in London, staying in the cheapest digs he could find, walking the streets, and exploring the British Museum. He caught the boat train for Paris the moment some cash arrived from June at American Express.

As he said to Emil, he was at the time "thirty-eight, poor and unknown." He had the carbons of *Moloch* and *Crazy Cock* with him; clearly he had still not given up hope on these early hopeless works. He had better clothes than he'd ever need in Bohemian Paris—clothes from his father, the failed master tailor—which in time he would have no choice but to sell. And he was cut off from friends and family for the first time in his middle-aged but still unfledged life.

He stayed in a series of cheap Left Bank hotels, marked up his maps of Paris, and walked the streets, looking for literary echoes. His final destination was always the American Express office at 11 rue Scribe, and always there was the desperate hope of news and money from June. Paris was feeding Henry's heart, but not his stomach. As March turned to April, he had received no more cash from June—only promises. He was on the point of utter destitution when Alfred Perlès, an Austrian writer who worked at the *Chicago Tribune* (and whom he had met in Paris in 1928 with June and the "lovely lesbian" Jean Kronski) turned up. Perlès was to become Henry's master of revels. He immediately invited Henry to share his modest room for a time, and began to teach him how to live by his wits. Perlès—or Fred or Alf or Joey as Henry called him—was to be an important friend for the rest of Henry's life, but he was never as important as during those early days when Henry was destitute in a new country, lonely for June yet also glad to be rid of her.

"Only get desperate enough and everything will turn out well" was Henry's Paris mantra. And he proved it true. *Tropic of Cancer* could not be written until Henry let go of literature, of New York, of all his ties to the tailor shop and his mother. It was to be "the last book," a book by "the last man on earth," a book to end all books. And it still feels that way.

Henry lived with Perlès in various cheap hotels, even slept in cinemas at times. He ran into an Indian messenger from the Cosmodemonic who gave him a job as houseman, which became a funny episode in *Cancer*. He hocked his beautifully tailored suits, the last vestiges of his patrimony; he cadged money and drinks from other expatriates. Finally, when June arrived on the *Majestic* in September 1930, Henry was so overwrought that he missed meeting her boat train. They went back to the Hôtel de Paris (where they had stayed in 1928) and for a short time were blissfully reunited. June promised everything, as usual, but it soon became obvious that she had really come with the hope of landing a movie job. Henry had written to her about meeting a woman director, Germaine Dulac, who might employ her, and June, ever the spinner of daydreams, had taken Henry's promises literally. When the dreams did not materialize, Henry and June began to battle hideously again. In a month or so, June sailed back to New York on borrowed money. Henry very nearly went with her, but once that impulse passed, he felt freed by her departure.

He began to work at his French, which, to the end, he spoke with a heavy Brooklyn accent. When the weather got wretched in Paris in November, he thought again of going home, but just couldn't raise the money. He was forced to stay on, to cultivate his friends, his notebooks, his letters—and eventually his luck began to change.

A pivotal event late in 1930 was his meeting with Richard Osborn, who would eventually be his link to Anaïs Nin. Osborn was an upper-class WASP Yale graduate from Connecticut who wanted to be a writer. Generous, crazy, intent on having a good time, Osborn was employed as a lawyer at the Paris office of the National City Bank, where Hugh Guiler, Anaïs Nin's husband, was also employed, supporting his wife's elegant bohemian life in Louviciennes. Dick Osborn, who loved bohemians and wanted to be one, impulsively invited Henry to live with him at 2 rue Auguste-Bartholdi, a smallish, pretty street of apartments and little shops not far from the Tour Eiffel and the Champs de Mars. Rue Auguste-Bartholdi still has an authentic turn-of-the-century bar on the corner and looks as it must have done in the thirties. Henry was to find his first happiness in Paris there, on a street named for the creator of the Statue of Liberty!

Given a free place to live, fancier than anything Perlès could offer, Henry could work at ease and walk the streets for inspiration. He went on compulsively reworking the already overworked *Crazy Cock*, but he also began to write some pieces in his newfound voice. The story "Mademoiselle Claude" dates from this time, and it signals the birth of the new Henry Miller. "If Mlle Claude is a whore, then what name shall I find for the other women I know?" he asks. The direct first-person voice is beginning to assert itself.

By the time Henry had been in Paris a year, he was surrounded by friends such as Dick Osborn, Alfred Perlès, and Wambly Bald (who wrote a column, *La Vie Bohème*, for the *Chicago Tribune* and gave Henry his first newspaper publicity). Perlès got Henry work writing articles for the *Tribune,* which gave him some much-needed confidence. He began filling the wall above his desk with huge sprawling charts and diagrams of the unwritten books that teemed in his brain. He was seething with inspiration.

On the last day of 1930, Henry had a near collision with mortality, which must have convinced him of divine protection. His taxi flipped over, but he walked away totally unharmed. Divine protection was to be abundant in the next year of his life—1931 was to prove for Henry what 1819 was for Keats: the *annus mirabilis.*

It was in 1931 that Henry began to find intellectual peers: Walter Lowenfels, the poet and critic, as bitter a satirist of America as Henry; and Michael Fraenkel, a publisher, philosopher, and writer. Fraenkel, the inspiration for Boris in *Tropic of Cancer,* believed that all current civilization was a celebration of the power of death. In order to combat this death force, a writer had to work anonymously, creating for the sake of creativity, not for the sake of reputation. Michael Fraenkel had collaborated with Walter Lowenfels on a pamphlet called "Anonymous: The Need for Anonymity," which expounded this theory, and Henry was very much under its influence for a time.

It is fascinating to me that Henry began *Tropic of Cancer* thinking he would publish the book anonymously. Anonymity is a great liberator—even if one later changes one's mind and acknowledges the book. I have often tricked myself into writing with candor by promising myself either not to publish or to publish under a pseudonym. Freed of modesty, freed of self-judgment, one can write with maximum passion.

"The cancer of time is eating us away," Henry declares at the beginning of *Tropic of Cancer.*

> Our heroes have killed themselves, or are killing themselves. The hero, then, is not Time, but Timelessness. We must get in step, a lock step, toward the prison of death. There is no escape. The weather will not change.

Clearly the passionate life force of *Tropic of Cancer* was partly provoked into being by Henry's desire to escape the prison of death. And anonymity was for a time his key.

During this critical period in Henry's writing life, June was mainly in New York. This was lucky, because Henry was still obsessed with her and she tended to be a difficult muse. During the early stages of the composition of both *Moloch* and *Crazy Cock*, she had demanded of Henry countless revisions to make herself look good. Of course no writer can function that way. With June gone, Henry was at last free to write.

Anaïs Nin came to supply Henry with the acceptance he needed. She became a beneficent mother-surrogate and perhaps his greatest love. Nin's passionate belief in Henry (not to mention her financial support) made this creative blossoming possible. Her journals, particularly the unexpurgated versions of their liaison, *Henry and June* and *Incest*, describe this period vividly and describe Henry better than he describes himself. Henry's own books about these Paris years—*Tropic of Cancer, Black Spring,* and *Quiet Days in Clichy*—deliberately omit his romance with the married Nin (and Nin's infatuation with June) and therefore only tell one side of what must have been one of the most extraordinary triangles in literary history.

Henry kept his promise to Anaïs Nin: he would not jeopardize her marriage in print. For a writer whose stock-in-trade was his own odyssey, this was a powerful renunciation and one that demonstrates how much Nin meant to him. Even years later, when their relationship turned hostile, he did not go back on his word.

Because of Henry's loyalty, we hear of the romance only from Anaïs's own pen:

> I've met Henry Miller.
>
> He came to lunch with Richard Osborn, a lawyer I had to consult for my D.H. Lawrence book.
>
> When he first stepped out of the car and walked towards the door where I stood waiting, I saw a man I

liked. In his writing he is flamboyant, virile, animal, magnificent. He's a man whom life makes drunk, I thought. He is like me.

Anaïs Nin immediately captures the essence of Henry, the exuberant life force coupled with the dreamy pensiveness:

In the middle of lunch, when we were seriously discussing books, and Richard had sailed off on a long tirade, Henry began to laugh. He said, "I'm not laughing at you, Richard, but I just can't help myself. I don't care a bit, not a bit who's right. I'm too happy. I'm just so happy right this moment with all the colors around me, the wine, the whole moment is so wonderful, so wonderful." He was laughing almost to tears. He was drunk. I was drunk, too, quite. I felt warm and dizzy and happy.

We talked for hours. Henry said the truest and deepest things, and he has a way of saying "hmmmm" while trailing off on his own introspective journey.

Henry is intrigued and attracted. He wonders if maybe she is "the kind of woman who doesn't hurt a man"— which indicates how scarred June had left him. Anaïs reports, in *Henry and June*, liking "his fierceness," but rejects "his desire, pointing at me . . . like a sword" because, as she says, "for me it can't be without love."

A few days later she discovers "that he knows the technique of kissing better than anyone I've met," and her "curiosity for sensuality is stirred." Yet when he offers his penis to her mouth, she is stricken: "I get up as if struck by a whip." She claims inexperience, which he immediately disputes. On some level he knows that he is to play Mellors to her Lady Chatterley. After all, they are both lovers of Lawrence and know only too well the roles they will be assigned by fate.

Within days, her husband, Hugo is worried: "You fall in love with people's minds. I'm going to lose you to Henry."

Henry's "animal feeling for life" attracts Anaïs even as she rationalizes that Hugo is "finer than any man I know." She presents Henry with little gifts—books, money, railway tickets. She longs to give him a home and an income, so he can write.

Bored with Hugo's tepid sexuality, she is intrigued with animal Henry. He seems the initiator into the life force. Then, all at once, June Mansfield Miller arrives, becoming at once Anaïs's rival, inamorata, and muse.

Anaïs captured June more vividly than Henry ever did, for Henry's writing, even at its best, is only ever about Henry. The complete solipsist cannot describe another person. To Anaïs, June is "the most beautiful woman on earth." She has "a startlingly white face, burning eyes."

> Her beauty drowned me. As I sat in front of her, I felt that I would do anything mad for her, anything she asked of me. Henry faded.

Anaïs Nin falls in love with June "like a man." She knows that Henry has no choice but to be besotted by her. Now Nin is besotted too. *Henry and June* is a remarkable document because of the vividness of its description of a woman's emotions while involved in a passionate love triangle:

> June. At night I dreamed of her, as if she were very small, very frail, and I loved her. I loved a smallness which had appeared to me in her talk: the disproportionate pride, a hurt pride. She lacks the core of sureness, she craves admiration insatiably. She lives on reflections of herself in others' eyes. She does not dare to be herself. There is no June Mansfield. She knows it. The more she is loved, the more she knows it. . . .
>
> A startlingly white face retreating into the darkness of the garden. She poses for me as she leaves. I want to run out and kiss her fantastic beauty, kiss it and say, "You carry away with you a reflection of me, a part of me. I dreamed you, I wished for your existence. You will always

be part of my life. If I love you, it must be because we have shared at some time the same imaginings, the same madness, the same stage.

Anaïs, June, and Henry begin a strange three-way flirtation, which is also a flirtation with literature—a ménage à trois of three married lovers who lard their relationship with lies. Every betrayal is forgiven if it provokes art, and Anaïs is the most artful dissimulator of all. Even in her notebooks, she seems to be dramatising herself for posterity. And yet she tells the story of a woman's sexuality more honestly than any writer who ever lived.

Anaïs practiced a sexual freedom which makes that of our own age seem timid. Open to her own bisexuality, adventurous in her open marriage, Anaïs presents herself as the true *picara* of sex despite—or perhaps because of—her comfortable alliance with her husband, Hugh Guiler. She admits that she is Donna Giovanna, desperate to seduce and abandon men, to wreak her revenge on a father who abandoned her. Henry was far more at home, whatever his reputation, with serial monogamy in the American fashion.

Henry's dependency on Anaïs appears to have been far greater than hers on him. For all his fictional boasting of his sexual exploits, his other partners appear to have been casual, sometimes paid, while she was deeply involved with a variety of men, including her husband and her two psychiatrists, René Allendy and Otto Rank. She was also, for a time, incestuously involved with her own father, a period she describes with great vividness in *Incest*. Nowhere before, to my knowledge, has a woman written so candidly of breaking the final oedipal taboo.

Before reading this document, I thought that Anaïs had what might be called the European aristocratic view of sex: now her sexual adventures seem utterly transformed. She was acting out her seduction and abandonment by a powerful, erotic father. And she lived what most women cannot even admit they dream. For all their self-boosting, her unexpurgated diaries constitute one of the landmarks in twentieth-century literature. Both as literary history and as the history of female sexuality, the diaries fulfill Henry's predictions that they would eventually be seen as one of the great works of our age. Perhaps unwittingly they show how much freer a woman's sexuality can be than a man's. While Henry and Hugo pined for Anaïs and wished to possess her, Anaïs was capable of juggling several men with minimal guilt.

In *Henry and June,* she chronicles the immense power June had over Henry. She understood his masochism and how it fired his work:

> And what does she do to Henry? She humiliates him, she starves him, she breaks his health, she torments him—and he thrives; he writes his book.

His book. There is more to say about his book. Why was it such an explosion? Why did it change the world?

Early in *Tropic of Cancer,* Henry gives us the key, the secret of its revolutionary charge:

> There is only one thing which interests me vitally now, and that is the recording of all that which is omitted in books. Nobody, so far as I can see, is making use of those elements in the air which give direction and motivation to our lives. Only the killers seem to be extracting from life some satisfactory measure of what they are putting into it. The age demands violence, but we are getting only abortive explosions. Revolutions are nipped in the bud, or else succeed too quickly. Passion is quickly exhausted. Men fall back on ideas, *comme d'habitude.* Nothing is proposed that can last more than twenty-four hours. We are living a million lives in the space of a generation . . .

Remember where the world was in 1931 and 1932, when Henry was writing this "last book." The Great Depression was spreading through America and Europe. The

Great War had left a generation of corpses and *mutilés*. Those who were not mutilated in body were mutilated in spirit or in pocketbook. National income had dropped 33 percent in the U.S. between 1929 and 1931. "Brother, can you spare a dime?" was on the airwaves, and the suicide rate was soaring as the employment rate was plummeting. For Henry, down but not out in Paris, the world was just now experiencing what he had been experiencing all along. Art would not suffice. What was needed was something stronger: a revolution in consciousness, the eternal truth that is omitted from books.

What was the nature of this truth? And why did Henry have to relate his picaresque journey through the Paris underworld to illuminate it? Because he had to go to the end of the night in order to explode with the truth he discovered there: that all freedom comes only with total surrender. Henry discovers in Paris that it is only when man has died in the world that he can begin to live in the spirit. When his back is to the wall, he bursts free of repression. At the bottom, he begins his ascent.

Henry's greatest philosophic insight follows that amusing episode in *Tropic of Cancer* in which he guides a young Hindu (a disciple of Gandhi) to a Paris brothel. The Hindu commits a terrible gaffe. He takes a shit in a bidet, mortifying himself before the madame and all her girls. The Hindu's mortification becomes Henry's epiphany. He remembers that

> For weeks and months, for years, in fact, all my life I had been looking forward to something happening, some extrinsic event that would alter my life, and now suddenly, inspired by the absolute hopelessness of everything, I felt relieved, felt as though a great burden had been lifted from my shoulders.

What burden is this? The burden of hope:

> Somehow the realization that nothing was to be hoped for had a salutary effect upon me. . . . At dawn I parted

company with the young Hindu, after touching him for a few francs, enough for a room. Walking toward Montparnasse I decided to let myself drift with the tide, to make not the least resistance to fate, no matter in what form it presented itself.

Once Henry gives up hope, once he frees himself from expectation, he can see the truth:

Nothing that had happened to me thus far had been sufficient to destroy me; nothing had been destroyed except my illusions. I myself was intact. The world was intact. Tomorrow there might be a revolution, a plague, an earthquake; tomorrow there might not be left a single soul to whom one could turn for sympathy, for aid, for faith. It seemed to me that the great calamity had already manifested itself, that I could be no more truly alone than at this very moment. I made up my mind that I would hold on to nothing, that I would expect nothing, that henceforth I would live as an animal, a beast of prey, a rover, a plunderer. Even if war were declared, and it were my lot to go, I would grab the bayonet and plunge it, plunge it up to the hilt. And if rape were the order of the day then rape I would, and with a vengeance. At this very moment, in the quiet dawn of a new day, was not the earth giddy with crime and distress? Had one single element of man's nature been altered, vitally, fundamentally altered, by the incessant march of history? By what he calls the better part of his nature, man has been betrayed, that is all. At the extreme limits of his spiritual being man finds himself again naked as a savage. When he finds God, as it were, he has been picked clean: he is a skeleton. One must burrow into life again in order to put on flesh. The word must become flesh; the soul thirsts. On whatever crumb my eye fastens, I will pounce and devour. If to live is the paramount thing, then I will live, even if I must become a cannibal. Heretofore I have been trying to save my precious hide, trying to preserve the few pieces of meat that hid my bones. I am done with that. I have reached the limits of endurance. My back is to the wall; I can retreat no further. As far as history goes I am dead. If there is something beyond I shall have to bounce back. I have found God, but he is insufficient. I am only spiritually dead. Physically I am alive. Morally I am free. The world which I have departed is a menagerie. The dawn is breaking on a new world, a jungle world in which the lean spirits roam with sharp claws. If I am a hyena I am a lean and hungry one: I go forth to fatten myself.

In *Tropic of Cancer*, Henry is writing of the life that comes after one has been declared dead, of the illumination that comes in the darkness of the pit, of the abundance that comes in the midst of deprivation. A man must go to the bottom and become a *clochard* to find the truth about life and death. Henry's message is not so different from Dante's or, for that matter, from that of any shamanic vision quest. Semistarvation in Paris equals forty days in the desert; the free meal is his manna; cunt is his illumination; God is dead; Miller is alive.

If *Tropic of Cancer* is Miller's *Inferno*, then *Capricorn* is his *Purgatorio* and *The Colossus of Maroussi* is his *Paradiso*. In an age when the average man has been reduced to a beggar-vagabond for his idiotic belief in Progress, Miller shows the way for the average man to endure his life, even to triumph over it.

The incessant march of history has come to this: starvation and the collective back to the wall. And what does Henry find? That if to live is the paramount thing, then he will live, even as a cannibal. And the cannibal finds God by feeding on his fellow man—and woman.

A rough message for rough times: *what is left out of books*. With your back to the wall, you either live or die. Perhaps the reason Henry loved the Paris episodes in *Fear of Flying* was because Isadora found there what Henry himself had found: totally humiliated, she found herself. She hit bottom and became free.

Why is hitting bottom necessary? Ask any recovering alcoholic. Only at the absolute bottom can illumination be found. Only at the bottom can you decide whether to live or die. Miller had been half alive for his first forty years. Now he decided to go whole hog. He decided to live.

It was no accident that he turned forty in that miraculous year he wrote *Tropic of Cancer*. It is only at forty that *homo adulescens*—the late-maturing man of the modern world—finally comes to grips with the live-or-die imperative that mortality imposes on all of us. Miller's eternal boyishness—a sort of sexual Peter Pan in Paris—has irritated many who are, in truth, as boyish as he. Readers tend either to passionately identify or passionately denounce. Either they are inspired by his surrender and the freedom it brings or they feel compelled to denounce it.

There is a curious parallel between Henry Miller's Paris hegira (and his eventual surrender) and the male initiatory ritual Robert Bly describes in *Iron John: A Book About Men*. To become his own man, Bly's uninitiated boy must go away on the shoulders of the wild man—a shaman covered in animal skins, a Robin Hood-Pan figure, an initiator into male mysteries—and partake of the secrets of the Wild Wood. There, men initiate boys into manhood. There, boys separate from their mothers so that they can eventually love them again—but differently, as grown men, not as children. There, boys gain the confidence, through the detachment from Mother, to become mature.

Henry's Paris was just such a descent into the wood of the wild man. It was his initiation, his break from Louise and June, his search for (and bonding with) wild men (Perlès, Frankel, Bald) who would help him sever the tie to his powerful mother and to overcome the meekness of his drunken father.

In Paris, Henry finally grew up. That was how he was able to find the voice of *Tropic of Cancer*. Rough, hairy, the voice of the wild man, *Tropic of Cancer* delights even as it disgusts. It is strong meat. It is like drinking sperm.

At night when I look at Boris' goatee lying on the pillow I get hysterical. O Tania, where now is that warm cunt of yours, those fat, heavy garters, those soft, bulging thighs? There is a bone in my prick six inches long. I will ream out every wrinkle in your cunt, Tania, big with seed. I will send you home to your Sylvester with an ache in your belly and your womb turned inside out. Your Sylvester! Yes, he knows how to build a fire, but I know how to inflame a cunt. I shoot hot bolts into you, Tania, I make your ovaries incandescent. Your Sylvester is a little jealous now? He feels something, does he? He feels the remnants of my big prick. I have set the shores a little wider, I have ironed out the wrinkles. After me you can take on stallions, bulls, rams, drakes, St. Bernards. You can stuff toads, bats, lizards up your rectum. You can shit arpeggios if you like, or string a zither across your navel. I am fucking you, Tania, so that you'll stay fucked. And if you are afraid of being fucked publicly I will fuck you privately. I will tear off a few hairs from your cunt and paste them on Boris' chin. I will bite into your clitoris and spit out two franc pieces. . . .

After passages as rough as this, Henry moves into a surreal flow of images:

Indigo sky swept clear of fleecy clouds, gaunt trees infinitely extended, their black boughs gesticulating like a sleepwalker. Somber, spectral trees, their trunks pale as cigar ash. A silence supreme and altogether European. Shutters drawn, shops barred. A red glow here and there to mark a tryst. Brusque the façades, almost forbidding; immaculate except for the splotches of shadow cast by the trees. Passing by the Orangerie I am reminded of another Paris, the Paris of Maugham, of Gauguin, Paris of George Moore. I think of that terrible Spaniard who was then startling the world with his acrobatic leaps from style to style. I think of Spengler and his terrible pronunciamentos, and I wonder if style, style in the grand manner, is done for. I say that my mind is occupied with these thoughts, but it is not true; it is only later, after I have crossed the Seine, after I have put behind me the carnival of lights, that I allow my mind to play with these ideas. For the moment I can think of nothing—except that I am a sentient being stabbed by the miracle of these waters that reflect a forgotten world. All along the banks the trees lean heavily over the tarnished mirror; when the wind rises and fills them with a rustling murmur they will shed a few tears and shiver as the water swirls by. I am suffocated by it. No one to whom I can communicate even a fraction of my feelings. . . .

And then, without even a beat, Henry goes from surreal poetry back to cunts:

> The trouble with Irène is that she has a valise instead of a cunt. She wants fat letters to shove in her valise. Immense, *avec des choses inouïes*. Llona now, she had a cunt. I know because she sent us some hairs from down below. Llona—a wild ass snuffing pleasure out of the wind. On every high hill she played the harlot—and sometimes in telephone booths and toilets. She bought a bed for King Carol and a shaving mug with his initials on it. She lay in Tottenham Court Road with her dress pulled up and fingered herself. She used candles, Roman candles, and door knobs. Not a prick in the land big enough for her . . . *not one.* Men went inside her and curled up. She wanted extension pricks, self-exploding rockets, hot boiling oil made of wax and creosote. She would cut off your prick and keep it inside her forever, if you gave her permission. One cunt out of a million, Llona! A laboratory cunt and no litmus paper that could take her color. She was a liar, too, this Llona. She never bought a bed for her King Carol. She crowned him with a whisky bottle and her tongue was full of lice and tomorrows. Poor Carol, he could only curl up inside her and die. She drew a breath and he fell out—like a dead clam.

First flesh, then vision, then flesh again. That is man's life as Henry sees it.

There is another important element in *Tropic of Can-*

cer that is always overlooked by its humorless critics—its wild humor. People have gazed so intently at the four-letter words that they have missed the laughs. And they have also missed the source of this humor: the outsideness of the outsider, the laserlike vision of the man or woman who has seen the world and knows that all it amounts to is two lumps of shit in a bidet.

In *Crazy Cock* and *Moloch*, Miller was still buying into literary myth. In *Tropic of Cancer*, he freed himself to see the absurdity of the world stripped of all myth and of all illusion. This totally irreverent angle of vision allows Henry to see things that nobody else would see until decades later.

Russia, for example, in the bloom of communism, he recognizes is just like America in the bloom of capitalism:

> They don't want to see sad faces in Russia; they want you to be cheerful, enthusiastic, light-hearted, optimistic. It sounded very much like America to me. I wasn't born with this kind of enthusiasm.

India, he understands, is threatened not by England, but by America:

> India's enemy is not England, but America. India's enemy is the time spirit, the hand which cannot be turned back. Nothing will avail to offset this virus which is poisoning the whole world. America is the very incarnation of doom. She will drag the whole world down to the bottomless pit.

America wants mindless enthusiasm; so does Russia; India, with her great spiritual culture, is about to be dragged into this fake ideal of progress which ends only in the slaughter of wars to end all wars.

Henry rejected belief in progress, belief in war, belief in meliorism. He opened himself to a more primal enthusiasm, an enthusiasm for admitting the light, since "only those who can admit the light into their gizzards can translate what is there in the heart."

All of *Tropic of Cancer* is a digression against death. The artists Miller admires—Matisse, Proust—are those in whom he also sees a great antideath spirit.

> In every poem by Matisse there is the history of a particle of human flesh which refused the consummation of death. The whole run of flesh, from hair to nails, expresses the miracle of breathing, as if the inner eye, in its thirst for a greater reality, had converted the pores of the flesh into hungry seeing mouths.

Because he is "immersed in the very plexus of life," because he is seeing life with the wild irreverence of one who has abandoned the quiet desperation of the proper breadwinning spouse, the useless anger of the disappointed believer in progress, Miller can cut straight to its core.

And what does he see? That man is a bag of guts, hungering, a chancred prick seeking a diseased cunt; that all human life comes down to shit. And out of shit comes philosophy.

What does he do with this vision of humanity, stripped of illusion? Does he despair, like Céline? Does he invent utopias and dystopias, like Huxley? No—he laughs a great, hearty Rabelaisian laugh and finds in the rotting matter at the heart of things a spiritual illumination!

> And so I think what a miracle it would be if this miracle which man attends eternally should turn out to be nothing more than these two enormous turds which the faithful disciple dropped in the *bidet*. What if at the last moment, when the banquet table is set and the cymbals clash, there should appear suddenly, and wholly without warning, a silver platter on which even the blind could see that there is nothing more, and nothing less, than two enormous lumps of shit.

I maintain that it is passages like this that many people find more obnoxious than the sexual passages. Miller dares

to equate shit with illumination! Miller dares not to believe
in progress! He dares not to believe the twenties' bromide:
"Every day, in every way I feel better and better." He
dares not to believe in "positive thinking." He is un–
American! Even if he were writing today, these attitudes
would make him a pariah.

Yes—the sex is also abundant, and it is unvarnished
by romanticism. But always, if you read it in context
(which is not the way most readers—even intellectual
ones—read it), the sex is about this same demystification
process. Miller strips the power from the mystery of cunt,
which heretofore has held him in such thrall.

This is Van Norden in *Tropic of Cancer*, but the need
to demystify the female organ could well be Henry's:

> "Did you ever have a woman who shaved her twat? It's
> repulsive, ain't it? And it's funny, too. Sort of mad like. It
> doesn't look like a twat any more: it's like a dead clam or
> something." He describes to me how, his curiosity
> aroused, he got out of bed and searched for his flashlight.
> "I made her hold it open and I trained the flashlight on it.
> You should have seen me . . . it was comical. I got so
> worked up about it that I forgot all about her. I never in
> my life looked at a cunt so seriously. You'd imagine I'd
> never seen one before. And the more I looked at it the less
> interesting it became. It only goes to show you there's
> nothing to it after all, especially when it's shaved. It's the
> hair that makes it mysterious. That's why a statue leaves
> you cold. Only once I saw a real cunt on a statue—that was
> by Rodin. You ought to see it some time . . . she has her
> legs spread wide apart. . . . I don't think there was any
> head on it. Just a cunt you might say. Jesus, It looked
> ghastly. The thing is this—they all look alike. When you
> look at them with their clothes on you imagine all sorts of
> things: you give them an individuality like, which they
> haven't got, of course. There's just a crack there between
> the legs and you get all steamed up about it—you don't
> even look at it half the time. You know it's there and all
> you think about is getting your ramrod inside; it's as

though your penis did the thinking for you. It's an illusion! You get all burned up about nothing . . . about a crack with hair on it, or without hair. It's so absolutely meaningless that it fascinated me to look at it. I must have studied it for ten minutes or more. When you look at it that way, sort of detached like, you get funny notions in your head. All that mystery about sex and then you discover that it's nothing—just a blank. Wouldn't it be funny if you found a harmonica inside . . . or a calendar? But there's nothing there . . . nothing at all. It's disgusting. It almost drove me mad. . . . Listen, do you know what I did afterwards? I gave her a quick lay and then I turned my back on her. Yeah, I picked up a book and I read. You can get something out of a book, even a bad book . . . but a cunt, it's just sheer loss of time. . . ."

If cunt is "sheer loss of time," then what is the sexual act? When we look closely at Henry's descriptions of sex, we see that he makes sex analogous to carnage and war. His descriptions of the sexual battlefield are remarkably similar to those of Andrea Dworkin in *Intercourse* or *Mercy:*

We haven't any passion either of us. And as for her, one might as well expect her to produce a diamond necklace as to show a spark of passion. But there's the fifteen francs and something has to be done about it. It's like a state of war: the moment the condition is precipitated nobody thinks about anything but peace, about getting it over with. And yet nobody has the courage to lay down his arms, to say "I'm fed up with it . . . I'm through." No, there's fifteen francs somewhere, which nobody gives a damn about any more and which nobody is going to get in the end anyhow, but the fifteen francs is like the primal cause of things and rather than listen to one's own voice, rather than walk out on the primal cause, one surrenders to the situation, one goes on butchering and butchering and the more cowardly one feels the more heroically does he behave, until a day when the bottom drops out and suddenly all the guns are silenced and the stretcher-bear-ers pick up the maimed and bleeding heroes and pin medals on their chest. Then one has the rest of his life to think about the fifteen francs. One hasn't any eyes or arms or legs, but he has the consolation of dreaming for the rest of his days about the fifteen francs which everybody has forgotten.

It's exactly like a state of war—I can't get it out of my head. The way she works over me, to blow a spark of passion into me, makes me think what a damned poor soldier I'd be if I was ever silly enough to be trapped like this and dragged to the front. I know for my part that I'd surrender everything, honor included, in order to get out of the mess. I haven't any stomach for it, and that's all there is to it. But she's got her mind set on the fifteen francs and if I don't want to fight about it she's going to make me fight. But you can't put fight into a man's guts if he hasn't any fight in him. There are some of us so cowardly that you can't ever make heroes of us, not even if you frighten us to death. We know too much, maybe. There are some of us who don't live in the moment, who live a little ahead, or a little behind. My mind is on the peace treaty all the time. I can't forget that it was the fifteen francs which started all the trouble. Fifteen francs! What does fifteen francs mean to me, particularly since it's not my fifteen francs?

Ironically, Miller seems offensive to many feminists because his perception is sited inside a man's head, but these same perceptions of sex fill feminist literature: loveless sex is war, brutal and bloody. In a way Henry's antiromanticism is very close to that of feminist literature. Henry has the same need to destroy romantic illusions and see the violence at the heart of heterosexual "love." He writes of demystified cunt and demystified sex in the same tone in which he writes of racism—as a madness to be blown away with humor:

A special feature in American skulls, I was reading the other day, is the presence of the epactal bone, or *os Incae,* in the occiput. The presence of this bone, so the savant went on to say, is due to a persistence of the transverse occipital suture which is usually closed in fetal life. Hence it is a sign of arrested development and indicative of an inferior race. "The average cubical capacity of the American skull," so he went on to say, "falls below that of the white, and rises above that of the black race. Taking both sexes, the Parisians of today have a cranial capacity of 1,448 cubic centimeters; the Negroes 1,344 centimeters; the American Indians, 1,376." From all of which I deduce nothing because I am an American and not an Indian. But it's cute to explain things that way, by a bone, an *os Incae*, for example. It doesn't disturb his theory at all to admit that single examples of Indian skulls have yielded the extraordinary capacity of 1,920 cubic centimeters, a cranial capacity not exceeded in any other race. What I note with satisfaction is that the Parisians, of both sexes, seem to have a normal cranial capacity. The transverse occipital suture is evidently not so persistent with them. They know how to enjoy an *apéritif* and they don't worry if the houses are unpainted. There's nothing extraordinary about their skulls, so far as cranial indices go. There must be some other explanation for the art of living which they have brought to such a degree of perfection.

Henry hated all racism, especially racism dignified with scientific theory—much in the air in the twenties and thirties, preparing the way for Hitler's Nazi doctors, "experimenting" on Jews. His scorn is obvious in this passage.

How can Miller have called Jews *kikes* and yet hate institutionalized racism? Easy. He hates all self-important rationalizations, and what could be more self-important than rationalizing racism by measuring skulls? When he makes fun of racists, of Jews, of Germans, of Frenchmen, of women, of himself, he shows no mercy. He punctures all pretension—including the favorite Jewish pretention that Jewish suffering is somehow sanctified above all other. Henry would be unforgivable if he didn't spread his satire around equally against all groups. But he makes fun of

gentiles no less than Jews, of cocks no less than cunts. Van
Norden in *Tropic of Cancer* is a walking cock as much as
Tania is a walking cunt. Gandhi's Hindu disciple is re-
duced to two lumps of shit in a bidet.

Nor does Miller excuse *himself* from the general low
level of humankind. He is a walking intestine when he's
hungry, a walking cock when he's horny. He, too, is a mass
of instincts that doesn't deserve to be cloaked in high
ideals.

Where have high ideals ever led humanity, anyway? To
the trenches of World War I? To the apple sellers on the
streets of New York? To the mad pseudoscientific racial
theories of the Nazis that promoted genocide? Henry
thinks humanity has less to lose by embracing the depths
than by pretending to the heights. A bag of guts, a cunt,
a cock, has a sort of primal beingness, the honesty of being
just what it is. Romanticism and high ideals have only led
humanity to slaughter.

Henry, the Victorian, the romantic, the Rousseauist,
the Whitmaniac, revolutionizes *himself* in *Tropic of Cancer*. He strips down to his essential nature. He admits he
is dust, grass, failing flesh—and when illusion is stripped
away, illumination comes.

But isn't a human being more than that? asks the
injured romantic in all of us. Of course. We are dust that
dreams. And sometimes we dream we are more than dust.
But in 1931 it was clear—I maintain it still is today—that
we have been more wounded as a species by our misguided
idealism than by an acceptance of the physicality at the
base of all our lives. Henry's vision of man as a horny cock,
a voracious gullet, is bracing. It still feels real after all these
years. His vision of woman reduced to her hungering cunt
may offend some feminists—and all those who think we
can "rise above" our physical natures—but it also has a
primal truth about it. And the truth is always liberating.

At the pivotal moments of our lives—passionate love,
childbirth, war, terminal illness—we *know* that we are
captive to our physical natures and that humbling knowl-

edge often brings illumination. The dark secret of oozing intestines is essential to the liberation of our souls.

Henry reduces the world to its basest elements so he can make fire. He strips his own illusions so he can remake his vision and his world:

> The wallpaper with which the men of science have covered the world of reality is falling to tatters. The grand whore-house which they have made of life requires no decoration; it is essential only that the drains function adequately. Beauty, that feline beauty which has us by the balls in America, is finished. To fathom the new reality it is first necessary to dismantle the drains, to lay open the gan-grened ducts which compose the genito-urinary system that supplies the excreta of art. The odor of the day is permanganate and formaldehyde. The drains are clogged with strangled embryos.

Henry understands that "even as the world goes to smash there is one man who remains at the core, who becomes more solidly fixed and anchored, more centrifu-gal as the process of disillusion quickens." That man is the artist. Henry is talking about Matisse here. But it is Henry himself who will come to be a rock in the midst of chaos. By the time he writes *The Colossus of Maroussi*, he will have learned not only how to come back from hell but how to enter paradise.

If you read *Tropic of Cancer* straight through today, you will find another book than the one usually talked and written about. The trouble is that *Tropic of Cancer* is seldom really *read*. Even as careful a reader as John Up-dike recently wrote to me (when I inquired of the influ-ence, if any, of *Tropic of Cancer* on *Couples*):

> Strangely, I don't believe I read either of the Cancers through . . . Just a peek inside and the perusal of a para-graph was, well, inflammatory . . .

In that, Updike, one of the most brilliant writers and readers of our time, was probably like most of us. We opened the book for inspiration and quickly closed it lest we be contaminated!

Tropic of Cancer is a book blocked off to readers by its incendiary reputation. It is hard to read, partly because of its plotlessness, but also because of our own prejudices. We have to break down our resistance in order to read it fairly.

Is it possible that a book can become so infamous it cannot be read? Absolutely. People dip their toes in and recoil in horror, thinking they have read the book and found it wanting. What is wanting is their own perception of it.

A book—any book—demands total immersion. With *Tropic of Cancer*, for a variety of reasons, such immersion has been impossible. A wall of preconceptions and prejudices surrounds it, prejudices born of years of litigation, years of sneak-reading, years of critical dismissal. For all those reasons, the book has become a sort of terra incognita. I urge you to lose yourself in it and read it straight through. I promise you will find a totally different book from the one you thought was there.

Read it as if you knew nothing whatever about it. Read it as if the four-letter words were as prevalent in literature in 1931–32 (when it was written), or 1934 (when it was first published) as they are today. You will come to realize that books can be banned from your mind even as they remain available on the shelves. You will come to realize that books can be burned without flames.

The judging of books without bothering to read them was to become the nemesis of Henry's writing life. He was to be dismissed first for his sexual shock therapy, his demystification of sex, then for his supposed New Age Guruism, and finally for his personal life—as if he were a sort of Humbert Humbert of the Pacific Palisades. James Joyce had the good or bad fortune—depending on one's point of view—to be embraced by academics who saw much to teach in his puzzles and portmanteaus. D.H. Lawrence always had the partisans of paganism on his side, even as the prudes shunned him. Gertrude Stein became our token lesbian and Virginia Woolf our token bisexual neurasthenic. But Henry had three strikes against him from the start. He pressed all America's buttons: open sexuality, the failure to believe in Progress, the courage to explode all things literary and let his own outrageous vision thrust through. He was punished for these sins by remaining unread by those people best suited to understand him. The books were there, but the will to read them with an open mind had already been tainted.

The four-letter words in *Cancer* distracted everyone but the most diligent from the truth of Miller's discovery: peace only comes to a mortal creature when he starts to see himself as part of the flow of creation.

The famous last section of *Tropic of Cancer*, where Henry sits watching the Seine and is finally at one with himself, is a clear statement of a man accepting his unity with the cosmos. The river is within him and without him. Knowing that, his course is fixed:

> After everything had quietly sifted through my head a great peace came over me. Here, where the river gently winds through the girdle of hills, lies a soil so saturated with the past that however far back the mind roams one can never detach it from its human background. Christ, before my eyes there shimmered such a golden peace that only a neurotic could dream of turning his head away. So quietly flows the Seine that one hardly notices its presence. It is always there, quiet and unobtrusive, like a great artery running through the human body. In the wonderful peace that fell over me it seemed as if I had climbed to the top of a high mountain; for a little while I would be able to look around me, to take in the meaning of the landscape.
>
> Human beings make a strange fauna and flora. From a distance they appear negligible; close up they are apt to

appear ugly and malicious. More than anything they need to be surrounded with sufficient space—space even more than time.

The sun is setting. I feel this river flowing through me—its past, its ancient soil, the changing climate. The hills gently girdle it about: its course is fixed.

Henry and June were sundered by the time *Cancer* came out and they divorced in 1934—by which time Anaïs was the emotional mainstay of Henry's life.

Tropic of Cancer lay in limbo for two years, waiting to be published. Henry had met Jack Kahane of Obelisk Press through the agent William Aspenwall Bradley in Paris, and Kahane believed in *Tropic of Cancer*. But as it turned out, he had more admiration than money, and he was frightened of publishing such a dangerous book. *Tropic of Cancer* only appeared after Anaïs Nin underwrote its printing expenses: It cost her 5000 francs. The money was borrowed from another of her smitten lovers, her second psychoanalyst, Otto Rank.

When *Cancer* eventually appeared in 1934, it was priced at an exorbitant fifty francs and had the printed caveat *"Ce livre ne doit pas être exposé en vitrine"* (this book may not be shown in windows) banded around its lurid, crab-festooned cover. To save money, Jack Kahane had let his fourteen-year-old-son, the future Maurice Girodias, design the cover. It shows a woman languishing in the claws of a crab. Girodias, who used his French mother's name to escape the anti-Semitism of Vichy France, was later to become the founder of Olympia Press and publish such classics as *Lolita* and J. P. Donleavy's *The Ginger Man*.

Lurid cover or not, *Tropic of Cancer* established Henry's reputation. The responses were slow to come, but Henry was indefatigable in promoting his own work, and eventually Ezra Pound, George Orwell, William Carlos Williams, Aldous Huxley, Edmund Wilson, Blaise Cendrars, John Dos Passos, T.S. Eliot, and Herbert Read all responded enthusiastically. Contemporary women writers like Kay Boyle and Anaïs Nin also saw the book as a breakthrough and did not fault its depiction of women. (Nin's criticism of Henry's view of women would come later.)

How did the publication of *Tropic of Cancer* change Henry's life? It certainly did not make him financially secure. (He was not to be that until the very end of his life.) But "the last book" consolidated his view of himself as a writer, strengthened his resolve to produce a great oeuvre, and gave him *himself* in a very basic way. It was as if the various parts of his personality finally came together: the passion of the writing seemed to impart a new strength to his soul. He had been reborn through *Tropic of Cancer*. Though much in it was a wildly heightened, surreal version of his life in Paris, though he was never as profligate as the narrator seems to imply, he did blast through to a new vision of life. He made peace with the wild man in himself, with his own mortality and his own sexuality. He was never to be the same afterward.

CHAPTER 5

The Last Man
on Earth

I want to kiss the man whose passion rushes like lava through a chill intellectual world.

—ANAÏS NIN, *HENRY AND JUNE*

the creation of a book is a rite of passage for the author even more than for the reader. It is a way of stripping down to the essential being, a self-analysis far more profound than any professionally guided psychoanalysis and a way of remaking oneself spiritually. It is for this act of self-transformation that writers write. And they are fortunate when they recognize this, because such self-transformation is the only truly dependable reward of writing.

After *Cancer*, Henry was released to write other things. *Black Spring*, a book he originally called *Self-Portrait*, remained "one of my favorite books" as he inscribed my copy in 1974. It is written in a sort of surrealist prose poetry. It is the most exuberant of his books, full of the colors, sounds, and smells of life. It reeks of his joy in Paris.

He was working on *Black Spring* even as he revised (four times at least) *Tropic of Cancer*, wrote endless letters to Anaïs Nin, and nearly lost himself in the book on Lawrence he was destined never to finish.

At this time—between the acceptance of *Cancer* by Jack Kahane in November 1932 and its publication in September 1934—Henry was living with Perlès in Clichy, having a passionate affair with Nin at her house at Louveciennes, on holidays (before her husband arrived) at her mother's apartment in Paris, at a series of Paris hotels, and elsewhere. The affair blossomed throughout the months of mad writing, the revisions of *Cancer*, Anaïs's two psychoanalyses, and through all her various writing projects, chief among which was her journal. The sexual current between Anaïs and Henry spurred them both to frenetic literary activity, proving how allied the forces of sexuality and creativity always are.

In August of 1934, Anaïs gave birth to a stillborn girl. Although she made it appear in her first published diary that the child was her husband's, Anaïs Nin's last great love, Rupert Pole, revealed to Miller biographer Robert Ferguson that "Anaïs knew the child was Henry's and should not be brought into the world." *Incest*, published late in 1992, confirms that the child was indeed Henry's and that Anaïs deliberately aborted it. She identified with the unborn child and imagined that it would be abandoned as she was by her father. Reading about the abortion, one feels that this event led inexorably to her growing estrangement from Henry. Anaïs told herself that she was making the sacrifice for Henry, the child-man-artist. Such sacrifices never come without repercussions.

A month after that empty birth in September, on the same day *Cancer* was published, Miller moved into 18 Villa Seurat, his first permanent writing home and his base for the next five years in Paris. The studio owned by Michael Fraenkel, rented by Anaïs, and known to Henry from an earlier stay, was the envy of other writers and artists for its skylight, its spaciousness, its artist neighbors (including Chaim Soutine and Salvador Dali). A house can be a confirmation of success to someone who has drifted for a very long time—and 18 Villa Seurat was just that to Henry. At last he felt he was an artist, not a bum. At last he had a published book and a studio to call his own. He fervently hoped that it would be his home with Anaïs.

The Villa Seurat, a sunny impasse in the fourteenth arrondissement, a modest but pleasant section of Paris, was named after Georges Seurat, who had lived and painted there. A little mews of small, brightly colored houses with big studio windows, it still seems inviting and warm, a hospitable place to live. There is no plaque commemorating Henry's years at Number 18, but perhaps that will come.

Another attraction of the Villa Seurat was Betty Ryan, an artist, then in her twenties, who had the studio under Henry's and at some point became Henry's friend and perhaps secret love. Betty Ryan was young, pretty, and employed a great cook (always important to Henry). She was a passionate Hellenophile. She claims that she and Henry fell in love talking about the wonders of Greece. Of course this relationship had to be kept secret from Anaïs, with whom Henry was "entangled and indebted." Anaïs held sway and sometimes Ryan had to go out with Henry "in mufti." Anaïs, meanwhile, still had a harem of lovers to juggle.

Anaïs did with Henry what many strong women do with the weak men they love: she mothered him. She did not trust him to be strong enough to support her in motherhood and she did not want to bring Henry's child home to Hugo. Despite some wavering, she maintained her marriage and her deepening affair with Otto Rank, which was also an affair with psychoanalysis.

Anaïs was so important to Henry that he would do nothing to risk her disapproval. When he figured out that monetary support brought with it an unexpressed infantilization and perhaps even contempt, he was devastated. And when she went to New York in the fall of 1935 to help Otto Rank open a psychoanalysis clinic, Henry was wildly jealous. By now Nin made no secret of the fact that she thought Miller was weak, and that she needed time away from him. In the coming years she would even begin to criticize his writing, something she had never done before. The relationship with Ryan, known only to Durrell and a few others, is seldom mentioned in connection with the Villa Seurat days. Why is this? Betty Ryan claims she burned her correspondence with Henry after their break. A very private person, she has been slow to confide in Henry's chroniclers. After three years of inquiries on my part, she finally wrote me of her connection with Henry and responded to my request for an interview. Living with her dog on the island of Andros, Betty Ryan was apparently moved to talk by the spate of books appearing about Miller. She is typical of the women Henry loved in that she is very strong.

The truth is that all the women Henry loved best in his life were strong; they accepted him only on their own terms. Chief among them was Nin. When she took off for New York to work with Otto Rank, she was following her own creative karma, and neither husband or lover could change her mind. Anaïs had an independence in her marriage to Guiler that she would have never possessed with Henry. She remained tied to Guiler all her life, but she always needed at least two men to reenact her oedipal drama.

Nin's independence both as a wife and as a lover seems beguiling. At first she appears a beacon of liberation for women, but perhaps she was more enslaved to men than most of us. Her freedom came at a very high cost: she was unable to publish her journals freely during her own lifetime. In a way she traduced her art for the sake of her deceptions. She knew that women can have their sexuality as long as they don't publish it.

I had an amusing encounter with Anaïs Nin once at the Poetry Center of the Ninety-second Street Y in Manhattan, where she was speaking after her edited diaries had begun to appear. At that point I had published one or two volumes of poetry and was writing *Fear of Flying*.

"Why did you edit the sexual parts out of your diary, Miss Nin?" I asked from the audience.

"Because I had observed," she replied coolly, "that whenever a woman revealed her sexual life, she was never again taken seriously as a writer." Nin was pragmatic. I was passionate and young.

"But that's precisely why we must do it," I said, unwittingly predicting my entire career. Nin did not comment further. I remember being disappointed by her lack of candor and thought she was being hypocritical. Now, I see that I was terribly green and brash and she was wise.

She was right, of course: if a woman expresses her sexuality in print, she is *always* exposed to attack. It was a situation she was destined to help change, but only after her death. I was to beard that particular dragon with my very first novel, and in many ways my reputation has never recovered.

In the winter of 1935, Henry, desolate without Anaïas, followed her and Otto Rank to New York. He ever after claimed that he "practiced psychoanalysis." It's not clear what he meant by this. After one practice session with Otto Rank, Henry was brash enough to believe he could do it on his own. Maybe he treated patients to his special Millerian philosophy, which was composed of Emerson, Zen, Lao-tzu, Rimbaud, and Lawrence. It was an intoxicating brew even when I knew him, but you couldn't really call it psychoanalysis.

But the real reason for Henry's presence in New York was his determination to capture Anaïs from her various men and make her his wife. She would have none of it. She knew Henry too well. Like many men, he was more devoted as a lover than a husband. Early in their relationship, Nin had longed to open herself utterly to him and she *had* contemplated leaving Hugh Guiler for him, but now she was in retreat. Her husband appeared: Henry disappeared. He threw himself into conquering literary New York, meeting e.e. cummings, Nathanael West, and James T. Farrell. He tried to sell *Tropic of Cancer* to Harcourt Brace and Simon & Schuster without success. He also had hopes of publishing in *The New Yorker* and *Esquire*; both turned him down. Driven back on himself, he finished *Black Spring*—a book filled with the Paris spirit, though completed in New York. The exuberance he had tapped in Paris was now within him, and he would never lose it. But it would take thirty years for publishers in his own country to catch up with him.

If we look at *Black Spring* as a key to this period in Henry's life, we see that he is integrating the New York of his youth with the Paris of his literary breakthrough. Some of the chapters deal with his early life ("The Fourteenth Ward," "The Tailor Shop") and some with present-day Paris "(A Saturday Afternoon" and "Walking Up and Down in China") but the tone of *Black Spring* is the tone of celebration—the celebration of being free at last, free to write, free to be a man.

In one of my favorite pieces, "A Saturday Afternoon," Henry describes a ride on a bicycle, stopping to pee at a urinal and what a man thinks while the wheels roll and the bladder empties. His mind flows over the books in his life, from Rabelais to *Robinson Crusoe*. He ruminates on writing. He understands that all writers' blocks are about fear of criticism.

> *Begin!* That's the principal thing. Supposing her nose is not aquiline? Supposing it's a celestial nose? What difference? When a portrait commences badly it's because you're not describing the woman you have in mind: you are thinking more about those who are going to look at the portrait than about the woman who is sitting for you. Take Van Norden—he's another case. He has been trying for two months to get started with his novel. Each time I meet him he has a new opening for his book. It never gets beyond the opening. Yesterday he said: "You see what my problem's like. It isn't just a question of how to begin: the first line decides the cast of the whole book. Now here's a start I made the other day: Dante wrote a poem about a place called H_____. H-dash, because I don't want any trouble with the censor."
>
> Think of a book opening with H-dash! A little private hell which mustn't offend the censors! I notice that when Whitman starts a poem he writes: "I, Walt, in my 37th year and in perfect health! . . . I am afoot with my vision. . . . I dote on myself. . . . Walt Whitman, a kosmos, of Manhattan the son, turbulent, fleshy, sensual, eating, drinking and breeding. . . . Unscrew the locks from the doors! Unscrew the doors themselves from their jambs. . . . Here or henceforward it is all the same to me. . . . I exist as I am, that is enough. . . ."
>
> *With Walt it is always Saturday afternoon.*

In *Black Spring*, Henry writes like a man recently freed to write, like a man to whom life is suddenly joyous: "I am delirious because I am dying so fast," he proclaims. "I am riding in full sunlight, a man impervious to all but the phenomena of light." And when he stops rolling on his "racing wheel" to take a pee, "it is all gravy, even the urinal."

As I stand there looking up at the house fronts a demure young woman leans out of a window to watch me. How many times have I stood thus in this smiling, gracious world, the sun splashing over me and the birds twittering crazily, and found a woman looking down at me from an open window, her smile crumbling into soft little bits which the birds gather in their beaks and deposit sometimes at the base of a urinal where the water gurgles melodiously and man comes along with his fly open and pours the steaming contents of his bladder over the dissolving crumbs. Standing thus, with heart and fly and bladder open, I seem to recall every urinal I ever stepped into—all the most pleasant sensations, all the most luxurious memories, as if my brain were a huge divan smothered with cushions and my life one long snooze on a hot, drowsy afternoon. I do not find it so strange that America placed a urinal in the center of the Paris exhibit at Chicago. I think it belongs there and I think it is a tribute which the French should appreciate. True, there was no need to fly the tricolor above it. *Un peu trop fort, ça!* And yet, how is a Frenchman to know that one of the first things which strikes the eye of the American visitor, which thrills him, warms him to the very gizzard, is this ubiquitous urinal? How is a Frenchman to know that what impresses the American in looking at a *pissotière*, or a *vespasienne*, or whatever you choose to call it, is the fact that he is in the midst of a people who admit to the necessity of peeing now and then and who know also that to piss one has to use a pisser and that if it is not done publicly it will be done privately and that it is no more incongruous to piss in the street than underground where some old derelict can watch you to see that you commit no nuisance.

I am a man who pisses largely and frequently, which they say is a sign of great mental activity. However it be, I know that I am in distress when I walk the streets of New York. Wondering constantly where the next stop will be and if I can hold out that long. And while in winter, when you are broke and hungry, it is fine to stop off for a few minutes in a warm underground comfort station, when spring comes it is quite a different matter. One likes to piss in sunlight, among human beings who watch and smile down at you. And while the female squatting down to empty her bladder in a china bowl may not be a sight to relish, no man with any feeling can deny that the sight of the male standing behind a tin strip and looking out on the throng with that contented, easy, vacant smile, that lone, reminiscent, pleasurable look in his eye, is a good thing. To relieve a full bladder is one of the great human joys.

Henry's mind rolls on, from *pissoirs* to books read in toilets, from the King James Bible to Rabelais building the walls of Paris with cunts, from dung to angels and back again. He calls for "a classic purity, where dung is dung and angels are angels."

A classic purity, then—and to hell with the Post Office authorities! For what is it enables the classics to live at all, if indeed they be living on and not dying as we and all about us are dying? What preserves them against the ravages of time if it be not the salt that is in them? When I read Petronius or Apuleius or Rabelais, how close they seem! That salty tang! That odor of the menagerie! The smell of horse piss and lion's dung, of tiger's breath and elephant's hide. Obscenity, lust, cruelty, boredom, wit. Real eunuchs. Real hermaphrodites. Real pricks. Real cunts. *Real banquets!* Rabelais rebuilds the walls of Paris with human cunts. Trimalchio tickles his own throat, pukes up his own guts, wallows in his own swill. In the amphitheater, where a big, sleepy pervert of a Caesar lolls dejectedly, the lions and the jackals, the hyenas, the tigers, the spotted leopards are crunching real human bones— whilst the coming men, the martyrs and imbeciles, are walking up the golden stairs shouting *Hallelujah!*

Without salt, we are unpreserved. Without obscenity, there is no divinity. Henry embraces dung so he can have angels.

It is this exultant acceptance of all life that he cele-
brates in *Black Spring*. Its mood is lighter than *Cancer*
though it continues many of *Cancer*'s themes. It urges
surrender and acceptance. This "message" still offends the
Miller antagonist, while those who understand his spirit
recognize that it is this very acceptance that is the essence
of his greatness.

"The great writers are the ones who don't judge," says
novelist, journalist, and screenwriter David Black, one of
our most sensitive contemporary interpreters of America's
love-hate relationship with sexuality.

Black understands that it is Miller's all-embracing
worldview that makes him unique:

> I discovered Miller late. Through Mailer I read Miller. I
> think Miller is the world-class American twentieth-century
> writer, the greatest. He has more life in him than anyone.
> Does he work all the time? No. But when I read him
> writing about Brooklyn, burlesque shows, different neigh-
> borhoods, a sense of life comes through in Miller. The man
> is filled with love of humanity. Reading Miller is closest in
> artistic experience to the pornographic carvings in India
> . . . They were showing all of life in this art.

Black Spring shows Miller's philosophy of acceptance
more than any other book. It is full of the joy of being
human. With Paris in his blood and bones, Miller can even
make sense of and come to terms with his crazy family, the
family that caused him such grief:

> However, *always merry and bright!* If it was before the
> war and the thermometer down to zero or below, if it
> happened to be Thanksgiving Day, or New Year's or a
> birthday, or just any old excuse to get together, then off
> we'd trot, the whole family, to join the other freaks who
> made up the living family tree. It always seemed astound-
> ing to me how jolly they were in our family despite the
> calamities that were always threatening. Jolly in spite of
> everything. There was cancer, dropsy, cirrhosis of the

liver, insanity, thievery, mendacity, buggery, incest, paralysis, tapeworms, abortions, triplets, idiots, drunkards, ne'er-do-wells, fanatics, sailors, tailors, watchmakers, scarlet fever, whooping cough, meningitis, running ears, chorea, stutterers, jailbirds, dreamers, storytellers, bartenders—and finally there was Uncle George and Tante Melia. The morgue and the insane asylum. The merry crew and the table loaded with good things—with red cabbage and green spinach, with roast pork and turkey and sauerkraut, with kartoffelklösze and sour black gravy, with radishes and celery, with stuffed goose and peas and carrots, with beautiful white cauliflower, with apple sauce and figs from Smyrna, with bananas big as a blackjack, with cinnamon cake and Streussel Küchen, with chocolate layer cake and nuts, all kinds of nuts, walnuts, butternuts, almonds, pecans, hickory nuts, with lager beer and bottled beer, with white wines and red, with champagne, kümmel, malaga, port, with schnapps, with fiery cheeses, with dull, innocent store cheese, with flat Holland cheeses, with limburger and schmierkäse, with homemade wines, elderberry wine, with cider, hard and sweet, with rice pudding and tapioca, with roast chestnuts, mandarins, olives, pickles, with red caviar and black, with smoked sturgeon, with lemon meringue pie, with lady fingers and chocolate eclairs, with macaroons and cream puffs, with black cigars and long thin stogies, with Bull Durham and Long Tom and meerschaums, with corncobs and toothpicks, wooden toothpicks which gave you gum boils the day after, and napkins a yard wide with your initials stitched in the corner, and a blazing coal fire and the windows steaming, everything in the world before your eyes except a finger bowl.

In this passage, Miller has finally accepted his family, accepted both their nourishment and their starvation of being, accepted their death-dealing and life-giving qualities, as part of one gestalt.

No one can equal Miller in evoking the physical side of life—food, hunger, illness, health—but always he breaks through the physical to the spiritual. They are intertwined, indivisible. Henry does not say people must always be happy and free of suffering. He does not expect to have no ugly feelings or violent thoughts. He accepts all the extremes of life—the rape fantasies and the murderous thoughts as well as tenderness and affection—and his acceptance gives the reader the gift of *self*-acceptance.

> Walking over the Brooklyn Bridge. . . . Is this the world, this walking up and down, these buildings that are lit up, the men and women passing me? I watch their lips moving, the lips of the men and women passing me. What are they talking about—some of them so earnestly? I hate seeing people so deadly serious when I myself am suffering worse than any of them. *One* life! and there are millions and millions of lives to be lived. So far I haven't had a thing to say about my own life. Not a thing. Must be I haven't got the guts. Ought to go back to the subway, grab a Jane and rape her in the street. Ought to go back to Mr. Thorndike in the morning and spit in his face. Ought to stand on Times Square with my pecker in my hand and piss in the gutter. Ought to grab a revolver and fire point-blank into the crowd. The old man's leading the life of Reilly. He and his bosom pals. And I'm walking up and down, turning green with hate and envy. And when I turn in the old woman'll be sobbing fit to break her heart. Can't sleep nights listening to her. I hate her too for sobbing that way. The one robs me, the other punishes me. How can I go into her and comfort her when what I most want to do is to break her heart?

Such admissions soften our hearts rather than harden them. Henry is one of us: he cannot control his fantasies.

Those who have condemned Miller have confused the word with the deed. Henry is not a rapist: he is a man honestly confronting the *imaginary* rapist in himself. In truth, his message is not so different from Freud's: let the unconscious bubble into consciousness and freedom will be the result. If we censor him, we are really censoring our humanity. It is only by admitting to our own murderous thoughts that we can be free of them, and only by exploring the whole range of our sexuality that we can understand its dark pull on our lives. Censorship is not the answer. Acceptance is.

There was little chance of above-ground publication for *Tropic of Cancer* or *Black Spring*. American publishing was still controlled by the Hicklin rule, a 1868 British judicial interpretation of obscenity as anything that might "corrupt those whose minds are open to such immoral influences, and into whose hands a publication of this sort may fall." U.S. Customs personnel regularly seized and destroyed all literature deemed obscene under this definition—including James Joyce's *Ulysses*, until Judge Wolsey exempted it in 1934, pronouncing it too "emetic" to encourage lustful thoughts.

Jack Kahane's Obelisk Press could never have published *Tropic of Cancer* in French either (for French obscenity laws were equally strict), but potentially "obscene" books could be published in France if they were in English and thus unavailable to corrupt the incorruptible French. Obelisk Press owed its very existence to this loophole. In his native country, however, Henry was a writer *non gratus*. He was too sensitive to rejection to bear this for long, and after an unpromising attempt to crack the American literary establishment, he sailed back to Paris in May of 1935, soon after Anaïs Nin and her husband had returned.

He settled again into 18 Villa Seurat and focused on trying to make himself famous. People who knew him at this period describe the Villa Seurat as a kind of Warholesque "Factory," with Miller writing, writing, writing and sending copies of his underground book to critics and authors all over the world. He was determined to make his reputation by sheer force of will (and postage).

Meanwhile, he was also working on *The World of Lawrence* (he would struggle with it through the forties), on *Max and the White Phagocytes*, on *Money and How*

It Gets That Way, on *Aller Retour New York* (an account of his recent trip to New York, which showed him again how America misused its artists), and on letters to Anaïs Nin, Michael Fraenkel, and many others.

The "June book," which was to become *Tropic of Capricorn*, was also beginning to grow its wings and claws. An attempt to make sense of his relationship with June would occupy Henry for much of the rest of his writing life, eventually inspiring four huge novels: *Capricorn, Sexus, Nexus,* and *Plexus.* And yet the theme of Henry's abasement before his women was all foretold in "Mademoiselle Claude":

> Where women are concerned I always make an ass of myself. The trouble is I worship them and women don't want to be worshiped. . . .

Anaïs Nin was the muse to whom Henry dedicated *Black Spring.* It was published in June 1936, by Obelisk, though it had first been under contract to Michael Fraenkel's tiny Carrefour Press. It is the second published book that cements a writer's identity. A first book may be a fluke, but with the second, one becomes a writer. *Black Spring* let Henry know that he had found his *métier.*

That winter, Henry and Anaïs made another brief trip to New York. Anaïs was ending her connection with Rank's institute and Henry was resuming his literary assault on his hated native land. *Tropic of Cancer* was garnering fame and readers around the world, making Henry an underground celebrity. But he was still irked to be unavailable in "Amurrica." He had conquered Paris, but "America winged and sexed" still eluded him. Though the breakthrough of Joyce's *Ulysses* in 1934 had given him and other writers some vague hope of having the customs ban lifted for books of "recognized value," it seemed unlikely to benefit *Tropic of Cancer.* As Edward de Grazia shows in his important study of censorship *Girls Lean Back Everywhere* (1992), *Ulysses* did not open the door for other sexually explicit books because it was admitted to the United States on the grounds that it was *not* arousing to the average reader. Not until 1962–63 would the Hicklin rule be overturned by the U.S. Supreme Court for *Tropic of Cancer*. Now I fear we are giving it new life in our various proposed legislations against pornography.

But Henry found another way into America for *Tropic of Cancer*. Frances Steloff and David Moss, the owners of the Gotham Book Mart in New York, met Henry in 1936 and became his most important patrons.

It is impossible to overstate the role of avant-garde booksellers in the spread of new works of art during the twenties and thirties. From Shakespeare & Company in Paris, to the Gotham in New York, important contemporary writers of that era came to us through the indispensable offices of open-minded booksellers, often women, who were truly the midwives of literary culture. (Once again women were more easily accepted in this role than in the role of creators in their own right.)

The story continues today with independent bookstores all over the U.S. who have the gumption to stock and hand-sell the unpopular, the new, the politically incorrect, the literary. Bookselling remains a business of passion and conviction, however much the corporate computer and unfair discounting practices that discriminate against the independents try to eliminate all passion from the process. As large media conglomerates expand their stranglehold on what can and cannot be published, new small presses also make their way into the world through the good offices of independent booksellers, who are still fighting to keep literacy alive in a world that seems to want to crush it on all sides.

Henry, like Joyce and Zola, was to be the beneficiary of such feisty booksellers and publishers all his writing life. Without Frances Steloff, Jack Kahane, Maurice Girodias, James Laughlin, and Barney Rosset, Henry Miller would be unknown to us today. I cannot help but wonder where all the future Henry Millers are, and whether we shall ever even know of their existence. It grows harder and harder to break through the indifference of "official" publishing with all its rationalizations for publishing ghostwritten celebrity books to the exclusion of almost everything else.

The years 1936 to 1938 were years of amazing fecundity for Miller. Both his inner and his outer life were unbelievably rich. While writing *Capricorn*, Henry also worked on one of his most delightful books, *The Hamlet Letters*, a correspondence (about almost everything but *Hamlet*) with his friend Michael Fraenkel. The play of Miller's mind in correspondence, the mischievous ideas about literature, the sprightliness of the writing, make this book (first published in very limited editions in 1939 and 1941 and published in abridged form in paperback in 1988) one of Miller's most revealing. Henry was made for the epistolary book and digression was his art form. In *The Hamlet Letters*, he ranges over every subject from Shakespeare to anti-Semitism, from Buddha to reincarnation. He reveals the sage at his most contemplative and entertaining. We are immersed in Henry's mind, which is like no other.

While this flurry of activity was going on, *Tropic of Cancer* began to make new friends for Henry—friends like George Orwell, Lawrence Durrell, and James Laughlin (then a Harvard student, later the founder of New Directions and one of Henry's publishers to this day). This is one of the most amazing results of publishing a first book: it reaches out into the world for the author and inevitably changes the author's life.

In time the Villa Seurat became a sort of magnet for creative people. An informal group of painters and writers gathered around Henry. They boosted each other's work and had wonderful times together. Among them were Betty Ryan, David Edgar, Hans Reichel, Alfred Perlès, Michael Fraenkel, Abe Rattner. The atmosphere was electric and Henry was the current that ran through it.

> Henry Miller radiated from No. 18. Radiated is the correct word. There was a quixotic mood of coercion hanging about the place, like an atmosphere. On approching, the

least sensitive visitor must have become aware of an exceptional presence. Even I who had by now known him for nearly six years, even I couldn't mount the stairs to his first-floor studio without experiencing a queer feeling of exultation and enthusiasm. I seldom entered without pausing outside the door for a minute or two to take in the familiar Miller noises within. Usually it was the clatter of the typewriter I caught. The door to the sanctum was peppered with notices and *avis importants:* "If knock you must, knock after 11 A.M."—"Am out for the day, possibly for a fortnight."—*"La maison ne fait pas de crédit."*—*"Je n'aime pas qu'on m'emmerde quant je travaille."* And so forth. He pinned these notes to the door because he hated to be pestered while at work. But he never fooled me: I always knew when he was *genuinely* out: I smelled it.

Anaïs Nin still visited Henry a couple of afternoons a week, when her husband came into town to take painting lessons with Hans Reichl. Their projects together were literary as well as sexual at this point. Hugo knew yet did not know or did not *let himself know* that he knew. Anaïs, for her part, did not know about Betty Ryan. She once imperiously ordered Ryan to knock on a pipe that went up from her apartment to Henry's studio should Hugo appear. What a busy place the Villa Seurat was.

Henry and Anaïs worked together on *The Booster,* a turgid publication of the American Country Club of Paris that was shanghaied by Henry's Villa Seurat circle and turned into a literary joke. (Imagine a country club publication being taken over by a group of surrealists!) Henry and his writer friends were able to get their hands on a printing press and they turned *The Booster* from puffery for rich expatriates to a genuine avante-garde magazine. They also produced the Siana series of books for Obelisk Press (*Anaïs* spelled backward). Georges Belmont's literary magazine *Volontés* and *The Phoenix,* an American journal devoted to D.H. Lawrence, also attracted Henry's abundant energy during his Villa Seurat days.

At what point did Henry give up all hope of marrying Anaïs? Probably not until the war broke out and they both returned to America. But he never ceased to credit Anaïs for his breakthrough as a writer. As late as 1939, he wrote to Huntington Cairns, a lawyer and admirer of Henry's work, who advised U.S. customs on censorship (and was therefore an important contact for Henry):

> I owe nearly everything to one person—Anaïs Nin. I want you to remember, if you survive me, what I have said and written about her Diary. I haven't the slightest doubt that one hundred years from now this stupendous document will be the greatest single item in the literary history of our time. Anyway, had I not met her, I would never have accomplished the little I did. I could have starved to death here, for all the French care.

In 1937, at the Villa Seurat, Henry made another of the great friendships of his life—with Lawrence Durrell. Durrell often joked that he had found *Tropic of Cancer* in a public toilet on Corfu, where it had been abandoned by a disgusted reader. The truth was that Barclay Hudson, a friend of his, had given it to him during a literary discussion in Greece. It changed Durrell's life—and Henry's. Durrell immediately—in August 1935—wrote to Henry: "I love its guts. . . . It really gets down on paper the blood and bowels of our time."

Miller immediately replied: "You're the first Britisher who's written me an intelligent letter about the book . . . it's curious how few people know what to admire in the book."

At the time Durrell discovered it, *Tropic of Cancer* was beginning its underground life, being admired by many and sold at the Gotham Book Mart, but receiving almost no official literary recognition.

"It is almost unobtainable," Henry wrote to Durrell, who answered: "I always imagine the book scorching through apathy like a hot knife in butter."

Miller was dazzled (as I was forty years later) at being understood by a kindred spirit.

As Henry described in one of his letters to me, he had to fight to have his book read. The world never knows it needs a new book. And only the insane tenacity of the author ever gets it to those who need it most.

Durrell responded to Henry in a way that was essential: "the only man-sized piece of work which this century can really boast of," he wrote of the book. And Henry loved him, as we always love everyone who understands us.

When Durrell first wrote to Miller in 1935, neither was known except to a coterie. The two were destined to influence each other, and to give each other courage.

Here is Perlès's account of the beginnings of their friendship:

> I arrived at the Villa Seurat somewhat out of breath. Lawrence Durrell was there with Henry. He had arrived fresh from Corfu, a handsome young fellow in his middle twenties with golden hair and a boyish face that made him look like a cherub. The two were drinking wine and seemed to be getting along splendidly. Durrell's wife, Nancy, was preparing food in the kitchenette at the back of the studio; she was tall and slender, like an elegant flamingo.
>
> Both Henry and Larry were in high spirits. They seemed to have recognized each other immediately as "old souls"—people of the same atavism who have everything in common with one another. They had been talking and drinking and making merry all day and by the time I arrived were already bosom friends. A veritable *coup de foudre à la russe.*
>
> The first evening with the Durrells (there were many more to follow) was an unforgettable event. Nancy had prepared a delicious dinner of filet steak (only the English know how to grill a steak so that it is neither underdone nor carbonized but just *à point*, as the French always say but never do), and we were in fine fettle as we settled down to the feast. We drank a lot of wine, but the wine didn't

make us drunk—we were intoxicated with one another. The conversation flowed like music. No one tried to monopolize the table talk: no tedious monologues, no indigestible intellectual pronunciamenti. Larry was scintillating and radiantly happy. He was the first truly civilized Anglo-Saxon I had come across since Henry Miller himself; he was sufficiently civilized to make his culture and erudition palatable—which is a great deal. Already a poet of distinction despite his youth, he had just completed his second book, *The Black Book*, "a chronicle of the English Death," he called it, which was to be published a few months later by the Obelisk Press.

The correspondence with Durrell (which began in 1935) and the face-to-face friendship (which began in 1937) were both important because these were the years that Henry finally found the courage to tackle the June-book in its ultimate form—*Tropic of Capricorn*. He had attempted this book in *Crazy Cock* and *Moloch*, and for years he had carried around the notes of his relationship with June, hoping he could effect their transformation into fiction. When the time came, however, he was better off forgetting his notes and letting the book rip. *Cancer* and *Black Spring* had prepared him to tackle his New York life with abandon. At last he was ready. He began by dedicating *Tropic of Capricorn* "To Her," and exploding with his own Abelard–like *historia calamitatum*, a flashback to his New York life in the twenties from his Paris present in the thirties.

What a difference a decade can make in a writer's life! With literature left behind, Henry was ready to capture "Her" forever. June had been the "She-Who-Must-Be-Obeyed," the Ayesha of his life (after Louise), the primal Lilith-Eve, the Sorceress, the torturer, the muse. He had to subsume life into literature in order to capture her and conquer her forever. The process of writing was essential to overcoming the obsession. What Henry says in his "coda" to *Capricorn* is true of every writer who ever lived:

It came over me, as I stood there, that I wasn't thinking of her any more; I was thinking of this book which I am writing, and the book had become more important to me than her, than all that had happened to us. Will this book be the truth, the whole truth, and nothing but the truth, so help me God? Plunging into the crowd again I wrestled with this question of "truth." For years I have been trying to tell this story and always the question of truth has weighed upon me like a nightmare. Time and again I have related to others the circumstances of our life, and I have always told the truth. But the truth can also be a lie. The truth is not enough. Truth is only the core of a totality which is inexhaustible.

"The truth can also be a lie." This is critical to Henry's whole concept of life and writing. He tries to tell the whole truth in *Capricorn*, the truth of June, of Louise, of Pauline, of the Cosmodemonic. He tires to rise above his New York existence and transubstantiate it into art—or something even higher: life. And what happens when his book is finished? He realizes he will have to write more and more books before he gets to the core of his story. And in fact he will write *The Rosy Crucifixion* (*Sexus*, *Nexus*, *Plexus*) about this same material.

What is *Capricorn* about? Outwardly, it is about how Henry rose (as Saul Bellow might say) from humble origins to complete disaster. It is a book about his people (those "Nordic idiots"), about his mother (with her "clutching womb"), the world of work in Jazz-Age New York and finally about Henry falling in love with his muse—a Venus who turns out to be Lilith. The meeting with the muse makes it possible for him to take his earthbound sorrows and transmute them into soaring words. The meeting with June comes at the very end of the book, but it is the basis for everything that comes before and after, the basis, in fact, of Henry's whole writing life. By capturing his mother in June, he is launched on his way forever, and he can never turn back.

Like every writer, Henry must build an elaborate tomb to bury the woman who embodies his obsession:

> Passing beneath the dance hall, thinking again of this book, I realized suddenly that our life had come to an end: I realized that the book I was planning was nothing more than a tomb in which to bury her—and the me which had belonged to her. That was some time ago, and ever since I have been trying to write it. Why is it so difficult? Why? Because the idea of an "end" is intolerable to me.
>
> Truth lies in this knowledge of the end which is ruthless and remorseless. We can know the truth and accept it or we can refuse the knowledge of it and neither die nor be born again. In this manner it is possible to live forever, a negative life as solid and complete, or as dispersed and fragmentary, as the atom. And if we pursue this road far enough, even this atomic eternity can yield to nothingness and the universe itself fall apart.
>
> For years now I have been trying to tell this story; each time I have started out I have chosen a different route. I am like an explorer who, wishing to circumnavigate the globe, deems it unnecessary to carry even a compass. Moreover, from dreaming over it so long, the story itself has come to resemble a vast, fortified city, and I who dream it over and over, am outside the city, a wanderer, arriving before one gate after another too exhausted to enter. And as with the wanderer, this city in which my story is situated eludes me perpetually. Always in sight it nevertheless remains unattainable, a sort of ghostly citadel floating in the clouds. From the soaring, crenelated battlements flocks of huge white geese swoop down in steady, wedge-shaped formation. With the tips of their blue-white wings they brush the dreams that dazzle my vision. My feet move confusedly; no sooner do I gain a foothold than I am lost again. I wander aimlessly, trying to gain a solid, unshakable foothold whence I can command a view of my life, but behind me there lies only a welter of crisscrossed

tracks, a groping, confused, encircling, the spasmodic gambit of the chicken whose head has just been lopped off.

Capricorn is remarkable for the honesty with which it details the role of sexual obsession in a writer's life. The muse comes to us dressed in human sexuality in order to extract us from time and allow us to enter timelessness. This could be Shakespeare writing about his Dark Lady: "You come to me disguised as Venus, but you are Lilith, and I know it."

This could be Petrarch writing of Laura, or Dante writing of Beatrice:

> It is Sunday, the first Sunday of my new life, and I am wearing the dog collar you fastened around my neck. A new life stretches before me. It begins with the day of rest. I lie back on a broad green leaf and I watch the sun bursting in your womb. What a clabber and clatter it makes! All this expressly for me, what? If only you had a million suns in you! If only I could lie here forever enjoying the celestial fireworks!

Henry is relating his progress from man to angel, from man to artist:

> These are the facts and facts mean nothing. The truth is my desire was so great it became a reality. At such a moment what a man *does* is of no great importance, it's what he *is* that counts. It's at such a moment that a man becomes an angel. That is precisely what happened to me: *I became an angel.* It is not the purity of an angel which is so valuable, as the fact it can fly. An angel can break the pattern anywhere at any moment and find its heaven; it has the power to descend into the lowest matter and to extricate itself at will. The night in question I understood it perfectly. I was pure and inhuman, I was detached, I had wings. I was depossessed of the past and I had no concern about the future. I was beyond ecstasy. When I left the office I folded my wings and hid them beneath my coat.

Without June, the muse, Henry the artist-angel could not have been born.

Montparnasse in the late thirties was being transformed even as the world was being transformed. German refugees were fleeing Hitler, bringing with them terrible stories of anti-Semitism. Henry's reaction to Hitler was not what you would expect from an anti-Semite. He despised Hitler and regarded his Jew-baiting as drivel. If confronted by anti-Semitism, Henry often claimed to be a Jew himself. He was a man always against the grain.

As war threatened and Paris became less and less secure, Larry Durrell, who was ensconced in his retreat on Corfu, kept inviting Henry to visit Greece, the paradise Betty Ryan had described to him on their first meeting at Villa Seurat. Henry eventually accepted, and the trip resulted in what may be Henry's most important book, *The Colossus of Maroussi*. But first Henry had to make the break with Paris.

He was terrified of war and violence, was cowardly about fighting, and hated both the Fascists and Communists equally. He also, of course, despised America. Only when the French mobilized for war was Henry finally motivated to leave Paris. He knew he was coming to the end of another period in his life, but for the moment didn't know where the next period would unfold. *Tropic of Capricorn* was done and Larry was urging him to bring it to Greece. Henry got as far as Bordeaux, but he was still not sure of his next move:

> *Hotel Majestic, 2, Rue de Condé,*
> *Bordeaux*
> *Sunday—*
>
> 　　　　　　　　　　　　　　*25th September [1938]*
>
> *Dear Larry & Nancy—*
> *I left Paris a few days ago to take a vacation after finishing* Capricorn *and having my teeth fixed. Found the country too dull and came on here just as things began to*

look really bad. Before leaving Paris I packed all my belongings carefully—Anaïs will take them to storage, unless war is declared so suddenly that she hasn't time. I have been in a very bad state up until last night when things looked so bad that I could begin to think of action. Sending you this by air mail—hope it will reach you before declaration of war. I am stuck here—no use returning to Paris because the city will be evacuated. Can't go anywhere from here as I haven't the money. (If an American gun boat comes along I may have to take it!)

I'd like to know what you intend doing—stay in Corfu or return to England to be drafted et cetera. Could you send me a telegram to the above address? Anaïs is still in Paris and Hugo is in London. Communications are already poor, interrupted. I am here with just enough to last about a week. I won't budge from here, if I can help it. There's no place to go to! Have written Kahane for an advance on royalties due, but doubt if he'll come across, he's such a tight bugger. I may be stranded here in this bloody awful place where I don't know a soul and never intended to be. No doubt I shall pull out all right— Jupiter always looks after me—but I'd like a word or two from you. Maybe I might find a way to get to Corfu—if it's safe there? If you don't reach me here try Kahane. I have two valises with me, a cane (bequeathed by Moricand) and a typewriter. If necessary I'll throw it all overboard and swim for it.

Everything would be O.K. if Anaïs could depend on receiving money from London regularly—but who can say what will happen to communications, banks, etc? If I need some dough in an emergency—if I have to make a break for it somewhere—can I depend on you for anything? I won't ask unless I'm absolutely up against the wall. I'm already on a war basis, ferreting about like an animal, not a thought in my head except to keep alive by hook or crook. The worse it gets the keener I will be. It's the tension, the inaction, the pourparlers, that gets me. Five minutes alone with Hitler and I could have solved the whole damned problem. They don't know how to deal with the guy. He's temperamental—and terribly earnest. Somebody has to make him laugh, or we're all lost! Haven't spoken to a soul since I left Paris. Just walk around, eat, drink, smoke, rest, shave, read papers. I'm an automaton. Fred was still at the Impasse Rouet—not called for yet. And without a cent as usual. Love to Veronica Tester—what a wonderful name!

Henry

[P.S.] If you lose track of me, if Paris is bombed & Obelisk wiped out, write to my friend Emil Schnellock— c/o Mrs. L.B. Gray, Orange, Va., U.S.A. Anaïs is at the Acropolis Hotel—160 Blvd. St. Germain, Paris (6ᵉ). She may come here. Everything depends on that boyo Hitler! P.P.S. I gave Kahane MS. of Capricorn *to put in vault of his bank. Have carbon copy with me—also* Hamlet *MS.*

A few months before, Henry had written to tell Huntington Cairns that he might head for Arizona or Easter Island or even India. He was very much at loose ends as the war threatened:

I am giving notice now that I will leave the Villa Seurat within the next three months, as I am obliged to do by law. If I can, I will ship a trunkful of my documents to Schnellock in Virginia, in advance of sailing. This is the end of another period for me. The end of my European adventure, perhaps. I don't know precisely what I'll do, but I plan to get to Arizona and stay there a while, and, if the money is available, make a whirlwind tour of the whole country, in order to write that book I have planned: America, the Air-Conditioned Nightmare. *After that, we'll see. Perhaps the Orient. Perhaps some remote, outlandish island. I would like to get to Northern India and then thence to Tibet, but at the moment I lack the courage for further hardships. But I have thought often of a place like Easter Island, or the Caroline Islands, where some of my German ancestors are reported to have settled long ago. I can do without civilized society, without art, with-*

out culture: I have enough inside me to last me the rest of my life.

His "Easter Island" would in fact turn out to be Big Sur, California.

Torn between destinations, in 1939 Henry settled on Greece, hoping he could wait out the war there. This proved providential. Greece was to become another spiritual locus in his life.

At forty-seven, Henry the sage was about to be born.

One senses the transformation from the opening pages of *The Colossus of Maroussi:*

> I would never have gone to Greece had it not been for a girl named Betty Ryan who lived in the same house with me in Paris. One evening, over a glass of white wine, she began to talk of her experiences in roaming about the world. I always listened to her with great attention, not only because her experiences were strange but because when she talked about her wanderings she seemed to paint them: everything she described remained in my head like finished canvases by a master.

The prose is suddenly simple, lucid, calm. Betty Ryan had described Greece to Miller as "a world of light such as I had never dreamed of," and that light is in the prose, as is the limpidity of Grecian waters. Suddenly the long, tortuous sentences of *Cancer* and *Capricorn*, full of outrageous and surreal contradictions, become short, clear, shimmering in *Maroussi*. The writer is sublimed into a seer. He is ready to give up chaos for serenity. He is ready to give up darkness for light.

If one looks at the evolution of Miller's books, from *Clipped Wings* to *Crazy Cock* to *Moloch* to *Tropic of Cancer* (and the other Paris books), to *Maroussi*, one sees a fascinating progression. The derivative pastiche of *Clipped Wings* gives way to mannered, self-conscious literary writing (*Crazy Cock* and *Moloch*), which in turn yields to madcap fuck-everything formlessness (the *Trop-*

ics, Black Spring, et cetera), which in turn transforms itself into the radiant clarity of *Maroussi.* And yet they are clearly all the work of the same writer, the same soul. That soul goes down to hell like Dante and ascends the mountain to find the gates of Paradise in Greece. New York is the entrance into the underworld, Paris the entrance into purgatory, and Greece the entrance into paradise.

Maroussi is Miller's central book. It explains everything that comes before and after. He was, as he once said to me, "always looking for the secret of life." And it was in Greece that he found his true calling as an author/sage whose mission was to liberate his readers.

As the Paris books are full of bloody womb images, the Greece book is full of images of illumination. The sentences themselves are different. Instead of twisting back on themselves like pretzels, they are clear and sharp. There are still lists—Henry's favorite trope—but they are not full-throttle, cacophonic Rabelaisian ones, they are brief and visionary:

> The tree brings water, fodder, cattle, produce; the tree brings shade, leisure, song, brings poets, painters, legislators, visionaries.

How different this is from the rambunctious list-making of *Cancer, Capricorn,* and *Black Spring*—full of wombs, shoes, fur, pus, wings, chancres, cancers, spiders, and vitriol . . .

The "supernal light" has transformed Henry.

> One would have to be a toad, a snail, or a slug not to be affected by this radiance which emanates from the human heart as well as from the heavens.

"The only paradise in Europe," he calls Greece—and for him this was true. In Greece his "heart filled with light"; he opened like a flower.

> I don't know which affected me more deeply—the story of the lemon groves just opposite us or the sight of Poros

itself when suddenly I realized that we were sailing through the streets. If there is one dream which I like above all others it is that of sailing on land. Coming into Poros gives the illusion of the deep dream. Suddenly the land converges on all sides and the boat is squeezed into a narrow strait from which there seems to be no egress. The men and women of Poros are hanging out of the windows, just above your head. You pull in right under their friendly nostrils, as though for a shave and hair cut en route. The loungers on the quay are walking with the same speed as the boat; they can walk faster than the boat if they choose to quicken their pace. The island revolves in cubistic planes, one of walls and windows, one of rocks and goats, one of stiff-blown trees and shrubs, and so on. Yonder, where the mainland curves like a whip, lie the wild lemon groves and there in the Spring young and old go mad from the fragrance of sap and blossom. You enter the harbor of Poros swaying and swirling, a gentle idiot tossed about amidst masts and nets in a world which only the painter knows and which he has made live again because like you, when he first saw this world, he was drunk and happy and care-free. To sail slowly through the streets of Poros is to recapture the joy of passing through the neck of the womb. It is a joy too deep almost to be remembered. It is a kind of numb idiot's delight which produces legends such as that of the birth of an island out of a foundering ship. The ship, the passage, the revolving walls, the gentle undulating tremor under the belly of the boat, the dazzling light, the green snake-like curve of the shore, the beards hanging down over your scalp from the inhabitants suspended above you, all these and the palpitant breath of friendship, sympathy, guidance, envelop and entrance you until you are blown out like a star fulfilled and your heart with its molten smithereens scattered far and wide.

Summing up what Greece taught him, Henry says, "I can see the whole human race straining through the neck of the bottle here, searching for egress into the world of light and beauty."

Maroussi shows Henry climbing up out of the bloody womb of time into the radiance of eternity. The book works on many levels. It is the odyssey of fallen man moving from darkness into light, from mortality to immortality, from mutability to permanence, from benighted materialism to enlightened spirituality. It also tells the story of the world at the exact fulcrum of the twentieth century. In 1939, this planet with its millions of war-bound inhabitants was crossing an inexorable divide from the pre–Nuclear to the Nuclear Age, from the illusion of species immortality to the conviction of species mortality, from the war to end all wars to the understanding that war would be with us always in various forms—both cold and hot. Henry's odyssey in *Maroussi* is exactly the odyssey the human race needed in 1939—but failed to take. It is prophetic that it concludes with the line "Peace to all men, I say, and life more abundant!"

Maroussi creates a new form for the spiritual travel book, building on and extending Thoreau. It astonishes me that so few of the people who have written about Miller have seen this. The sex of the Paris books has blinded them. They do not even *look* at *Maroussi*.

Mary Dearborn acknowledges the beauty of *Maroussi*'s prose, but she dismisses the book in a few lines: "[H]is recounting of one spiritual experience after another tends to bore readers who are not taken up with mysticism."

Of course, "mysticism"—the very word has become pejorative—is always boring to those who believe only in materialism. "Boring" is in itself a codeword for fear—as any psychoanalyst can tell you. There is a whole school of journalists and critics who will dismiss as "New Age claptrap" everything from *Maroussi* to *Walden* to the *Tao Te Ching* to Shirley MacLaine's bestsellers as if there were no difference in quality or in kind.

Probably the fear of enlightenment is greater in some people than the attraction toward it, but some of us are drawn to it, while others stubbornly turn their backs, claiming the light does not exist. One cannot argue about the possibility of enlightenment any more than one can argue about the existence of god and goddess. It requires a leap of faith, an act of amazing grace. Miller made that leap of faith in Greece. Many of his chroniclers cannot follow him.

Even Robert Ferguson, who is a somewhat less grudging and bitter critic of Henry than Mary Dearborn, says of *Maroussi* that "a second rebirth, coming so soon after the first one in Paris with *Tropic of Cancer*, might seem like one rebirth too many." But spiritual experiences are cumulative. They gather like waves and result in breakthroughs. Creative life does not proceed by accumulating anthills of "facts." Rather there is a slow accretion of experience, of learning one's craft, of growing spiritually, until suddenly, seemingly out of nowhere, one soars to a new level. If you've experienced it, you believe it. If you haven't, you disbelieve.

Of all Henry's biographers, Jay Martin best comprehends Miller's mission to free his readers. He records the sense of liberation and ease Miller felt in Greece. After the frenzy of the Paris years, where he wrote and wrote to empty himself of the bitterness of his past, he was finally able to draw a long breath of life and light. He returned to America a new person. In a sense, his soul had been shriven.

Perhaps *Maroussi* is played down by Miller's biographers because it is "a book without sex," as one of his Greek friends predicted. It doesn't fit the Miller stereotype, so it is safer to ignore it than to acknowledge that Miller was multifaceted, both as a human being and as a writer. In this age of electronic sound bites and media stereotyping, few public figures are allowed complexity, complication, or chiaroscuro. Miller is seen as the antic goat, nothing more. How can we notice that his central book is full of sea and sun, not slime and sperm? It would make our precious point of view seem wrong! The truth is that Miller was on a spiritual journey his whole life—and Greece was at the heart of it.

In Greece, Henry mingled with poets and philosophers and traveled to ancient sites—Poros, Nauplia, Epidaurus, and Mycenae—with George Katsimbalis, whom Henry was to immortalize as *The Colossus of Maroussi*. Like Henry, Katsimbalis was a great talker as well as a writer. As he led Henry on a spiritual and literary journey, he also captivated him.

Henry turned serene, almost seraphic in Greece, and all his friends noticed the change. He began his lifelong romance with the wisdom of the ages—yoga, Zen, the I Ching. His friend Ghika (whom he called Giks), the painter from Hydra, predicted that Greece would change Henry: "If you came to Greece as a Parisian bohemian, you have become a pilgrim," he said. "Henceforth your writing must be different." *Maroussi* was to prove Ghika right.

In September 1939, Henry's publisher at Obelisk Press, Jack Kahane, died, and Miller's modest monthly stipend from *Tropic of Cancer* and *Black Spring* was interrupted. Durrell was going to fight with the Greeks against Italy; Paris was in chaos, preparing for war. Like it or not, it was time for Miller to return to America. He always fled war when he could, knowing its uselessness. Just three weeks before his forty-eighth birthday on December 26, all Americans were told to leave Greece, and Henry's friend George Katsimbalis, the mad word-spinner, took Miller to see a fortune-teller.

Like the fortune cookie he later gave me ("your name will be famous in the future"), the prediction he received was also destined to come true: Henry was to be a joy-giver, fated never to die, but simply to disappear from the earthly sphere like Lao-tzu. The prediction was truer than Henry would know, even in his own lifetime, for though obscurity and struggle awaited him in his homeland, he had already written most of the books that would bring him immortality. All except *Maroussi*, which he wrote in New York upon his return.

When Henry arrived in his native city in January 1940,

he was as broke as when he had left ten years earlier, unknown to the general reading public and still without a nurturing mate.

Anaïs had also fled Europe and returned to New York, but she was ill and didn't meet Henry's ship, the *Exocharda*, when it docked. She was, anyway, retreating from Henry with each passing year.

This was no triumphal return from abroad. Henry had published only one book in the States, *The Cosmological Eye*, a miscellany of pieces brought out by James Laughlin of New Directions in 1939, and it had not done at all well even in literary circles. Henry was afraid and ashamed to see his elderly parents, terrified of being wholly unable to write in America, terrified of being claimed by the Cosmodemonic New York he had fled.

New York was a city of failures and defeats for him, and yet somehow he was able to sit in its midst and write *The Colossus of Maroussi* and some of his best essays (*The World of Sex* and "Reflections on Writing") in Caresse Crosby's apartment on East Fifty-fourth Street. She was the widow of Harry Crosby of The Black Sun Press, and another returned expatriate—albeit a solvent one.

Henry began *The Colossus* between the winter and spring of 1940, and it covers the period in Greece that immediately preceded it. It feels like a book that was written in a blaze of inspiration. It is not labored, but clean and true. Henry Miller's letters to Anaïs Nin from Greece have the same clarity. Greece had focused his energies. He was almost fifty, and ready to enter the next phase of life.

During Henry's New York sojourn another important literary event occurred that illuminates Miller the writer. Always desperately hard up, and unable to sell his work to mainstream publishers, Henry was tempted to try his hand at pornography-on-demand, writing for a rich collector at a dollar a page. He proved as unsuited for this "job" as for the others he'd taken in his life, and, like them, he lost it.

He did turn out a few pieces, some of which have unfortunately been published posthumously as "Sous les Toits de Paris," "Rue de la Screw," and "France in My

Pants" in *Opus Pistorum* (1983), but his "career" as a paid pornographer was to prove Vladimir Nabokov's maxim that pornography lovers insist on their smut being "limited to the copulation of clichés." "Style, structure, imagery should never distract the reader from his tepid lust," Nabokov says in *Lolita.* Henry couldn't write pornography for long. The porno collector found him "too poetic."

This shows how little most censors, critics, and even sober First Amendment specialists understand about the impetus to write about sex. As Nabokov says in his afterword to *Lolita,* "no writer in a free country should be expected to bother about the exact demarcation between the sensuous and the sensual." Life contains both, and in order to evoke it, writing must also contain both.

But the porno fancier is seeking something else altogether—a masturbatory aid. Too much poetry distracts him from his single goal: an efficient orgasm. Henry's goals were always far less single-minded and far less efficient. The sex in his books was there just as the spirituality was—to awaken, to enlighten, to bring the reader to his senses. Those who confuse the Paris books with pornography clearly do not know how tedious and repetitive pornography really is. Those who accuse Henry of putting in the sex "to sell" do not realize that in his case the sex was an impediment to his "career." But he had no choice. He wrote what "the voice" dictated.

The posthumous publication of Henry's small output of for-hire pornography has, sadly, further besmirched his reputation—not only because it is sexual, but because it is so dreary, dull, and badly written.

At the same period, in 1940, in New York, he wrote his truest book about the uses of sex in literature. It is a brief essay entitled *The World of Sex,* and in it Miller discusses the various responses to his sexual books. He explains that people either despise them or see them as liberating, but that very few readers can make sense of the way the sexual and the spiritual are interrelated. Henry speaks of his oeuvre as if his place in literature were already established.

For me *The World of Sex* remains the last word on the

still misunderstood subject of sex and spirituality. Like Flaubert, Henry did not choose his subject matter, he submitted to it. That he wrote *The World of Sex* hard on the heels of *Maroussi* and the pornography-for-hire experiment is fascinating. Henry could *only* be himself. That is surely one definition of genius.

In New York, Henry at last found the courage to visit his parents, who were old, poor, ill, and very glad to see him. The empathy he felt for them, the transformation of his feelings of anger, also had a profound effect upon his writing and his life to come. His parents finally accepted him, not because of his work—by their standards an underground writer was a failure—but as their son, which is perhaps more important.

Maroussi was turned down by ten publishers, including Blanche Knopf, and it finally came out with a small, financially strapped San Francisco press called Colt. Although Henry was rejected again and again, he still would not allow Penguin Books to bowdlerize *Tropic of Cancer* just to get it published in America (an offer that came to him at this time). Some hostile Miller critics imply that he would do anything for money, but the fact is that his stubborn individualism always made his economic life very difficult. He simply could not compromise with the taste of the mainstream. He couldn't even publish in *The Kenyon Review, Esquire,* or *The New Republic.* He was so far ahead of his time that even the little magazines and literary quarterlies were afraid of him. And *The New Yorker* turned up its aristocratic nose at his work. Nor could he get a grant from the Guggenheims. Henry has a wry take on grants in his coda to *Air-Conditioned Nightmare.* Though he "answered all questions faithfully" and "submitted names of persons of good repute" who would vouch for the fact that he was neither a "moron, adolescent, insane or alcoholic," he did not get the grant. Of the list of nineteen professors, journalists, and psychologists who made the grade in 1941, when Henry Miller didn't, not one has been heard of since.

As a paradigm of the plight of the creative artist in America, Miller's life is nothing short of terrifying. Always rejected by both the literary establishment and the literary antiestablishment, broke until he was a relatively elderly man, he had no choice but to live on the margins and like it. Had he been a chronic depressive, he probably would not have survived. But Henry's great good luck was his temperament—"always merry and bright," as he said— and he went on writing for the sheer joy of it.

So Henry "the failure" was in fact the greatest success. If climbing one's own mountain against all odds is the mark of spiritual success, Miller was a dazzling success. His tenacity is exemplary. And no one needs tenacity more than an American writer who cannot cut his conscience to the taste of the times—that is, any writer of value.

When *Maroussi* was turned down almost everywhere, when his short pieces could find no home in magazines, Miller asked his new literary agent, John Slocum of Russell and Volkening, what on earth *would* sell in America? Desperate to be read in his native land, Henry needed to know this. Slocum canvassed the publishers, who all seemed to want Miller, the returned expat, to write a book on America.

What a coincidence! He had been thinking of a book on America for a while, and in his head had called it *The Air-Conditioned Nightmare*. The book, as he envisioned it, would have fifty chapters, with illustrations by his artist friend Abe Rattner, and would be based on notebooks he'd keep on a trip across the United States.

But Doubleday, the contracting publisher, didn't see it his way. They didn't want an illustrated book—too expensive to produce. And they didn't want to give Henry enough money to do the tour of the United States. They wanted a guarantee of no pornography and advanced him $500 for the book, the trip, the whole project.

It was scarcely enough to cover half his expenses, traveling modestly. But Henry had things to say about America that had to find expression, and *The Air-Conditioned Nightmare* was fated to be written.

His timing, as usual, could not have been worse. When Henry finished *The Air-Conditioned Nightmare* on Christmas Day, 1941, he had in his hand a broadside attack on America just in time for America's entry into World War II. He knew that the book would not only never be accepted for publication, but might get him locked up as a traitor like the Japanese-Americans who were currently being interned in camps. It was hardly a propitious moment to publish rough truths about America.

Henry and Rattner made their 250,000 mile car trip through America between October 1940 and October 1941. "A year wasted!" Miller wrote of that period. But the book is far from a waste, even though *The Air-Conditioned Nightmare* would not be published till 1945 in hardcover, not till 1970 in paperback. Miller revised it in 1944 at Big Sur. Read today, it is an amazing prophecy of things to come. It is almost as though Miller foresaw the eighties turning nineties: "We have two American flags always: one for the rich and one for the poor."

The American passion for materialism and the treadmill of mediocrity it creates is anatomized:

> The most terrible thing about America is that there is no escape from the treadmill which we have created. There isn't one fearless champion of truth in the publishing world, not one film company devoted to art instead of profits. We have no theatre worth the name. . . . We have no music worth talking about except what the Negro has given us, and scarcely a handful of writers who might be called creative.

Miller saw through to the heart of American hypocrisy—saw it was a country founded on misplaced theories of freedom that had allowed all its ideals to become nothing more than "the biggest profits for the boss, the utmost servitude for the workers. . . ."

But Miller saved his most scathing barbs for the treatment of the American artist:

> The dreamer whose dreams are non-utilitarian has no place in this world. Whatever does not lend itself to being bought and sold . . . is debased . . . the poet is anathema, the thinker a fool, the artist an escapist, the man of vision a criminal . . .

"I feel at home everywhere, except in my native land," Miller told a Hungarian friend, a recent émigré to New York:

> America is no place for an artist: to be an artist is to be a moral leper, an economic misfit, a social liability. A corn-fed hog enjoys a better life than a creative writer, painter or musician. To be a rabbit is better still.

The Air-Conditioned Nightmare reads like a page out of our own times. It predicts the utter debasement of art and literature to forms of commerce. And *The Nightmare Notebook*, Henry's notebook during the trip, which was later published with his and Rattner's watercolors, is full of life and insight into Miller's way of thinking—his list-making, his search for the secret of life, his search for an America he could love—under all that hate.

It is typical of writers to burn with the next book while finishing the book on the desk. Even as Henry wrote *The Air-Conditioned Nightmare*, he chafed about his *next* book, which he had been carrying in his heart for ten years: *The Rosy Crucifixion (Sexus, Nexus, Plexus)*, his final settlement of the debt to June. He had only begun the story in *Capricorn*, he felt. Now he must tell it all.

What is this drive to write? Surely not for fame or money—which are far more easily gained in less disciplined, less lonely pursuits—but in search of that ecstasy one feels while in the trance of creation, that unity with self, with heart, with Mother. It becomes more necessary than life. It is meditation, balm, release.

"Writing is an act of healing," says the novelist and critic Doris Grumbach. Every real writer feels this. The fate of the book is almost irrelevant. And thank goddess for that, because the energy to write is needed long before the applause (more likely rotten tomatoes or mute indifference) comes along.

To write is to live in a time warp between creation and response. The labor of writing must be borne long before the reaction, if any. Often, as in Miller's case, the true response is many decades off.

Henry was still imagining himself in love with June on *The Air-Conditioned Nightmare* trip. He says as much in his *Nightmare Notebook:* "Where are you sitting now? . . . I love you!" he writes in an imaginary telegram to June from Hollywood. And he signs himself: "Valentine Valentino." He was determined to embark on a great Proustian saga that would make sense of his great love and finally release him from it. But first he had to settle down and find a home, and this time it was the West that would call him.

During the *Nightmare* journey, Henry had become fascinated with Hollywood, which was, in that period, a haven for writers, artists, European émigrés. "A Hollywood conception of Hollywood," he wrote in the notebook. "Familiar faces—from Paris, Vienna, Cracow, Berlin. Everybody is here. Looks lousy. But the sky is bright. One hopes . . ."

Miller hoped to find work on the film gravy-train, though he was soon to prove as unsuited for that as for other forms of knuckling under to bosses. Besides, his reputation had preceded him to Los Angeles. Women expected him to be a goatish stud and Hollywood businessmen thought he would be too pure an *artiste* to sell out and become just another schmuck with an Underwood.

They were both right and wrong. Henry was still a romantic about women and servicing "Hollywood wives" was not his idea of romance. He was not about to become a Hollywood writer-for-hire, either. His temperament couldn't have been less suited. And his skills as a dramatist were all reserved for his own life.

But painting, miraculously, saved him.

During the lean years in Hollywood, between 1942 and 1943, when Miller was shacking up in Beverly Glen with his friends Margaret and Gilbert Neiman and striking out as a potential Hollywood hack, he turned to watercolor painting, which he had loved since the twenties when Emil Schnellock first gave him lessons.

Henry had seen many of the best painters at work, and he himself had the innate freedom of the artist. When he wrote, he worked; when he painted, he played—and everyone could see the joy in the results. Joy was to rescue him once again. In 1942, in Los Angeles, Henry painted for love, not money. He followed his bliss and his bliss always provided for him.

A trip to an art-supply store in Westwood put him in touch with Attilio Bowinkel, a dealer in painters' supplies, who gave him materials and then displayed the resultant watercolors in his window. When they were snatched up by Arthur Freed, the MGM producer and art collector, Henry was so elated that he began to paint as demonically as he once had written. When the Neimans moved to Colorado, Henry turned their Beverly Glen cottage into a studio and eventually into a gallery where he sold his own work.

This beggar-artist was opening his palms to the heavens, and the heavens were answering. In 1943, he wrote his famous "open letter to all and sundry," asking for handouts of cash and clothes. The letter was published in *The New Republic* and caused a stir. Even today, people remember it—either with disapproval or amusement.

Henry was an ironic beggar:

> Anyone wishing to encourage the watercolor mania would do well to send me paper, brushes and tubes, of which I am always in need. I would also be grateful for old clothes, shirts, socks, etc. I am 5 foot 8 inches tall, weigh 150

pounds, 15½ neck, 38 inch chest, 32 inch waist, hat and shoes both size 7½. Love corduroys.

The New Republic called Henry "one of the most interesting figures on the American literary scene" (though apparently they didn't find him interesting enough to showcase his work). His fame was as a character, not a writer—and to some extent this remains true even today.

Perhaps it is Henry's view of money that makes him seem so odd. He had no pride about money because he had ceased to accept the American view that poverty is moral turpitude. When he did have money, he shared it with everyone. When he had none, he expected others to share with him. He was generous as only one who does not believe in material things can be. Giving it all away was his religion. As the sages predict, it always came back.

Some Miller "experts" claim the myriad limited editions of his essays and books were made with hope of gain—but nothing could be farther from the truth. Anyone who has made beautifully printed books and pamphlets knows that the process is painstaking and far from economically remunerative. One does it for the love of hot type on rag bond, the desire to blend various senses: sight, touch, and the music of words.

A writer and a painter who came out of the same Paris that produced Picasso, the surrealists, the small presses of Sylvia Beach (Shakespeare & Co.), Harry Crosby (Black Sun), and Nancy Cunard (Hours), Henry truly cared for the look of books—the synthesthesia of books—in a way that was obsolete in publishing even then. There is a great American tradition of self-publishing that goes back to Whitman and before. Henry was aware of this tradition, and aware that he was part of it. That some of the books, letters, lists, and watercolors have become collectors' items is serendipitous. The American writer who "sells out" hardly does so through limited editions. In fact, when Henry was finally offered a screenwriting contract from

MGM in 1943, he refused it, preferring to live by his watercolors, with the angel as his watermark.

In this he knew himself well. He would have been incapable of dealing with the psychological situation of the Hollywood writer-for-hire, the constant rewrites at the behest of the "suits," the constant attempt to second-guess a fickle public, the committee decisions, the fear, the chronic covering of one's rear. Henry must have sensed he'd never be able to stand it. And he was right.

But he needed to settle down, have a home, a woman, a place to write, and in 1943 security still eluded him. He wanted to get on with writing his trilogy about his tumultuous romance with June, and for that he needed a calm life. (The irony of writing is that the most tumultuous books require the most regular lives.) He had been rebuffed by two young women he had recently become infatuated with; his watercolor income, which had started like a downpour, had suddenly dried up; and he had no hope of a permanent home. He was feeling his age and, like many writers, he began dreaming of a paradise for artists—and of a patron to free him to create. Everything he needed was given to him.

An anonymous donor set up a modest trust fund for him, much of which, characteristically, he immediately gave to Anaïs Nin and others. He then found his next earthly paradise in Big Sur. After that, he found the woman who was to give him the greatest gifts of his later years: his daughter Valentine and his son, Tony.

Henry came to Big Sur initially because of Jean Varda, the sculptor, but stayed because of the sky, the birds, the fog, the mountains. As he wrote to Anaïs Nin:

> *I have a sort of Paradise here, as to scenery, but the work involved is almost too much. I live up a steep road, over a mile long, away from the highway. Three times a week the food and mail arrives, and I drag it up with the last ounce of energy in me. Coming down to get it, I feel*

elated. Always I think I am in the Andes, the view so magnificent.

Henry found in Big Sur a landscape to which his soul responded. "It is a region where extremes meet, a region where one is conscious of weather, of space, of grandeur, and of eloquent silence," Henry writes in *Big Sur and The Oranges of Hieronymus Bosch*. This was his place to contemplate eternity, the next stop on his spiritual journey after Greece. "And who can say when this region will once again be covered by the waters of the deep?" he asked.

Henry settled here, between earth and sky, between time and eternity, to make the next stage of his journey. "Here the redwood made its last stand . . . [Big Sur has] the look of always. Nature smiling at herself in the mirror of eternity."

The city boy from Brooklyn and Paris was beguiled by the grandeur of the Pacific Coast. It was to be his last earthly stop.

CHAPTER 6

Heart Filled with Light: Big Sur, Earthly Paradise, and After

In the last reaches of being there is but one true marriage; each person wedded to himself.

—HENRY MILLER IN A NOTE TO
BILL PICKERILL, SHORTLY BEFORE HIS DEATH

■ stayed in Henry Miller's Big Sur studio one night in 1974. Henry was already living in Pacific Palisades, and I was his daughter Valentine's guest in the old homestead on Partington Ridge.

It was one of the most glorious, cold, foggy and uncomfortable places I've ever stayed. Henry's "studio" was a shack with practically no insulation, and my then-lover and I clung to each other to keep warm. We were too cold to get up to go to the bathroom, too cold to sleep, except fitfully. The wind whistled through the slats of the cabin. The damp settled in our bones. And I had the most amazing dreams—undersea dreams, sailing dreams, flying dreams. Henry's paradise was about as comfortable as the Andes, but spiritually it was magical. You felt that if Big Sur did not exist, Henry would have invented it—as he invented Brooklyn, Paris, and Greece.

Writers and places constitute a strange synergy. Do we absorb the energy from the place, or do we find the place when our own energy is right?

Big Sur seems to have taught Henry many spiritual lessons. Both the arduousness of the life there (and the beauty) and the strange way he came to find his home were lessons he needed. He wanted a home, but could not afford one, and then he discovered what we all discover on spiritual journeys:

> When you surrender, the problem ceases to exist. Try to solve it, or conquer it, and you only set up more resistance. . . . The most difficult thing to admit, and to realize with one's whole being, is that you alone control nothing. . . .

The home in Big Sur came to Henry in an almost magical way. He described the process to Anaïs Nin:

> I told you I am getting a piece of property—a home. It
> came about strangely. It *is* almost impossible to get land
> or house here. There was a neighbor on the hill where I
> lived, a Mrs. Wharton, who seems to understand me—
> without reading the books. She is supposed to be a Chris-
> tian Scientist—but she's outgrown that. She's the only
> person I know who uses the word Reality as I do. That's
> our meeting ground . . . [S]he is virtually offering me her
> place. . . . [T]he price is ridiculous. . . . Sometimes I think,
> in offering me my dream, she is only teaching me another
> lesson. She says, for instance, in explaining her willingness
> to relinquish it, that it is now inside her, can't be lost.
> . . . Have I not become more and more aware latterly that
> the things I deeply desire come without struggle?

After the house came watercolors, came devoted
friends like Emil White, the Austrian book dealer—"boon
companions" the like of whom he had not known since his
Paris days. All he needed was another June. Henry's romances in the second part of his life always seemed to be
attempts to conjure the past, just as his early romances had
been attempts to conquer his mother.

He hadn't been happy with the first June, and he
wasn't destined to be happy with the second. She turned
up like a sort of mail-order bride, provided by a friend in
New York who had known the first June.

Henry's romance-by-letter with June II (June Lancaster) seems inexplicable to anyone but another writer, who
knows that the disease of our kind is to invent our lovers
out of whole cloth, so that they may become characters in
our books. Henry did this often and expertly. He decided
to fall in love and then conveniently invented the person
to fall in love with.

True, he needed certain reference points: the name
June was one. June Lancaster had been a taxi dancer and
an artists' model. She had what Henry called a "meta-
morphic" personality—meaning that he thought he could
shape her according to his needs—and she was young
enough to be his daughter. This was a May-December

relationship, one of a series that was to form a repeating pattern throughout the latter part of Henry's life.

A friend of Miller's, Harry Herschkowitz, went to New York to "interview" (and mattress-test) her on Henry's behalf. He also apparently tested various other potential mail-order Mrs. Millers. Harry triumphed, and brought June II to Big Sur, where, despite her beauty and sensuality, she didn't last long. Miller could whip himself up into a frenzy of long-distance infatuation, but even he could not counterfeit lasting love. And June II was too undomestic to be much help in as rugged a place as Big Sur. Without indoor plumbing or running water to cook and wash, Big Sur required a pioneer-woman spirit for survival. June II didn't have it.

Lepska did. At least for seven years or so.

The pivotal women in Miller's life were always highly intelligent—and certainly this was true of Janina Lepska, now known as Lepska Warren, Henry's third wife. There is little about Lepska in his writings, but the watercolors he painted of her (recently published in *Henry Miller: The Paintings. A Centennial Retrospective*) depict her as a serious, Athena-like blonde and himself as a floating, Chagall-inspired lover.

He first met Lepska in 1944, while on a trip East to visit his mother. Louise was being operated on for cancer, and Henry arrived like the dutiful son he really was. Then, with his mother out of danger, he visited Lepska at Yale, where she was studying philosophy, and where Henry had an important literary pen pal in Wallace Fowlie. It wasn't long before the romance between Henry and Lepska became serious and they headed out West together, marrying in Denver in December 1944, with Henry's friends the Neimans as witnesses.

Henry recorded the marriage in a watercolor called *Marriage sous la lune* (1944). It shows a blue crescent moon above a jagged mountain range, and a twinkling six-pointed star that says "Lepska."

"There was a near conjunction of Venus with the moon on the day we were married," Lepska Warren writes of the watercolor. "At that elevation, everything was luminous." The lovers returned to Big Sur and took up life in their Spartan paradise.

We have a glimpse of the idyllic beginning of their marriage in one of Henry's letters to Larry Durrell:

> Going to bed now. End of a quiet Sunday at Big Sur. My Polish wife, Lepska, has just been telling me stories of Poland. I've only learned two words of that language so far—Good Morning: sounds like Gin Dobrie. . . . Every day we take a sun bath. It's like Spring now. Amazing climate and gorgeous scenery. Something like Scotland, I imagine. It's one of the few regions in America you would like. I must describe it to you some day. One of the features of it are the vultures. The other is the fogs. And the third is the lupine which is like purple velvet over the mountain sides. There are also four crazy horses which I meet on my walks through the hills. They seem glued to the spot. And two of them are always in heat. I have a wonderful cabin, you know, dirt cheap—ten dollars a month. I have a young wife (21), a baby on the way proba-bly, food in the larder, wine *à discrétion*, hot sulphur baths down the road, books galore, a phonograph coming, a radio also coming, good kerosene lamps, a wood stove, an open fireplace, a shower, and plenty of sun—and of course the Pacific Ocean, which is always empty. Alors, what more? This is the first good break I've had since I'm living in America. I open the door in the morning, look towards the sun rising over the mountains, and bless the whole world, birds, flowers and beasts included. After I have moved my bowels I take the hound for a walk. Then a stint of writing, then lunch, then a siesta, then water colors, then correspondence, then a book, then a fuck, then a nap, then dinner, and so to bed early and up early and all's well except when I visit the dentist now and then.

Henry's fame—and notoriety—were growing in a cult-ish sort of way; he had many helpers and admirers—almost too many—but money continued to be tight.

When Valentine, his second daughter, was born in 1945, he was still sending out begging letters for baby food, money, and clothes. Watercolors and handouts continued to be a more reliable source of income than his books. He was nearing sixty and a father of three.

In the forties, the press began circulating rumors of Henry Miller's "cult of sex and anarchy" at Big Sur, and admirers kept arriving on the rugged coast looking for same. Henry complained of these tourists and hangers-on, but often invited them in to talk and eat, and it fell to Lepska to cook and entertain them. She must have felt like Madame Tolstoy with the Tolstoyans.

Whatever its myth, life at Big Sur was difficult, and Henry and Lepska quarreled over the children, the visitors, their differing views of how life should be run. There is no question that Lepska understood and admired Henry as an artist, but that doesn't mean she found it easy to share his life. In his later years, Henry often seems to be using women as appliances to make himself more comfortable. A monumental selfishness, ironically, accompanies the blossoming of the sage.

Henry adored Val and Tony and spent time with them that he never spent with his first child. He was an enchanted, middle-aged father, and he once confessed to me that the greatest defeat of his life after Lepska left was his inability to care for his children totally. He was astounded, he said, by the power of women to raise children. "The greatest wrestler or boxer in the world would be worn out in one week if he had to take care of two little children. Feed them! Put diapers on them. Wipe their ass," Henry said to me with sheer amazement in 1975. He thought that if the next generation were left to men, the human race would surely perish.

The years 1944–48 were important ones for Miller in many ways, but, creatively, they were less fertile. The birth of Val and Tony and the flowering of the reputation of his Paris books were important to him, as was the defense of his literary reputation by French intellectuals such as Sartre, Camus, and Gide. Henry wrote *Sexus, The*

Time of the Assassins, and *The Smile at the Foot of the Ladder* in these years, but one gets the feeling that he was mostly rehashing old experiences. Why was he delving again into his marriage to June—the first June—in *The Rosy Crucifixion* trilogy? The books are full of wonderful digressions on writing and all manner of other things, but the relationship with June hardly seems a sturdy enough theme on which to base a whole trilogy. Was Henry written out? Or did he lack a new muse?

There is also a sense in *Sexus*, *Nexus*, and *Plexus* that Henry is imitating himself, trying to repeat what had been so fresh, new, and explosive in *Cancer*, *Capricorn*, and *Black Spring*, and which now has become stale. Often the sex in *The Rosy Crucifixion* is formulaic, and the women seem robotic. They have become nothing but isolated holes, begging to be filled. Henry did not fulfill his early promise with these books. It seems that at this point, Henry had no shit-detector: he did not know his good writing from his bad.

Both Anaïs Nin and Gore Vidal have commented trenchantly on the sloppiness that began increasingly to invade Miller's writing. In a letter of 1937, Nin assails Miller for his tendency to reduce "all women to an aperture," and she calls this "a disease." In a brilliant essay on "The Sexus of Henry Miller," written in 1965, Gore Vidal faults not only Miller's "hydraulic approach to sex" but also his tendency to reduce all characters except his autobiographical protagonist to "shadows in a solipsist's daydream." The criticism is apt. Henry's writing is nowhere more uneven than in *The Rosy Crucifixion*.

After the liberation of Paris, Maurice Girodias, the son of Henry's first publisher, Jack Kahane, wrote to Henry with the good news that his early books were selling. They were being constantly reprinted, probably for the GI market, and Henry had accumulated more money in royalties than had passed through his hands in his whole life. (No trip to Paris at this time would have been complete without the purchase of *Tropic of Cancer* and *Tropic of Capricorn*. One edition even bound them together in paper covers with *Jane Eyre* printed on the front!) For the briefest of moments, Henry was rich in France—the owner, in name only, of a fortune in French royalties that, for a few months, was worth an astonishing $40,000. But before he could collect this small fortune or move to France and spend it, the franc was devalued and his royalties all but evaporated.

Everyone wanted a piece of Henry's uncollectible fortune—his ex-wife June, the IRS, freeloaders who arrived in Big Sur to sit at the master's feet, old friends from Paris like the astrologer Conrad Moricand, whom Henry wrote about in the "Paradise Lost" section of *Big Sur and the Oranges of Hieronymus Bosch*.

Henry's financial life reads like a surrealist farce. Even when he had money, he sometimes couldn't get his hands on it, and when he didn't have any, the fates or his watercolors provided. He really needed the philosophy he espoused—the philosophy of the *Tao Te Ching*, the eternal ebb and flow of riches, both spiritual and material. His life was almost a constant lesson in letting go. He had to cultivate the detachment of the Zen sage, or go mad.

By 1949, the Paris books were appearing in sufficient numbers in the United States—smuggled in by returning Americans—to bring Henry a new burst of attention from the postwar generation of writers and readers.

The Happy Rock, printed by Bern Porter in California in 1945, shows the way Miller's reputation was growing in postwar years. Dedicated "to the freedom of the Press—should there ever be any," this little volume contains an odd assortment of selections from Kenneth Patchen, Nicholas Moore, Wallace Fowlie, Lawrence Durrell, William Carlos Williams, and others.

Porter was a Berkeley physicist who established his own small press with the exclusive purpose of furthering Miller's career. *The Happy Rock* is a strange festschrift, but one that shows how much Miller's work meant to many literary people, and how, despite the relatively small numbers of his books available in his native land, he was transforming the culture.

It is a fallacy of our benighted publishing industry that numbers and sales figures predict the "importance" of books. The truth is that many of the most significant books of our time were either printed in tiny first editions by hitherto unheard of presses—*Ulysses* appeared in 1922 in an edition of 750 copies—or not printed at all until many decades after their composition, like Anaïs Nin's diaries. The millions of copies of *Scarlett*, the so-called sequel to *Gone with the Wind*, and Danielle Steele's old wives' tales, will have vanished into the landfill when Miller's banned, smuggled books are still being read. Life is short, art is long, and freedom of the press moves forward like the light from vanished stars. Often the author is not around to enjoy the fruits of creation. No wonder the most important discipline the writer must cultivate is detachment.

Perhaps this was why, when Miller finally found himself famous for books written years earlier, he did not quite believe he had entered the realm of the kosher literary gent, and continued to publish with tiny presses and to live at the margins of "official" literary culture. Official literary culture had never been kind to him, had never understood him or granted him the barest livelihood from his work, even during his most productive years, and he truly felt he did not belong with its supposed worthies.

This must also account for much of the distressing unevenness of Henry's work. He never received any useful, practical criticism or enjoyed any nurturing editorial relationships. He was either an embattled, rejected author or the object of cult adulation. In order to continue working, he was forced to take a fuck-everything attitude toward the literary world. Either that, or slit his throat. He *had* to be defiant. As late as 1975, Henry said to me: "I read the literary pages and my name is never mentioned, it seems." (Even today a quick check of major universities and colleges, including Columbia, UCLA, Reed, Bennington, and Barnard, reveal no courses in Miller, and no Miller titles show up even in survey courses.)

It was Henry's fate to change the culture from underground, as it were, and never to be given official credit for doing so until well after he was dead. He vacillated between defiance and detachment, and had little trust in the advice given to him about his writing, even when it came from beloved friends.

Larry Durrell didn't like *Sexus* any better than I do. He cabled Henry that it would completely ruin his reputation and that he should withdraw it from publication. Henry flatly refused to do so, and even forgave Durrell the slur on his work. When Durrell wrote to Henry "what on earth possessed you to leave so much twaddle in?" Henry calmly replied:

> Larry, I can never go back on what I've written. If it was not good, it was true; if it was not artistic, it was sincere; if it was in bad taste, it was on the side of life.

It is possible that Henry might have felt this way even if he had encountered a caring editor whom he felt he could trust, but I wonder whether his narcissism would have permitted an editor to function. It was not in the cards for Henry to be able to trust anyone, because his best work was so far ahead of its time—and his worst work, as with many writers, was horrendous self-parody. Henry wrote the only way he knew how—out of a blind, brute desire to get it all down. The next stage—the shaping and honing and selecting—was in a sense denied him, because he had no choice but to write headlong and pell-mell. His fear of not writing at all was too great. He was creating a new level of honesty in his work and sometimes grace went with it, as in *Maroussi*, and sometimes grace went out the window, as in *Sexus*. What mattered to Henry was not grace but truth: he was so afraid of the silences and indecisions of his early career that he published too much sloppy, repetitive, unedited work.

I think time will prove his unmethodical method just. Even *Sexus*, *Nexus*, and *Plexus*, my least favorite Miller books, have wonderful moments. But I also think it is unfortunate that Henry, perhaps because he was forever embattled, had to choose between truth and grace. Is grace, perhaps the province of the serene?

We think too little of the conditions artists need in order to make the best possible use of their creativity. We expect our most talented people to blossom despite all odds.

Most of Lepska's and Henry's quarrels were over child rearing. Henry was indulgent, and to him Lepska was a Germanic (she was in fact Polish) disciplinarian like his mother. They parted in 1951. The next year Henry fell in love with Eve McClure, a woman many of his friends considered the best for him of all his wives. Eve was an artist, and she and Henry met by letter and by book, as Henry was to meet so many people in his life. Eve's admiration of his work, her beauty, her willingness to take care of him and Val and Tony, made her, for a while, the perfect wife. Lepska had decamped with a biophysicist who came to visit Big Sur—and in time Eve was to decamp as well. Henry and all his contradictions cannot have been easy to live with. His books were open, but he was often closed to his wives. He was intimate with everyone but the women he loved—perhaps with the exception of Anaïs, whose secret was her unavailability.

During Henry's relationship with Eve (who was twenty-eight to his sixty when they met), his fortunes as a writer finally began to change from cult status to superstardom. And Eve was there as his helpmate during this transition. They began to live together in Big Sur on April Fool's Day, 1952, and left for a seven-month tour of Europe on December 29, 1952. They arrived in Paris on New Year's Eve, to find Henry enormously famous. He was suddenly a target for paparazzi, adulated for books that had been written decades ago but had only recently captured the attention of the public as scandalous bestsellers—a curious fate for any writer. One is at once gratified by recognition and bitter that it did not come when it was most needed.

After the fifties, Henry was never really a poor man again. But by then his best work was behind him. The money he had been unable to collect from Girodias in the late 1940s was eventually replaced by royalties on the French editions of some of his early books. From then on, Henry was continually reprinted in France, in Germany, in Japan—everywhere but at home. As soon as he had money he tried to share it with everyone.

Georges Belmont reports that when he arrived in Paris with Eve, the first thing he said was: "*Do you need money, Georges? I have plenty.*" He couldn't wait to get rid of it. His inner abundance was such that he believed that the more he gave away, the more he actually had. Many people claim to believe this; few live by it.

Henry always said that censorship had the opposite effect the authorities decreed. And this was surely true in his case. The Paris novels of the thirties had been selling steadily all over the world, but it was his being prosecuted for "pornography" that would finally make Henry world-famous—for all the wrong reasons.

First, there had been *L'Affaire Miller* in 1946, when a Frenchman named Daniel Parker sued Henry's publisher, insisting he suppress the French version of *Tropic of Capricorn* on the grounds that it was pornography. A group of distinguished French intellectuals led by Maurice Nadeau sprang to Henry's defense, caused a stir, and in the process made Henry a household word and a bestselling author in France. Then, in 1949, *Sexus* was published in France and banned as pornography without benefit of intellectual protest from the likes of Sartre, Gide, and Camus.

Henry defended himself pretty well. Here's one story—as he told it to me in California in 1975:

> I was in France on a visit there and I'm informed one day that I must go to court in the Palais du Justice—do you

know where that is? And this is a court like we don't have.
It's a preparatory court before the trial and in this preparatory thing there's only a judge there with a clerk taking the
notes and you and your lawyer, and you have the freedom
to tell the judge everything you want about the thing. How
he should look at it, what you think, and so on. You can
speak your mind freely, you understand, he will ask questions too. And so I went through that. Incidentally, I was
so excited, you know, nervous, that I pissed in my pants.
I asked my lawyer, "Can't I go to the can? I have to go."
He said, "Just do it in your pants." Yeah! And it went all
over the floor, you know? The judge must have seen it and
I had to go on with the whole thing. The good thing was
the clerk sitting at a separate little table while the judge
was on the dais at another desk, talking down to me. I'm
sitting down below. And the clerk is always regarding me.
When the judge asked me a question this little clerk
watches me closely. I'm aware that he's hanging on my
words. So the thing is just about over and the judge says,
"Oh yes, now Mr. Miller, one more question. And I want
you to take your time answering it. I want to ask you, do
you honestly believe now . . . do you honestly in your own
heart and soul believe that a writer has the right to say
anything he likes in a book?" And I knew this was a great
moment so I didn't answer that. I was pondering it, pondering it, but I knew right away what I was going to say
and the clerk is watching me like a rabbit. And finally I
look up at the judge and I say, "Your Honor, I really do
think that an author has the right to say whatever he
likes." And the clerk judge comes down and I stand up, he
greets me, puts his arms around me, kisses me on each
cheek and he says, *"Would that France had more men like
you."* And then he says you know, of course, that you're
in honorable company, don't you know . . . François Villon, de Maupassant, he mentioned a whole string of writers, do you see? Isn't that marvelous?

I try to piece this very Henryish narrative together
with what I know about the history of the censorship of

Henry's books. Is he talking about *Sexus*? Or had he conflated the *Sexus* case with another of the many obscenity prosecutions he suffered? It appears that the only obscenity prosecution in which Henry was actually summoned to appear occurred in Brooklyn in 1962. But his books were always being banned somewhere in the world and Henry must have dreamed of judges.

The story Henry told me is therefore another example of Henry's mythmaking. It may contain some garbled recollections of the *Sexus* banning in Paris, but it has all the ingredients of a typical Henry story: a protagonist, an antagonist, a moral. And the protagonist calls himself "Henry Miller," but the historical coordinates are among the missing. Or at least among the woolly.

Also note the conjunction of abstract ideas and quotidian details! He talks about free expression while pissing on the floor! This is typically Henry: a classic purity, as he said in *Black Spring*, where dung is dung and angels are angels. Also, it's a terrific story. Especially the peeing in the pants and the kiss from the judge. That Henry would construct such stories gives us further insight into his books. Henry was the hero of his own life. His pants were damp. His cheeks were wet. But what's a hero for?

Henry's long trip to Europe with Eve in 1953 was one of the great times of his life, despite his distress at finding Europe so changed since his expatriate decade. He visited old haunts. In Paris he saw Man Ray, Brassaï, Belmont, Léger. And he went to Wells, England, where his old pal Alfred Perlès now lived with his wife, Anne. Eventually Henry and Eve returned to California and he married Eve in 1953.

Henry was a marriage addict, though once married he had a tendency to become cut off emotionally from his wives. He was happiest in pursuit, in courtship, in anticipating the delights of bonding, and always somewhat prone to move away from the intimacy of the bond itself. He had made his great bond early in life to a mother who, he claimed, never showed any affection for him. And he tended to become uncomfortable with closeness. Once the lover of his dreams was installed as a mate, he fled.

Psychoanalysis would perhaps have changed this pattern, had Henry wanted to change it strongly enough. So much of his writing about men and women was triggered by—and was a retelling of—the tempestuous relationship with June, that one feels he needed this central conflict in his life, that it was essential to his creativity.

One often sees this pattern in the lives of writers, who, of course, merely document the human condition: a pivotal unhappy relationship that recapitulates the pivotal unhappy relationship of childhood, and a creative life wedded to the past, to the constant winding and unwinding of this same ball of yarn. The oedipal struggle, disguised in a new relationship, is played out endlessly, even to the edge of doom. This was certainly the case with Henry. It seems never to have been resolved until, long after Louise Nieting Miller's death, Henry reinvented her as the loving mother of his dreams, the mother he encounters in paradise in "Mother, China, and the World Beyond" in *Sextet*.

It was in the fifties that all Henry's stories started to come full circle: Barbara, his first child, came back to him; June, his second wife, became his correspondent; Lauretta, his retarded sister, became his ward after his mother's death of cancer in 1956, and Louise's death itself consolidated his position as the head of the family and provider of stability for all the others.

This was an odd position for Henry to find himself in, since in many ways he remained childlike all his life. It is this childlike quality that accounts for the naïf wondrousness of his watercolors and for the open-heartedness of many of his essays on watercolor painting, places, and people. It also accounts for the openness of his response to new people in his life, which continued up to his death.

It is important to see just how responsible Henry could be. After his mother's death, he saw to it that his sister Lauretta was eventually moved to a home in California. He saw to it that June was minimally looked after (by his fans

James and Annette Kar Baxter). He was reunited with
Barbara, and eventually, in his will, made her equal legatee
with Val and Tony.

Miller's family feelings were quite conventional in his
later years; he tried to be responsible for those whom life
had left behind—Lauretta and June particularly. To the
end of his mother's difficult life, he did not want her to
know that he had divorced the mother of Val and Tony
and married Eve. He was afraid of her disapproval even
then.

I am sorry to have to report that he was not the unmiti-
gated monster feminist critics of the seventies made him
out to be. He was just a man—unanalyzed, full of contradictions, imperfect—but able to express the conflicts of
life and sexual politics with unparalleled honesty. I would
have shunned him as a husband as Nin did, because he was
a devourer of women, but as a friend he could be loving
and kind. He never claimed to be an angel; he saw himself
as a bundle of human foibles who had somehow wandered
into earthly paradise.

That Henry was a difficult husband is attested to by the
collapse of his marriage to Eve, who, for all her nurturing
nature, eventually found the strain of being Henry's wife
too great. Responsible for the children, the ex-wives, the
correspondence, inclined to drown her anxieties in drink,
Eve became Henry's victim in a way that June and Anaïs
were able to avoid. Henry was a difficult man unless he was
kept in a state of perpetual yearning. He didn't mean to be
difficult, but his life was so full of complexities, and he had
so many needs, that he used people. But they came back
again and again to bask in the radiance of his life force. He
always required various male "boon companions" to take
care of him (in Paris, Perlès, Belmont, and Fraenkel had
done such duty, and in Big Sur, it fell to Ephraim Doner
and Emil White).

Yet he could be cold to those women who really cared
for him, who gave him what he claimed he most needed.
It was for the unavailable ones that he reserved all his heat.

In 1959, at Nepenthe in Big Sur, Henry began an affair

with a young woman named Caryl Hill. Eve was an eyewitness to it, and was thoroughly humiliated. It plunged her further into alcohol abuse. Though later Henry was to be deeply remorseful about his marriage to Eve (especially after she took her own life in 1966), at the time he seems to have been oblivious to the effects of his behavior. In certain ways Henry could be incredibly insensitive to those around him, and women as vulnerable as Eve were the ones to suffer. The women who took off and made a new life, like Lepska, were the survivors of the Miller myth.

Henry seemed to know this about himself, for he loved Françoise Gilot's *Life with Picasso* and sent it to several of his ex-wives, as if daring them to expose him as a humbug and a narcissist. Henry loved spirited women who did not knuckle under to him. He loved honesty and feistiness even at his own expense, and was contemptuous of those who played the victim. One of the things he liked about my writing was the acid, satirical way it depicted men—from the woman's point of view. Henry knew he had been cruel to many women, and he knew he deserved to be exposed. Perhaps he felt that *Fear of Flying* exposed his own romantic cons. He was a sexist, but a repentant one.

In 1960, as his relationship with Eve was ending, he took off for Europe to be a judge at the Cannes Film Festival and he arranged for Caryl Hill to meet him in France. He went first to Germany to see his German publisher, Ledig Rohwalt, and there met Rohwalt's young, beautiful assistant, Renate Gerhardt, with whom he began a passionate affair. By the time he got to Cannes and met Caryl Hill as planned, he was already in love with Renate.

Renate proved ultimately unattainable and so held Henry's heart hostage. Henry wanted to marry her, but she was too practical. She had two boys, and was not about to give up her life in Europe to become Henry Miller's beleaguered helpmate. Eventually Renate started her own publishing firm and Henry sent her money to help finance it, though he had his usual share of financial difficulties. His letters to her show him dizzy with love in typical Henry fashion, signing himself "St. Valentine," and hypnotizing himself as in the early June-days, Anaïs-days, Lepska-days, Eve-days, *und so weiter.*

One feels a kind of hollowness in Henry's loves as he grows older and older. It is as if he is falling in love with love, or with love remembered. He needs the adrenaline high of being "in love," the image of himself as St. Valentine, the jump start to his animal spirits and his creativity that "love" provides. But the romantic round has a sort of forced quality to it—all except for the suffering part.

In 1961, Henry made another trip to Europe to press his suit with Renate, but he failed to convince her to join her life with his. On the way home, he stopped in New York, where his past claimed him in the form of June— now a beaten, emaciated "old" woman (she was only 58!), who looked to the now-famous Henry as her savior.

June's side of the story is a tragic one. She wound up alone, impoverished, hospitalized for madness, released to dire poverty. It would be fascinating to tell her tale in a novel. Anaïs Nin began it in *Henry and June,* and Philip Kaufman sensitively extended it in the movie of the same name. But there is another whole era of June's life after Paris, and it would make a wonderful, if tragic, saga. Henry never wrote it; the truth is, he never saw June as a separate person. The woman who inspired most of his writing was, when he found her again, a wraith, a will-o'-the-wisp. Henry had to look at the fact that he had devoted his imaginative life to someone who now seemed an apparition. Did this fateful meeting make him understand his own self-deceptions? Apparently not.

By 1961, Henry was at last famous in his own land and an American bestselling author. This was largely due to the efforts of Barney Rossett's Grove Press and because of a changed publishing climate, which, in turn, was to transform the American novel.

The story of Henry's books and the law would make a long and revealing volume in itself. His books were banned in many countries with differing legal traditions and liberated by means that were both astonishingly complex and costly. The legal aspects of Henry's career have been well-documented in Edward de Grazia's *Girls Lean Back Everywhere*, Charles Rembar's *The End of Obscenity*, and E.R. Hutchison's *Tropic of Cancer on Trial*. After *Ulysses*, *Tropic of Cancer* is the book that opened the bedroom door for American writers and for the world. Few people who write about novels seem to remember how short a time it has actually been since fiction was released, and allowed to enter the precincts of the bedroom. As recently as 1960, Alfred Knopf recommended to John Updike that he excise some of the racier bits in *Rabbit, Run* and Updike did so without a backward glance (though he reinstated the cuts in later editions).

1960 is indeed a pivotal year for the freeing of American literature from prudery and threat of legal assault. It was in 1955, after all, that Nabokov's *Lolita* was published by the Olympia Press in Paris because no American publisher would take it. When it appeared in the United States from Putnam's in 1958, it caused a sensation, shooting to the top of the bestseller lists in part because the public wrongly mistook it for the memoirs of a pervert. (Nabokov has some witty things to say about this—and the whole question of sexuality and literature—in his brilliant afterword to *Lolita*.) *Lolita* began to change a publishing climate that had kept Miller out of American publishing for three decades. And *Lady Chatterley's Lover* made the weather even warmer. But it was the many American litigations concerning *Tropic of Cancer* that finally freed our literature. And it was Grove Press, led by Barney Rossett, which finally took the risk of publishing *Tropic of Cancer* and thereby establishing the relatively new legal principle that a book of literary merit might not be suppressed just because it excited lustful desires. *Ulysses* weakened the effect of the Hicklin rule on American jurisprudence, but it was the litigation over *Tropic of Cancer* which established Justice Brennan's doctrine that sexual excitation alone was not enough to warrant the banning of a book. That doctrine has since been weakened in turn by a Supreme Court that has made "community standards" the most important test.

It is interesting to note that the puritanism of our culture has a tendency to condone pure smut but to vigorously attack artful, good writing that has a strongly sexual element. "Nothing infuriates the vigilante so much as the combination of sex and intellect," says Charles Rembar in *The End of Obscenity*. And it is true even today that an issue of *Screw* provokes less fury than a book like *American Psycho* or *Vox*. Madonna's *Sex* has had an easier passage into the world than the Mapplethorpe images she is purloining and betraying.

The sexomania of our culture is such that it simultaneously slavers and condemns. I have in mind an image of pious southern senators leaving a prayer breakfast at the Reagan White House to view—with an eye to censoring—pornographic movies, then buggering their aides, boffing their secretaries, and passing laws preventing the rest of America from doing the same. Sex in America is definitely not for hoi polloi.

At the beginning of my career I was always amazed that some critics of *Fear of Flying* (and subsequent books) resented Isadora not so much for her lustful thoughts as for her lustful thoughts coupled with her bookishness. It is as if the puritan sexomaniacs want their sex purely smutty—free from all traces of "culture," ghettoized in a sort of Forty-second Street of the mind. Is that because they are more threatened by literate lust?

Miller's books always seem to raise similar hackles. This is why, I suspect, the academic community has yet to take him seriously and subject him to intelligent literary scrutiny.

Barney Rossett, by his own account, fell in love with Miller's work in his student days and had been trying to publish Miller for some time at Grove Press. But Miller shied away from publication in America. Why? The reasons appear to be more complex than is usually assumed. First, Miller was afraid—afraid of arrest, afraid of being branded "the king of smut" (as he wrote to Rossett), afraid of burying books like *Maroussi* under a deluge of scandal, afraid for his children, and for his own loss of privacy (which, in fact, accelerated with his growing fame).

But I submit that Miller also felt guilty about his Paris books, guilty about the way his fiction had sucked June dry and spat her out as a husk of an old woman, while he rode on to adulation. He had mixed feelings about his sexual books. How could it be otherwise, when these books were propelled by such conflicting, tempestuous, oedipal emotions? There must have been a part of Miller that felt the punishment (the banning of his books in his mother-land) fit the crime (the betrayal of his mother).

Writers of revealing books normally have a welter of disturbing feelings about them, and sometimes these feelings are resolved by sabotaging their own work in various ways, both conscious and unconscious. Fame raises ambivalent responses, and many people, feeling themselves unworthy, are driven toward various forms of self-destruction—drugs, drink, lawsuits, disastrous money-losing schemes.

Miller had long been ambivalent about having his work published in his own country. He was well-known and widely published abroad, and in some ways it suited him well to be an underground writer in America. But he finally succumbed to Barney Rossett's ever-escalating offers for *Tropic of Cancer* and *Tropic of Capricorn* because of the precarious copyright status of the books published in Paris and the threat that another publisher would bring out an unauthorized, possibly expurgated edition. Barney Rossett agreed to pay not only for the books but for the cost of litigation, and the litigation proved to be extensive and expensive.

By the time *Tropic of Cancer* was published in America on June 24, 1961 (and sold 68,000 copies in the first week), Henry had made his peace with his fate as a writer.

"The game of writing, living, being—has come to be for me the end in itself," he had written to Barney Rossett. And it was true. He also told Rossett "that one's true fame is kept alive by the good opinion of a thinking few," and that "a sudden increase in fortune . . . would undoubtedly cause more harm than good." He saw American culture as "moving steadily in the opposite direction of Whitman's vision," and he expected little from the furor of the *Tropics* than to be established in the minds of his compatriots as the apotheosis of the dirty old man.

His prophetic vision was astoundingly precise. The extensive litigation over the *Tropics* fixed Miller in the public's mind as the author of "filthy, disgusting, nauseating" trash. Of course the public could not wait to get their hands on such stuff. And the *Tropics* sold like mad the more they were denounced. Sexomania in action.

A number of important literary intellectuals sprang to Miller's defense in the United States and to the defense of the First Amendment but, as in the later Rushdie affair, it proved easier for them to defend him than to read him. By the time the dust settled, Barney Rossett had sold a ton of books and incurred a ton of legal costs. And Miller had become just what he predicted he'd become—the "king of smut."

Tropic of Cancer sold 100,000 copies in hardcover and a million in paperback, caused the arrest of many booksellers, cost Grove Press at least $100,000 in legal fees, and established Henry Miller as a household word. Even when he was finally "vindicated" by the United States Supreme Court in 1964, he was doomed to live out his final decade and a half in the shadow of that ignoble reputation.

It was the final irony that, after the many prosecutions of his books all over the United States, it fell to Henry's own Brooklyn to sue him for having conspired with Barney Rossett to offer for sale "a certain obscene, lewd, lascivious, filthy, indecent, sadistic, masochistic and disgusting book" called *Tropic of Cancer*. Before this ugliness ended in 1964, Miller had been issued a warrant for arrest, threatened with extradition from California to Brooklyn, and had been forbidden to travel abroad for the duration of the legal action. Though it ended with a victory of sorts, Henry was certainly proven right in his reluctance to publish in the United States. That his books now languish largely unread by a generation that takes their existence in print for granted is, I suppose, the final irony.

Henry was wise enough to know that "success" did not bring peace. The royalties on his Paris books caused him endless accounting and tax worries. He had predicted as much in a letter to Barney Rossett: "I see no way to protect anyone through money, through security of any kind." And it surely proved true in his case. His last years were burdened with the immense loss of privacy that fame brings, and the sense of being an imposter for having become notorious because of books written long ago.

In 1963, Henry was even driven out of his beloved Big Sur by the fame he had given it in *Big Sur and the Oranges of Hieronymus Bosch,* and by the end of his marriage to Eve, had moved first to a flat, then to his last earthly address at 444 Ocampo Drive in Pacific Palisades. At first he shared his home with Val and Tony, their mother, Lepska, and her new husband. Later, he lived there alone, or with a series of caretakers.

Surrounded by his children, by interviewers, movie stars, directors, producers, and all the parasites the famous find themselves playing host to, Henry entered the last period of his life—the period when I was to meet him.

He seems to have made his peace with his fame by capitulating to its distortions and making them worse.

In his last years, he allowed books like *Henry Miller: My Life and Times* (1975) distributed by Playboy Press for Bradley Smith, its editor and publisher, to show him playing Ping-Pong with nude groupies or nuzzling a bikini-clad Israeli beauty—and these pictures certainly helped to trivialize his reputation. It was as if he were rushing to become a caricature of himself.

And yet *My Life and Times* also has wonderful things in it. It is a kind of illustrated autobiography, seen from the point of view of the ancient sage who regards the world as a joke—which, I suspect, is where long life leads.

"Let us do our best, even if it gets us nowhere," Henry

wrote in the "Notice to Visitors" he had posted at Big Sur. He almost always took his own advice and got nowhere. But often he was led astray by vanity and ego. It was the faulty shit detector again, and he often could not tell the con man from the prophet. His discrimination about people was almost as poor as his discrimination about his work.

After Val and Tony left home in 1964, and even Lepska took off with her new husband, Henry was lonely and looked to his old tonic—new love—to save him. When he met a twenty-seven-year-old Japanese gamine, Hoki (Hiroko) Tokuda, at a party given by his doctor, he fell madly in love with her looks, her Oriental mystery (mostly invented by him) and her singing and piano playing (an old aphrodisiac).

Hoki was unavailable—the essential ingredient. She came and went mysteriously. This, as always, provoked the necessary yearning in Henry. He became "the gorilla of despair beating his breast with immaculate gloved paws," as he scribbles on one of the "Insomnia" series of watercolors he painted from the depths of his infatuation with her. He was "the germ of a new insanity," "a freak dressed in intelligible language," and there was "a splinter buried in the quick of [his] soul."

Henry was, in short, in love.

His tribute to this May-December romance was *Insomnia or The Devil at Large*, written in his own hand, published by a small New Mexican press called Loujon and then by Doubleday in 1975, and accompanied by a series of hallucinatory, yearning watercolors covered with fragments of poetry. Henry was "shaking cobwebs out of the sky." Or rather, inventing a lover out of his own yearning. His late illustrated books show his constant desire to blend genres, to show the slant of his own handwriting, the faces of his ancestors, his children, his wives, his friends, and the rainbow hues of his watercolors.

It's important to remember that Henry comes out of the same Paris as Picasso, Man Ray, and Léger: mixed media, surrealism, automatic writing are part of his artistic heritage and he displays that heritage especially in the illustrated work of his last years.

Hoki found him too much like a grandfather to be attracted, but when she needed a green card, she relented and married him. The pictures of old Henry and young Hoki were duly carried by all the news magazines. They fitted in nicely with the pop persona of a dirty old man.

Insomnia is a lovely book, if slight, a wonderful paean to love-as-madness, hallucination, and despair. That Henry was still Pan enough to yearn so violently is a sort of tribute to the green fuse within him. His heart never dried out like a walnut. He remained moist to the end.

Or almost to the end. When I met him in October 1974, he was still overflowing with enthusiasm, with conversation, with the ability to yearn. Hoki had departed. (She now runs a nightclub called Tropic of Cancer in Tokyo.) He was in love then with Lisa Liu and Brenda Venus. And many other pretty ladies (like Twinka Thiebaud, and other friends of Val's and Tony's) came to cook for him, care for him, and keep the flame.

I was drawn to Henry because he gave me immense encouragement at a difficult time of my life, but I stayed because he was such a warm fire, such a force for life. His head and his heart lived on the same planet. Anaïs Nin had discovered this quality about him long before the rest of the world did. In an amazing "Boost for *Black Spring*" published in 1937 in *The Booster*, Nin wrote:

> Like all the hardy men of literature Henry Miller lives on two planes: either in the peaty soil, among the roots of things, or amidst the ecstasies. Like some hybrid out of ancient myth he walks the earth surefootedly and is one with the earth; but he can also depart the earth at a bound and soar to unheard-of realms, and, if it please him, remain there forever. The region in between, which is flimsy and unreal, which nourishes neither the body nor the soul, that region he never enters, thank God. He lives either on

the earth or in the mystery—*never in the salon of the mind*. Others around him are writing in a kind of black void, writing to compensate for their lack of virility. Their insanity is like a whirlpool with a hole in the center, an eddying round a void. But in *Black Spring*, the insanity is produced by an excess of life; it is like a surcharged top spinning wildly, experience ending not in crystallization but in a fantastic spiral ecstasy.

Always there is the smell of the street, the smell of human beings. Even in the upper galleries of metaphysics it smells of truth, of honesty and of naturalness. Depths reached by clairvoyance, not by cohabitation with ideas. It is always a man exploring the heavens; not a spirit hovering over the earth with wilted, offended wings. In one and the same instant he seizes upon man the animal and the dream which obsesses the poet. Always the flesh and the vision together. At moments he stands shouting like a prophet, cursing, vilifying, denouncing, seeing into the future with the same intensity with which he installs himself in the present. He is at one and the same time the man sitting contentedly at a café table and the restless, ghostly wanderer pursuing his secret self in an agony of duality and elusiveness.

Nin, who knew him both as colleague and lover, got him exactly right: *always the flesh and the vision together.* This is something few of the people who have dissected Miller without having known him personally can understand. He gave off heat like a roaring fire. He was more alive than most people ever are, and when you were near him, he shed his light and life force on you.

Surely he did unkind things in his life. But the minatory and grudging tone of his critics, which basically uses the cheap journalistic technique of contrasting his stated beliefs with his behavior and pronouncing him a hypocrite, is far worse than he deserves. Any of us would seem like hypocrites viewed that way, even the greatest saints. So what if he was not Gandhi with a penis? Even Gandhi was not Gandhi in that sense. Only angry adolescents expect their parents to be perfect, and, finding them human, pronounce a death sentence.

In the end, Miller's character doesn't matter. His art—flawed but powerful—does.

CHAPTER 7

Must We Burn Henry Miller? Miller and the Feminist Critique

Laws and traditions are not overthrown by a logistical performance, however good. It takes dynamite of one sort or another.

—HENRY MILLER, LETTER TO SIXTEEN-YEAR-OLD WILLIAM BECKER, JULY 18, 1966

It is no secret that a great deal of rhetorical rubbish has been written on the subject of Henry Miller, sexist. My conviction is that it has done little good either to the understanding of Henry Miller or toward the destruction of sexism.

Kate Millett, author of *Sexual Politics* and other important books, is not the main offender here. She, in fact, acknowledges Henry as a surrealist, an essayist, and an autobiographer, and many of her own fictions and nonfictions owe something to his unmethodical methods.

It is Millett's journalistic popularizers, particularly in England and to a lesser extent in the United States, who do both her and Henry an injustice in setting the terms of their opposition so grossly. Kate Millett is too much the artist not to understand that Henry Miller is more than just a misogynist. But her *Sexual Politics*, which, like Henry's *Tropics*, more people discussed than actually read, left an indelible mark on Miller criticism.

Millett makes a brilliant case for Henry Miller's autobiographical protagonist as a textbook study of patriarchal attitudes, but she fails to go farther, to explore the source of those attitudes, namely the male terror and envy of female power. (To be fair, this is not the province of her book.) Millett is out to prove that Miller is not "liberated" but that he is enslaved—and surely she is right in this. "Miller," she says, "is a compendium of American sexual neuroses, and his value lies not in freeing us from such afflictions, but in having had the honesty to express and dramatize them." Right again. "What Miller did articulate was the disgust, the contempt, the hostility, the violence and the sense of filth with which our culture, or more specifically its masculine sensibility, surrounds sexuality. And women too; for somehow it is women upon whom this onerous burden of sexuality falls."

Millett's analysis remains illuminating. But only its grossest elements have entered the debate about Miller. How can we use Henry's work to understand the roots of sexism and thereby eradicate them? How can we fight sexism without burning books? Some feminist zealots have damaged the movement for equality between the sexes by means of an oversimplification of analysis: all men are brutes and all women must be gay to be free. Zealotry is the enemy here, not feminism; and zealotry always fuels backlash.

In the last few years, we have been faced with a massive backlash against women's equality before even half the wrongs against women have been righted. Perhaps backlash is inevitable against all movements, and surely women's movements have characteristically ebbed and flowed, but dare we attempt constructive criticism of our own movement? Dare we look at the ways we may have aided the backlash with our own intransigence? Now, with a welcome third wave of feminism approaching, can we be honest enough to acknowledge that women are full of diversity and contradiction? Women, like men, come in all flavors—gay, straight, and indifferent. Women, to be free, must embrace diversity, not conformity.

In responding to these ebbs and flows, I fear we have not attacked the problem of making feminist reform stick. Female solidarity is the key. If we truly want to end this repetitive cycle of feminism and backlash, we must acknowledge the underpinnings of misogyny, the whore/ Madonna split in Judeo–Christian culture and how its setting man against woman and woman against woman has warped us all psychologically.

To blame Henry because he had the courage to articulate it honestly from the male point of view is clearly a case of killing the messenger.

Artists are forever accused of advocacy when they are trying to be mirrors of society, mirrors of the inner chaos of the self. Male chauvinist critics are forever assailing women's books for being full of rage against men and society—as if this were not inevitable, when one is seeking an honest expression of women's feelings. Let us be smarter than these two-bit polemicists. Let us understand the war between the sexes so that we can end it.

Henry Miller had the courage to ride his rage to the outermost limit and present an unforgettable picture of the world at war between cock and cunt. As Millett says, he is not a free man but a slave, and I think even Henry would be the first to agree with her notion of enslavement. He actually articulates this slavery himself in *Insomnia* and other books. But he did eventually get free, beyond the body, beyond the sex war, beyond the whore/Madonna split. His freedom came with the book most ignored by his critics: *The Colossus of Maroussi*. He transcended sex and war, as we all must, man and woman both, to become entirely human. And he came, at last, to forgive his mother—as we all must.

Mary Dearborn, a gifted writer who has written a fascinating but highly damning biography of Miller, strongly bears the marks of the feminist critique. It confuses her response to Miller the man and the writer to the point where she seems to vacillate between attacking him for anti-Semitism, veiled homosexuality, and not-so-veiled sexism, and praising him for his scathing honesty and for "being on the side of life." Her point of view lurches so wildly at times that one wonders why she chose to immerse herself in Miller's life and work. She hates him, yet she is fascinated by him. She denigrates his craft, yet praises his honesty. She is also confused about the difference between art and advocacy. It is as if Shakespeare were recommending regicide in *Macbeth* and suicide pacts in *Romeo and Juliet*.

Dearborn is not alone in her ambivalence. I have certainly felt it too. Anyone immersed in Miller must. Most critics, both academic and popular, are equally confused about the difference between art and advocacy. Feminist novels have been destroyed by the literary establishment because their "givens" were not granted.

In some ways, controversial women writers bear the brunt of this confusion between art and advocacy, because not only are they outside the societal norms of conformist behavior, they are also outside the societal norms of rebellious behavior. The male rebel-artist's way is never open to us. Henry is banned, deprived of publication in his native land, made literally a beggar for his art, but inevitably he becomes a hero because of his very rebellion and renunciation. Rebellious women tend to vanish, to be dropped out of the review media, the anthologies, the college courses. Witness the de facto ban on Andrea Dworkin, in effect for many years; the official eclipse of the once wildly popular Edna St. Vincent Millay; the obsolesence of Anna Wickham, Laura Riding, Muriel Rukeyser, and others too numerous to list.

There is some sign that this is changing in popular art. Feisty women private eyes, trained female killers, and outlaw women are beginning to populate our movie screens and bestseller lists, but they, too, are stereotyped from a male point of view. And only rarely do they outlive their plots. With a third wave of feminism gathering, we must honestly look at the fact that, since the seventeenth century, for every rise of feminism there has been an equal and opposite reaction. Patriarchal attitudes go underground, change terminology, but do not vanish: on the contrary, women creators *do* vanish—except for those few tokens that prove the rule.

We must ask why. And perhaps Henry Miller's work is a clue to that puzzle. Like any underclass, women are denied not only their rights to parity in the arts, but the right to their own subject matter. Their anger is deemed unacceptable, their sexuality hemmed in by male definitions, their place in the academy determined by males or male-identified women. Women critics and academics (who are often defending their token status) tend to be even less kind to them than men. Even the spate of feminist academics seems not to have benefited the position of contemporary woman creators—many of whom remain eternally beyond the pale—unless they espouse the trendy "politically correct" positions that will doom their work to be ephemeral.

Even if we look at Henry Miller vis-à-vis his female contemporaries, we see that his reputation eclipses the reputations of everyone from Anaïs Nin to Kay Boyle. Nin poured much of her essence into helping Henry fulfill himself as a writer. As for June, the writer she might have become was also submerged in Henry. When she arrived in Paris to find Henry involved with Anaïs Nin and writing *Tropic of Cancer*, she felt cast aside. And she was always furious with Anaïs Nin for rewriting history in her expurgated journals.

And what of Louise Nieting Miller, who is remembered mostly for her rages? What if those rages had been put on paper in her own hand, thereby powered by her own rage to live beyond her time? We shall never know. Women of Louise Nieting Miller's generation were rarely writers as well as mothers. We have in place of what she might have written her son's immense creation in response to her rage. Her rage was his motor, his motor-mother.

It is impossible to break the barriers of convention unless one is propelled by rage, a fuck-everything attitude toward literary censors that says, in effect: let them ban or burn me, publish me or punish me—whatever happens I must get down on paper *what is left out of books*. Henry's history as a writer was utterly dependent on his finding the courage to fuck everything.

First he cuts himself off from New York, from his family, from his first wife, Beatrice Wickens, and their daughter, Barbara. Then he takes up with June the taxi dancer, June the rebel, the renegade, the debtor, the conniver, the flagrant and unapologetic bisexual. Then he goes to Paris and becomes a bum, a beggar, a kept man. Under conditions of utter self-abnegation, stripped of his dignity, of all his supports, the Paris book explodes.

I have compared Henry's odyssey to the male initiatory odyssey described in *Iron John: A Book About Men*: a descent into the underworld to find the wildman in oneself and "steal the key from under the mother's pillow." Many women have been offended by Bly's book, thinking it excludes them from the quest for selfhood, but in truth the initiatory odyssey it describes is no different for women in today's world. Female heroism depends on a similar sequence of events. Women must claim their sexuality (and their wildwoman) in order to claim their creativity. But claiming sexuality has never been easy for women. One's own self-censorship is hard to break through, and, if one breaks through, the world is still brutal in its denunciation. Even Aniïs Nin has only published her sexuality from the grave.

The reasons that led to my writing *Fear of Flying* were remarkably parallel to those that led to Henry's writing *Tropic of Cancer,* and it seems he intuitively knew this when he "discovered" my first novel. He felt the kinship between us even though he could not then know how parallel our lives had been: bourgeois families; a renounced first marriage; a second marriage that made possible a flight to Europe and provided both subject matter and muse; many attempts to write "literary" books; and then an explosion, a fuck-everything, a descent into the cave of the wildman (or wildwoman) in the self.

Most commentators stop here in their exploration of both Henry and me. But, releasing the wild one, as Bly knows—it can be male or female—is only the beginning. The wild one takes the hero-writer down to the depths. Then the ascent must begin. And the ascent is everything. Most writers, most heroes, never make it. Henry did.

We live in a time of immense gender-anxiety, a time when both women and men are searching for new definitions of gender and there is such testiness on the subject of femaleness and maleness that it often seems the sexes do not know how to act with each other at all. Witness our current debates about definitions of date rape, sexual harassment, feminism, and backlash.

If this happens in life, imagine how much worse the problem is in literature! Literature presupposes certain societal agreement about what constitutes reality, and there is no such agreement between men and women today. Men live in one world of privilege, women in another world of want.

Literature mirrors this. At one extreme are Andrea Dworkin's fictions anatomizing female abuse; at the other is Bret Easton Ellis's evocations of male violence and brutality. How can such divergence make for a common literature? How can such divergence make for a common voice?

It wasn't always this way. When I began searching for my voice as a writer, it was absolutely clear what a writer's voice was supposed to sound like: male.

As a literature student at Barnard in the sixties, I studied the prescribed curriculum and it was at least 95 percent male. I remember using a book on Emily Dickinson that was from a series subtitled American *Men* of Letters. (Nobody seemed to get the joke.) The Modern American Novel meant: Bellow, Roth, Malamud, Updike. Modern poetry meant: Yeats, Auden, Pound. Even at a college founded by feminists, which prided itself on its affirmation of all things female, there was no question raised about the patriarchal nature of the curriculum. Not yet.

When in 1962, a famous male critic, the late Anatole Broyard, came to my writing class at Barnard and asserted: "Women can't be writers; they don't have the *experience* to be writers," not one female voice was raised against him. We all sat there—we budding female writers—with our eyes modestly downcast, listening to the male voice of authority telling us what we could or could not write. Nobody laughed out loud. Nobody challenged him. And nobody thought it strange at all that a man should be dictating to a room of promising young women writers, many of whom have by now published dozens of distinguished books. Why were we so timid? Why did we find it so difficult to raise a voice?

In my first poems, I assumed a male poet's persona. In my first attempts at fiction, I assumed the voice of a male madman. I loved Nabokov and this male madman's voice was my homage to him. None of this was conscious, of course. I struggled for several years after college and graduate school, searching for a voice that was mine—since I seemed to know even then that no writer is truly born until she finds a voice.

Sylvia Plath's *Ariel* and Anne Sexton's *To Bedlam and Part Way Back* were important books in my life because they released me to find my own experience valid, to stop slavishly imitating Auden and Roethke and become a *woman* poet, taking pride in her own femaleness. That was a long road to travel, because femaleness was mocked, disregarded, and invisibilized by the New Critical Orthodoxies of the academic world in which I found myself. It was not easy for a woman to raise an authentic voice. There were no models, except Colette and de Beauvoir, who were almost unavailable in my college days.

As a young teenage poet—thirteen, fourteen, fifteen years old—I adored Dorothy Parker and Edna St. Vincent Millay, found their work in my mother's bookshelves and appropriated their books to my own room. I loved Parker's mordant wit and Millay's female lyricism. I identified with these poets in a special way that encouraged me to think I could write myself. I did not know their status (or lack thereof) in the "literary world." How could I?

I arrived at Barnard to find these poets considered not kosher. Who among women poets *was* kosher? Elizabeth Bishop, Marianne Moore—women who neutered their voices, who did not wear their ovaries on their sleeves. At that point, I did not have the historical (*her*storical some would say) perspective to understand that these women poets whom I loved had undergone the usual invisibilization process that women creators are treated to under patriarchy. I was given Pound, Eliot, Auden, and Roethke to study and I did so—dutifully and well—but I could never identify much with the women poets allowed into the canon. I was not sophisticated enough to understand that perhaps that was precisely why they—and not the others—were allowed into the canon: so that young women would not identify with them and come to believe they could be writers themselves. Instead, everything was done to make it appear that writing was a male preserve.

I got a degree in literature with honors, won numerous fellowships to graduate school, and toiled for two years on an appropriately unreadable master's thesis about women in the poems of Alexander Pope. It was typical of my generation of women graduate students to express their nascent feminism in searching for traces of androgyny in male writers accepted by the orthodox canon. It would only be the next generation of feminists who would have the guts to rediscover invisibilized writers—from Aphra Behn to Kate Chopin, from Charlotte Perkins Gilman to Adelaide Crapsey. Surely the rehabilitation of Parker and Millay must be at hand.

I give all this background to show what a torturous road I had to travel to find the voice of *Fruits & Vegetables*, my first book of poems, or *Half-Lives*, my second. I had to throw out my literary education and accept my own life. Whatever may be said of my first two books of verse, they do break through to an authentic female voice. This, in itself, was against the odds, and a triumph of self-liberation.

I then sweated for several years on a derivative Nabokovian pastiche called *The Man Who Murdered Poets*. When I brought it to Aaron Asher, my then editor at Holt, a man who had published an unknown young woman poet twice before being rewarded with a novel, he wisely said: "Go home and write a novel in a voice you've discovered in those poems." That remark proved to be the boot in the pants I needed to release *Fear of Flying* from my psyche.

Writing the book was terrifying, another exercise in self-liberation. I truly never expected the book to see the light of day. I wrote with the wind at my back, full of fear and trembling, promising myself that if it were never published—I didn't expect it to be—I would at least be proud of myself for having tried. The book's ending cost me the most sleepless nights. I had internalized the paradigm of the sexual heroine who dies for her sexuality—a paradigm unchallenged in books as diverse as *Madame Bovary*, *Anna Karenina*, Kate Chopin's *The Awakening*, Mary

McCarthy's *A Charmed Life,* and even her *The Group.*
You will find the same paradigm in such comparatively
recent movies as *Fatal Attraction* and *Thelma & Louise.*
If you examine sexy heroines in recent literature you will
see that either they lose their lives or their children for
expressing their sexuality. Sue Miller's *The Good Mother*
punished the heroine for her sexuality by allowing her to
lose her beloved child.

As I sat writing and rewriting the ending of *Fear of
Flying* (twelve times in all), I found myself wanting to kill
off my rebellious alter-ego Isadora, or make her pregnant
and have her lose the baby to a botched abortion. After all,
she had left her "good" husband and gone off with a "bad
boy." Didn't she deserve something terrible?

I did not know why I was drawn to such catastrophes.
How could I know that I myself was a walking paradigm
of sexism? How could I know that I had internalized the
values of patriarchy and was expressing them even in this
supposedly liberated and liberating (as it eventually
proved to be) book?

Patriarchy is within us; that is why it proves so inexorable. We must eradicate it first within ourselves; after that
we may be able to eradicate it in the world.

The only way feminism will ever triumph politically is
if all women—young, old, gay, straight, black, white—
understand that solidarity is our only choice. We may not
always agree about everything, but to fight each other to
the death—however compelling the surface reasons—is to
relinquish our power, to give it away to the patriarchy. My
generation of women—aging baby boomers—has, alas,
sometimes fallen into this trap. We have divided along
essentially meaningless lines. The fact is that all women
are politically oppressed under patriarchy, just as all men
are spiritually oppressed, and only our honesty can save
us. First we must see the problem inside ourselves; then we
must see it in society; then we must fight to change it.
Perception is everything here. All change starts with perception.

Ultimately Miller can be a stronger force for feminism

than for male chauvinism. His writing consistently shows a ruthless honesty about the self, an honesty that even women writers would do well to emulate, because honesty is the beginning of all transformation.

Despite the decade of backlash we experienced during the eighties, despite the success of the divide-and-conquer technique used against feminist progress, I think we are on the verge of a brave new world of equality between the sexes. This is because I see the next generation of daughters—the young women born in the seventies and eighties—and I see that they take for granted a new level of freedom, a new level of choice and self-determination. They will *not* sit quietly while an authority figure tells them what to write. They are already feisty arguers and advocates. They have only to learn the all-important lesson: that it is wisest not to conspire against their sisters, however tempting it may seem.

Every time I read an article or book in which a woman trashes another woman, I think: *Fool!* You don't realize you have been programmed to attack women and coddle men. You don't realize you are the walking embodiment of male chauvinism—even though you have the anatomy of a woman.

Henry Miller's openness to women's writing started at the beginning of his life (Marie Corelli, Emma Goldman, Madame Blavatsky), and never ceased. He passionately advocated the historic contribution Anaïs Nin's diaries made, even after their estrangement. When I met him, he was full of admiration for women creators and intellectuals, and he strongly promoted not only my work but that of Suzanne Brøgger, the Danish writer whose *Deliver Us From Love* (1976) was full of polemics against monogamy, the nuclear family, and rape that had made her a heroine with Scandinavian feminists. Despite his quarrels with Nin, he publicly reunited with her. And he was more able to absorb the lessons of female creativity than many women are. In his Paris days, when Henry discovered Anaïs Nin's writing and celebrated that discovery in the essay "Un Etre Etoilique" (*The Cosmological Eye*), he knew at once he was in the presence of something female, revolutionary, and destined to change the world.

> The contrast between this language and that of man's is forcible; the whole of man's art begins to appear like a frozen edelweiss under a glass bell reposing on a mantel-piece in the deserted home of a lunatic.

Henry recognized at once that all male literature was frozen compared to the fecund delta of female prose. He absorbed Nin's writing and let its influence enliven his own art. He understood that Nin had put her finger on a revolutionary change in the nature of writing in the twentieth century. Henceforth the novels of our time would be autobiography and documentary, as Emerson had predicted when he spoke of novels giving way to diaries or autobiographies. The line between fiction and fact would blur. Just as the epic gave way to the novel in the mid-eighteenth century, so the twentieth century was the age of autobiography, an age in which fiction itself would give way to first-person chronicles based on fact:

> More and more, as our era draws to a close, are we made aware of the tremendous significance of the human document. Our literature, unable any longer to express itself through dying forms, has become almost exclusively biographical. The artist is retreating behind the dead forms to rediscover in himself the eternal source of creation. Our age, intensely productive, yet thoroughly un-vital, un-creative, is obsessed with a lust for investigating the mysteries of the personality. We turn instinctively towards those documents—fragments, notes, autobiographies, diaries—which appease our hunger for life because, avoiding the circuitous expression of art, they seem to put us directly in contact with that which we are seeking.

Henry Miller predicted the art of our age—and even our journalism, film, television, and visual arts—all based on the exploration of personality and the blurring of the line between fiction and fact. It was Henry's ability to seize upon this tendency in his own work, to make the most of both it and the androgyny of his own personality, that made him a radical and prophetic writer. In a sense, he points toward a future of feminized art. His novels may dissect sexism, but his essays and meditative books show a man profoundly in touch with the feminine side of his own nature, releasing the heat of the feminine principle to melt the frozen patriarchal world.

Just as Henry discovered the truth of what made Anaïs Nin a revolutionary writer, Anaïs understood Henry's contribution perhaps better than anyone. In *Henry and June*, the unexpurgated diary of her affair with Henry Miller and June Mansfield Miller (not published till 1987), she remarks on her first feelings while reading *Tropic of Cancer:* "He has left softness, tenderness out of his work, he has written down only the hate, the violence."

Anaïs believes he has done this because the violence of love is easier to express than the tenderness. "But the man who leans over my bed is soft," she writes "and he writes nothing about these moments."

It is the violence of Henry's writing about women that has so angered feminist commentators, just as the violence of much women's writing—Andrea Dworkin's, for example—about men has so angered male commentators. But it is the role of the artist to express this violence. Art *is* pagan, wild, red in tooth and claw. It must be, in order to reflect the chthonic side of nature. It follows the furies, the bacchae, the dybbukim—or it is not truly art. No one has enunciated this view of art more clearly than the controversial critic Camille Paglia, in her brilliant and troubling book *Sexual Personae*. Paglia's abrasive public persona and her regrettable tendency to trash other women makes her hard to accept. But some of her wildest ideas are provocative and much needed: "I see sex and nature as brutal pagan forces," says Paglia. And she challenges orthodox critical canons that attempt to sanitize art and literature, and, in the process, deeply misread them.

Whether one agrees with Paglia's views of maleness

and femaleness or not, her analysis is a brisk tonic for the misinterpretations perpetrated by feminist criticism of Miller. Since sex is indeed a violent pagan force, we cannot blame the artist who attempts to mirror this force. Similarly, women who write about female sexuality, female rage, female vulnerability to rape, ought not to be attacked for mirroring life accurately. We must stop demanding of our artists, male and female, that they sweeten sour nature, that they cook what is meant to be raw. To do this is to demand a Walt Disney theme-park treatment of all our art.

Theme parks are one thing, art another. And it would be tragic if, in the name of "family values," we so sanitized art that it was suitable only for children and therefore could no longer mirror the passions of real life. For years, censorship in America was founded upon the Hicklin rule, which insisted books and films be judged according to whether they would be a possible corrupting influence on minors. This has regrettably hampered the production of grown-up art—in all genres.

In a way, this same censorship is already prevalent in television and movies—two art forms whose immense promise has been utterly traduced, especially in America. Books and the visual arts alone have been allowed the power to disturb, to upset, to inspire controversy. And always, there are censors preparing to take away this freedom. The book industry, run by bean counters who buy shelf space in bookstores as toothpaste manufacturers buy space in drugstores, has begun seriously to dilute freedom of choice. Next time you stand in an airport bookstore and notice that you can choose only between A and B, think how restricted is your access to disturbing books. Try even today to find Henry Miller in the average mall bookstore. He most probably is not there.

"These choices are market-driven," the cynic says, "they stock what sells."

Not quite. A million decisions, made before the fact, determine subject matter, breadth of distribution, and the tenor of expression. In the name of "market forces," your freedoms are being eroded. You are the proof that the market-driven censorship has worked when you say, "They stock what sells."

We cannot pass over the subject of one sex's ability to crush the other without touching at least briefly on the issues raised by Women against Pornography and the Andrea Dworkin and Catharine MacKinnon–drafted model statute that seeks to punish pornography as a crime against women.

Dworkin and MacKinnon define pornography as:

> the graphic sexually explicit subordination of women through pictures and/or words that also includes one or more of the following: (i) women are presented dehumanized as sexual objects, things, or commodities; or (ii) women are presented as sexual objects who enjoy pain or humiliation; or (iii) women are presented as sexual objects who experience sexual pleasure in being raped; or (iv) women are presented as sexual objects tied up or cut up or mutilated or bruised or physically hurt; or (v) women are presented in postures or positions of sexual submission, servility, or display; or (vi) women's body parts—including but not limited to vaginas, breasts, or buttocks—are exhibited such that women are reduced to those parts; or (vii) women are presented as whores by nature; or (viii) women are presented being penetrated by objects or animals; or (ix) women are presented in scenarios of degradation, injury, torture, shown as filthy or inferior, bleeding, bruised, or hurt in a context that makes these conditions sexual.

The statute seems clear and specific and impossible to oppose unless you look at the history of sexual censorship all over the world. Alas, this history demonstrates that sexual censorship is *always* used to mask political goals. Frequently, it is not about sex at all.

People like Edward de Grazia, who have chronicled the censorship wars both in the U.S. and abroad, have shown that the suppression of books can often be linked to more than the reasons initially given. A few examples: D.H. Lawrence's *The Rainbow* was banned in 1914–15 supposedly for obscenity, but in reality because of Lawrence's antiwar sentiments and the fact that he had a German wife at a time when many people were virulently anti-German. Radclyffe Hall's *The Well of Loneliness* was banned in 1929, supposedly for lewdness and obscenity, but really for presenting lesbian characters in a favorable light. Countless books on contraception and sexual technique were banned, again supposedly for obscenity, but in reality because they enabled women to control their fertility or their access to pleasure. Writers like Margaret Sanger and Havelock Ellis were persecuted for these "sins."

Whatever the laws on the books, they tend not to be enforced by feminist intellectuals like Dworkin and MacKinnon, but by police yahoos. It is the societies of busybodies who fear—yet slaver over—sexuality, and the politicians who pander to them, who wind up determining what we can read or see. Wherever sexual laws exist, they will sooner or later be used to repress dissent.

One would think that the viciousness of the attacks on Emile Zola, Oscar Wilde, Radclyffe Hall, James Joyce, Edmund Wilson, and Robert Mapplethorpe would convince MacKinnon and Dworkin that *any* law governing sexual behavior or sexual representation in words or images eventually gets used by Big Brother to silence opposition. Homosexuality itself has historically been attacked as a loss of "family values."

I do not think we can afford to have any sexually repressive laws on the books at all, however benign or protective they may at first seem. I can easily foresee a day when parents who have taken nude pictures of their adorable babies will be arrested for child pornography. All that is needed is another House Un-American Activities Committee—an ever-present danger in the country that invented the First Amendment, but doesn't seem to understand it. Its very point is that we must tolerate cer-

tain obnoxious words and images simply in order to protect our larger freedoms.

Although I remain a First Amendment fundamentalist, I respect the courage of those feminists who have come
forward to illuminate the nature of pornography as a sym-
bolic form of violence against women. Abusive images of
women are ubiquitous in our culture, and these images do
serve to condone society's abuse of women. But it seems
that some feminists have allowed themselves to be manipulated by a cynical right wing, led by evangelical groups.
The attack on pornography that began under the auspices
of the woman-hating Reagan administration was clearly
politically motivated, and those feminists who endorsed it
were, alas, politically naïve.

Disturbing as it is to be surrounded by images of
abused women, it is equally disturbing to be surrounded
by the pretty young females who dominate our visual
media. It is as if old women did not exist, or were somehow
obscene. Women are forced to homogenize their public
images in public life. As long as they are forced to be
"feminine" to be heard and seen, and as long as "feminin-
ity" is defined as young, pretty, soft, and perfumed,
women will have no way to assert the full range of their
selfhood in public or private life.

A distressing conformity is imposed upon us all. Pornography is only part of the problem. Advertising, movies,
television, and romance novels also overwhelmingly present only one face of woman. Until I look at the TV screen
and see women allowed to go without makeup, without
dyed hair, showing their true age, and as long as First
Ladies are forced to prate of cookie baking and to stand by,
or behind, their husbands, we shall have a society in which
it is a dishonor to be a complete woman. These things are
just as damaging as pornography. And I would like to see
the entire female population rise up against them. But I
would not create codes of censorship or legislation against
specific images of women.

All women today live like those African-Americans of
an earlier generation who used to feel obliged to bleach

their skin. Whatever we are is not enough. Why aren't we fully human unless we are blonde, slim, and have no excess skin on our necks? To be a woman is to be always in the wrong. If we can change this, we can surely change pornography. If we can change this, there will no longer be titillation in the image of an abused woman.

Historically, politicians care less about pornography than they care about their power bases. Once they achieve power through pushing the "hot button" of porn, they tend to use that power to crush dissent from *any* source.

Even though we must raise society's consciousness about the many ways in which images of female abuse pervade our culture, there is a greater danger in legally equating such images—or words, for that matter—with acts. Some feminists believe the pornographic image is, in itself, an act of violence (see Susan Griffin's *Pornography and Silence: Culture's Revenge Against Nature* for a lucid exegesis of this idea), but I believe it is deeply dangerous to the First Amendment to equate an image with an act for any purpose whatsoever.

The image of an abused woman is not the same thing as an abused woman. Words are not deeds. If we allow such laws to be promulgated in order to protect women, I think it will not be long before they are used against women as a way to prevent their free expression of their very real grievances.

Imagine a society in which novelists and poets could only write nice things about women. How would we show the very real suffering of women in our culture? Suppose we could never write about sadomasochistic relationships? How would we show that sadomasochistic relationships are often the rule, not the exception? How could we change society if we could not chronicle it honestly?

Even if we are horrified by "snuff films," and by images of violence against women, I think we would be better off changing minds and hearts by a vigorous campaign of consciousness-raising than by altering our laws to interpret a representation of an act as the act itself. If we do that, we are well on our way to promulgating *fatwas* that condemn authors to death, or to lopping off hands and heads like Moslem fundamentalists.

Let Henry rail against the enormous womb. Let women writers rail against the various crazy cocks (and cunts) in their lives. Let the culture be aerated by controversy and debate. But let us not start punishing even the sleaziest creators of images for the harm that might come from ideas.

"Every idea is an incitement," wrote Justice Oliver Wendell Holmes in 1925. He was speaking about sedition, but he might as well have been speaking about pornography. Any text may cause action—sometimes destructive action. Once we punish writers and publishers for their words, we have opened the door to the obliteration of the word.

At present we have an incomplete feminist revolution, one in which women are still institutionalized as the second sex but are beginning to break out of their prison. A thousand censors and guards stand at the gates to silence their valid anger, but at least the Bill of Rights still protects their power to voice it. Overturning the Bill of Rights will hurt feminism more than it will hurt male chauvinism. Laws follow consciousness, and changing consciousness transforms society. This is a better sequence of events than the sequence that relies on suppression of expression to bring about what must eventually be a Pyrrhic justice. If we erase the First Amendment in the name of gender justice, such "justice" will surely backfire.

Ours may be the first culture on earth that has attempted the bold experiment of letting differing groups have their not always equal say. This is unprecedented in human history. Hierarchical animals that we are, we do not take easily to equality. It's too soon—merely two hundred years in the case of the Bill of Rights—to toss away this experiment without carrying it to its conclusion. It may yet bear fruit.

So how shall we write honestly about men and women in a culture where we have, as some have said, two sexes divided by a common language? I think we must grant the

sexes the same freedom of expression that multicultural-
ists grant to differing cultural groups in our heterogenous
culture. We must acknowledge that men and women have
a different emotional experience of life, experience sex
differently, mothering differently, fathering differently,
love differently, rage differently. And we must grant each
sex its honest expression of feeling. In a sense, this is what
both the women's movement and the men's movement
have asked for. Easy as it is to mock the excesses of these
movements, each asks for something authentic: to have its
sex's view of the world declared valid and significant.

Why are we so threatened by this eminently reasonable
demand? We can, I hope, distinguish the desire to validate
emotional truth from the desire to crush the opposite sex.

The fact is that we are in transition from patriarchy to
a new sort of society, one which I hope will combine the
best elements of matriarchy and the best elements of patriarchy, and, in the process, make both words obsolete.

Equalarchy is what we seek, but that does not mean we
ask each sex to be identical. The world has been ruled by
men's emotions for the last several thousand years. Now
we are trying to create a society that equally validates
women's emotions. We are still a long way from it, as many
recent events have shown, from Willy Smith's rape trial to
Clarence Thomas's hearings for the Supreme Court.

Henry Miller's writing, with its open expression and
final transcendence of male rage and its ability to recognize
female creativity, is a good place to begin searching for the
honesty both sexes must find. Shall we burn Miller? Better
to emulate him. Better to follow his path from sexual
madness to spiritual serenity, from bleeding maleness to
an androgyny that fills the heart with light.

CHAPTER 8

Sexomania/ Sexophobia, or, Sex-Libris

The readers of my books fall usually into two distinct classes—those who are disgusted by the strong element of sexuality and those who rejoice in discovering that this element forms such a large ingredient. . . . Only a few discerning souls seem to be able to reconcile the so-called contradictory aspects of my being as revealed through my writing.

—HENRY MILLER, *THE WORLD OF SEX*

n 1974, a publisher wrote to Miller to ask him whether he would be interested in conspiring with me on a book to be called *A Rap on Sex*. Margaret Mead and James Baldwin had just published *A Rap on Race*, and it seemed a likely and promotable idea.

Miller didn't mince words in responding to this possibly lucrative proposal. "I think it stinks," he wrote back. "In the first place I am not an expert [on sex] as you dub me and secondly, though it may well be profitable, there is something about the idea that stinks."

So much for those commentators who say that Henry would do anything for money or that he put in the sex to make it sell. As he said repeatedly, he would rather not have written unpublishable books:

> Here I was begging the Muse *not* to get me into trouble with the powers that be, *not* to make me write out all those "filthy" words, all those scandalous, scabrous lines, pointing out in that deaf and dumb language which I employed when dealing with the Voice that soon, like Marco Polo, Cervantes, Bunyan *et alii*, I would have to write my books in jail or at the foot of the gallows . . . and these holy cows deep in clover, failing to recognize dross from gold, render a verdict of guilty, guilty of dreaming it up "to make money!"

What did sex mean to Henry Miller and why was he willing to risk everything to describe it so vividly in his books? Most of his contemporaries—Margaret Mitchell, Sinclair Lewis, Ernest Hemingway, F. Scott Fitzgerald, Gertrude Stein, Virginia Woolf (to name just a few)— made the conscious or unconscious decision to facilitate publication by referring only obliquely to sexual acts in their books. In the decision to be explicit whatever the price, Miller stands in a tiny crowd: D.H. Lawrence, James Joyce, William Burroughs. Why was depicting sex more important to him than anything else? What did he think sex was? Why did he think it mattered so deeply to human life?

He answers the question clearly in *The World of Sex:*

> Sometimes in the recording of a bald sexual incident great significance adheres. Sometimes the sexual becomes a writhing, pulsating facade such as we see on Indian temples. Sometimes it is a fresco hidden in a sacred cave where one may sit and contemplate on things of the spirit. There is nothing I can possibly prohibit myself from doing in this realm of sex. It is a world unto itself. . . . It is a cold fire which burns in us like a sun. It is never dead, even though the sun may become a moon. There are no dead things in the universe—it is only our way of thinking which makes death.

This "cold fire" of sexuality was equivalent to the life force for Miller. It was what he had in common with Lawrence, and why he labored so long and so maddeningly over *The World of Lawrence.* He shared with Lawrence the pagan sense of sex—sex as primal flux, sex as the gyre of birth, sex as the DNA of existence, the matrix of all creativity. Miller used the word *sex* in a cosmic, not a genital sense. And he was surprised to discover that the world did not agree with him.

But he did not start at this point.

He started in Brooklyn, full of the same sexual neuroses and inhibitions that bedeviled the rest of his contemporaries. That was why he was so keen to free himself. Only the most enslaved of us longs with such intensity to be free. Working his way through letters, vignettes, *Clipped Wings*, *Moloch*, and *Crazy Cock* to the new life of *Tropic of Cancer,* he gradually liberated himself to partake of life's cosmic sexual dance, thereby coming to understand that only by such participation could freedom be won.

The only way Henry could write, finally, was by listening to the divine dictation of the Voice. He had to write what that Voice dictated, or risk writing nothing at all. He did not choose his subject matter; it chose him. He discovered he was nothing but a medium, a channel, and he let language flow through him.

What was sex to him? It was precisely this flow, this flux, this seeming chaos out of which life springs. If he suppressed it, he would suppress *all* expression. He had no choice but to write about sex.

Miller's book on Lawrence, written and rewritten in the early thirties, was abandoned after the publication of *Tropic of Cancer* (though never definitively: he continued to work on it through the mid-forties). It was finally published in 1980, becoming his last book rather than what he had intended to be his first. *The World of Lawrence* gives us many important clues as to Miller's understanding of sex and its role in his writing.

Is *Lady Chatterley's Lover* obscene? If so, how is this obscenity justified? Miller asks. No justification is necessary, he concludes: "Life is obscene and miraculous, and neither is there any justification for life."

> Obscenity is a divine prerogative of man, and is always to be used carelessly, heedlessly, without scruple or qualms, without religious or aesthetic defense. When the body becomes sacred, obscenity comes into its own. Purity of speech is as much bosh as purity of action—there is no such thing. Obscenity is stomped down when the body is degraded, when the soul is made to usurp the body's proper function.

In discussing Lawrence, Miller does a mini-survey of the history of civilization and its varying attitudes toward sexuality. He notes how sex changes from an open, natural act to one performed in shameful privacy as Christianity overtakes the pagan world. He blames Christianity and its dualism for our culture's rejection of the body and all its wants.

"Obscenity," he notes, "figures large and heavily, magnificently and awesomely, in all primitive peoples. . . ." Miller observes that in so-called primitive cultures, where people are in touch with their instinctual selves, religion and ritual always contain powerful elements of both sex and death. Why? Because sex and death are fiercely important parts of life, evoking our deepest pleasures and our deepest fears.

Why is sex important? The answer is so obvious as to need immense obfuscation and denial to be ignored. Sex is important because it is at the very root of life.

> The savage is not a sick man. The savage retains his sense of awe, mystery, his love of action, his right to behave like the animal he is . . .

That animal, lacking the self-consciousness which names things, puts no veil between itself and sex, between itself and death. Sex just *is*—namelessly. So is death.

> Sex is the great Janus-faced symbol of life and death. It is never one or the other, it is always both. The great lie of life here comes to the surface; the contradiction refuses to be resolved.

At the front of *The World of Lawrence* is one of Miller's distinctive diagrams, the kind he used to guide himself while writing. He draws a tree of life at whose base are the words: "GRAVE = WOMB." Below that: "Mother Earth." Below that: "He embraces his animal nature in a primal frenzy for livingness." Up above, where the tree begins to open heavenward, are these words: "Fear of death becomes fear of life. By embracing death the artist restores life."

Miller is ostensibly referring to Lawrence here, but he more likely is referring to himself. Miller never wrote about another writer (Rimbaud, Lawrence, Nin, me) without writing about himself. And the same, no doubt, may be said of all of us.

When we embrace sex, we are also symbolically embracing our own mortality. Fear of sex is therefore also the fear of death. And for many men, the fear of woman is equivalent to the recognition of mortality. It is woman's fecundity that reminds man of the everlasting dance of birth and death.

Miller himself states this baldly:

> Ah, and man's coition, how ironic, mocking, comic it is in the last analysis—man lying on top of woman, dominating her, subjugating her, man the great fighting cock, the strong master of the world. He triumphs cruelly when he enters her and makes her obey, but it is the short triumph of a moment or two, just enough for nature to play her role, to wreak her havoc; and woman submits, submits so willingly (this alone ought to make him suspicious of her), submits so easily (and not just with him but with any one . . . the great whore that she is) because she is accomplishing *her* destiny. . . . The moment the child is born, however, she is through with man; as far as she is concerned now, as woman, he is finished, he can croak.

This is a perfect summation of misogyny—the same misogyny that justified blaming Eve for the expulsion from Paradise, burning witches, denying women the vote, denying them, even today, equal legal rights, equal pay, equal health care, equal right to have total control over their own bodies, equal right to life and limb in public and private spaces.

If woman is womb, the misogynist reasons, she is also tomb. If woman is life, she is also death. But the "primitive," the "savage," accepts this dichotomy unjudgmentally, making woman both the goddess of life and death; Kali; the Great Mother; Venus of Willendorf; the Goddess-Creatrix of the universe and everything in it. Woman is also the door to death, and to the afterlife. How much less primitive is the primitive than we are! The primitive is neither sexomaniac or sexophobic: both these states are aspects of one another. The primitive embraces the whole spectrum of his or her humanity.

We know now, as Miller and Lawrence could not— except in the truth of the unconscious—that the equation of woman with death is a patriarchal slander, made to deliberately discredit one half the human race.

> Patriarchal societies are founded upon a crime, the crime is not the murder of the father, as Freud would have us believe. It is the rape and scorn of the mother.

Miller's equation of womb with death is not an inevitable one; it is patriarchal one. By extension, it implies that only the wombless members of the human race can embody an imperishable spirit. It therefore designates men alone as prophets, preachers, and artists. Women are condemned to be vessels—vessels of birth and also vessels of death.

We are so used to this worldview that we forget we could easily see the world otherwise, if we chose. We could see woman and man as two halves of an organism that can, in harmony, produce and sustain life. We could see deity as androgynous, as in fact the Hindus do. We could see death as inherent in all living things, not only in the female of the species. We could go beyond the trap of patriarchy, the rosy pseudomythology of supposedly perfect ancient matriarchies, and try to create a world in which sex was not allied with death and therefore did not have to be discarded in the discarded body of a woman.

But as yet we do not have such a world. We are still dealing with the ignominious world of patriarchy, whose tentacles have entwined themselves around all our minds. Sex, in this world, is death, is woman, is disease.

These false ideas have been reinforced in our time by the plague of sexually transmitted diseases that announced itself right after the sexual revolution. A causal connection was made between sexual freedom and disease, a causal connection we never stopped to question. The sexual revolution was made the cause of AIDS because such causation fitted in perfectly with our puritanical notions of retribution for pleasure. Whether the AIDS virus evolved "naturally" or was deliberately invented by a governmental germ-warfare lab to squelch homosexuality and free sexual expression by heterosexuals, it has become a political force to be reckoned with. (See David Black's challenging book *The Plague Years*, published in 1986, for a study of the way AIDS fulfills our sexual stereotypes.) Sex has again become the root of all evil—and with it has come a ferocious backlash against women, against gays, against blacks, against Hispanics, against all those who do not conform to a white male ideal of sexless and bloodless spirituality.

Even though Miller was trapped in a misogynistic worldview, he was still able to see spirituality in woman; he was still able to see sexuality as a force for life as well as death. Though he can express almost textbook vignettes of misogyny and does so in *The World of Lawrence*, he can also accept fecundating female sexuality, as in his essay on Anaïs Nin, "Un Etre Etoilique," and elsewhere. Miller is, in fact, perfect proof that male rage is part and parcel of patriarchy, that the need to dominate and symbolically or literally kill the mother is at the root of all patriarchal evil.

Miller understood that fear of sex projected onto the woman was one of the ills of society. He struggled with this fear and then transcended it. Again, he says this of himself, using what he writes about Lawrence as a code:

> . . . Strindberg remained a misogynist whereas Lawrence (perhaps because of his latent femininity) arrived at a higher or deeper understanding. His abuse goes out equally to man and to woman; he stresses continually the need for each to accentuate their sex, to insist upon polarity, so as to strengthen the sexual connection which can renew and revive all the other forces, the major forces that are necessary for the development of the whole being, to stay the waste of contemporary disintegration.

Both sexes, Lawrence felt, Miller felt, were equally to blame for the sexual degradation of modern life.

> . . . and the real cause lies deeper than this surface war between the sexes. . . . The real cause issues from the evil seed of the Christian ideal . . .

In this *aperçu*, Miller shows himself in perfect agreement with such feminist thinkers as Mary Daley, writing in *Beyond God the Father* and other books, who analyze the whore/Madonna split in our culture, a split that has fed the fires of unending sex war between woman and man, and has led to a puritanical rejection of both sexuality and woman as being merely screens for death.

A new paradigm for the sexes is needed, one that sees women and men holistically rather than as battling armies. Such paradigms exist, but they have been deliberately buried for centuries, first by Judeo–Christian brainwashing—and now by Moslem brainwashing.

No one is really looking at the problem in terms of root causes. It is our own worldview that we must change, preparatory to changing the world. This is why I fear that the reductive, antisexual view of Miller's work—whether by male chauvinist prudes or feminist prudes—is merely another symptom of the distorted worldview he was seeking, above all, to change.

When he looked at Lawrence, Miller understood himself:

> His hatred of his own mother, of her influence, and the Church's influence, is the admission of defeat at women's hands.

He also revealed his own definition of sex by revealing Lawrence's:

> a sensuality rooted in a primitive apprehension of one's relation with the universe, with woman, with man. Sensuality is the animal instincts, which he wanted to bring out

again; sexuality, the false cultural attitude which he
wanted to overthrow.

Perhaps we should call it Sex (with a capital *S*) to
differentiate it from the smarmy world of porno parlors
and stroke books with which, in our puritanical, sexomaniacal culture, it is nearly always confused.

Anyone who writes about sex in a puritanical, sex-
hating, sexomaniacal culture falls into the trap of being
equated with those who peddle the frivolous titillations of
sex-for-sale. Once a writer says "sex," the reader projects
his own view of sex upon the word. Changing definitions
is always the hardest task for any writer. One is often
accused of exactly what one is attempting to change.

This was the case with Lawrence, with Miller, with
Joyce. Joyce and Lawrence have been rescued by the academics, but Miller has been caught in a trap of timing: first
he was unprintable; now he is politically incorrect.

Unfortunately, there is a strong anti-sex tendency in
contemporary feminism, a tendency that fits in nicely with
the differently rooted anti-sex tendency of puritanism and
reactionary politics. It is ironic that a contemporary feminist movement that began with such free spirits as Emma
Goldman and Margaret Sanger—whose sense of sex as life
force was not so different from Miller's or Lawrence's—
should now have evolved such an anti-sexual cast.

How on earth did this occur? How on earth did rejection of the penis, the equation of all maleness with violence
and rape, and the deep mistrust of heterosexuality become
dominant themes during the second wave of the feminist
movement? How did a movement rooted in the same liber-
tarian ethos as anarchism and free love become, fifty years
later, a sort of anti-sex league?

There were various reasons. First, it was historically
necessary to liberate both female and male homosexuality
from stigma and to raise consciousness about the omni-
presence of rape and violence against women in our culture. These were—and still are—worthy aims. But a false
causal connection was made between heterosexual male-

ness and rape. Because male heterosexuals are often rapists, maleness itself was equated with rape. This would only be true if patriarchal attitudes were immutable forces of nature, the very forces of nature modern feminists seek to dispute. Feminists, who claim that all men are rapists, are thus caught in a tautological trap. But as a result of their equation of maleness with rape, only lesbianism or impotence became wholly acceptable politically. Any man was guilty of rape until proven innocent. Not only did this *reductio ad absurdum* serve to alienate from feminism millions of women who continued to sleep with men, but it also, sadly, made feminism appear to be a fringe ideology rather than the belief of the majority of both women and men, which, in fact, it is. This unfortunate misrepresentation has been more useful to the enemies of feminism than to its proponents.

In a sane world, lesbianism would not be seen as superior to heterosexuality, but as another, equal, choice. Just as male homosexuality would be one viable choice—neither penalized by tax laws nor property laws—lesbianism and lesbian motherhood would both be given full legal protection. But political belief would not rest only on one's behavior in bed, in love, in pair-bonding. The personal *is* political, but politics has a rainbow of colors, including shades of gray. By identifying itself so uncompromisingly with the lesbian nation, feminism unwittingly played into the hands of the evangelical right wing.

Of course, it is easy to understand why lesbian feminists are freer politically than women who live with men, are freer to choose their lives, even under patriarchy. They need not please or pander to men—an admirable independence. They are outsiders with nothing to lose, so they cannot easily be co-opted by patriarchal attitudes. Heterosexual women are always in danger of being sold out by their sexuality.

But by linking politics with sexual orientation, the second wave of feminism fell into a trap: in a sex-hating, woman-hating culture, it was unknowingly reinforcing the same Judeo–Christian dualism that excoriated women's fertility because of its association with death.

If women want to be truly free to embrace all options, they must abolish dualism first. To insist that all men are rapists, all penises violent organs, and only like-minded lesbian lovers are capable of a peaceable queendom, is to fall hopelessly under the influence of the dualistic heresy.

Two sexes are posited, one good, one bad. The patriarchal paradigm sees men as good, as pure, as spiritual, and sees women as vessels of mortality. The matriarchal paradigm sees men as violent killers, armed with clubs and cocks. Neither paradigm is new, hopeful, or has a prayer of defeating dualism. Both paradigms continue the age-old war.

Let us try to imagine a new paradigm. Imagine a culture in which sexual orientation and politics were dissociated, in which women might bear children parthenogenically, by artificial insemination, or even the old-fashioned way, with a known father with whom they cohabited. Just as health care and styles of birthing vary, people would be able to choose natural uterine birth, artificial uterine birth, or eventually father-birth by means of soon-to-be-invented artificial wombs.

Suppose that men and women could also choose various forms of pair-bonding, of differing legal weights—a suggestion Margaret Mead made years ago. (People would marry for different lengths of time depending on their intention to bear children or not. There would be three degrees of marriage: one for students or beginners in life, one for householder-parents, and one for older people whose children were grown.)

Suppose that lesbian women and gay men could have the identical three degrees of marriage. Then imagine that gender became totally neutral as an economic and legal issue, that men and women (gay or straight) were finally totally equal under the law.

People would form pair-bonds out of desire rather than economic and legal need, and children would be equally parented by all sexes. Men would not need to escape the mother, and women would not fear domination or abuse by the father. Eventually, we would have a variety of forms of child-rearing. Father-reared children would be as numerous as mother-reared children. Children of gay couples would suffer no stigma, and eventually we would have a society of immense diversity. No child's right to love and security would depend upon conformity to out-moded ideals of the patriarchal family. The truth is we cannot afford the luxury of patriarchal ideologies. We must accept sexual diversity and learn to nurture all the too-numerous babies born on this fragile planet.

This will take an immense revolution in consciousness, but nothing *except* such a revolution can save our world. We can no longer afford nostalgia for patriarchy, with its unwanted and abused children no one has time to rear with love. It is essential that we become a multisexual society, one that accepts all varieties of parenting. We must also foster the idea that not everyone need be a biological parent. Some women and men are clearly much happier being childfree.

In truth, Miller's cosmic view of sex has never been more needed. We have gone through a decade of backlash against the sexual revolution, against women's rights, against gay rights. During this decade we have also experienced a population boom and a widespread attack on reproductive freedom. Now the tide is beginning to turn. This decade has already become one of social ferment, of feminism and change. Let us not make the mistakes we made in the last such decade—the sixties. Let us not equate sexuality with a narrow promiscuity, but rather learn to see it in a cosmic Millerian sense. It is critical that we expand rather than narrow our notions of sexuality. And Miller can guide us. Sexuality can be an attitude, an openness to the world, to the cosmos beyond.

In his fascinating book *The Secret Museum: Pornography in Modern Culture*, Walter Kendrick surveys the role of sexuality in Western culture and its expression in art and literature.

He observes that there was a drastic difference between the ancient and modern worlds in their attitude toward sexuality. Across the lustiness of Catullus and Ovid, the happy and lighthearted eroticism of the Pompeian frescoes, the good-humored sensuality of Chaucer, the sexuality of Rabelais, even of Byron (who in this respect is a far more eighteenth- than nineteenth-century figure) fell the shadow of the Victorian Age and the banishment of the obscene to the rare-book room. "Though the nineteenth-century invented 'pornography,' it did not invent the obscene," says Walter Kendrick.

While most cultures, as Kendrick points out, did not give equal access to the obscene to all groups, the art of all cultures expressed it. The rise of bourgeois culture in the nineteenth century condemned sexuality to the Secret Museum. What had been joyous and healthy to the Greeks, licentious and full of opportunities for biting satire to the Romans, full of life and the possibility for ridicule to Chaucer, Shakespeare, Donne, Fielding, and Byron, became now furtive and secretive, pathologically devious.

We are not yet free of the spell of this nineteenth-century sexophobia. The common view of Miller, above all, shows us this. It also proves to us that sexomania and sexophobia are but two sides of the same coin, mirror images of each other.

In our sex-hating culture, we look to blame sex for everything from AIDS to abortion-on-demand. We are in the grip of Mrs. Grundy and Mr. Comstock still. And the so-called sexual revolution of the sixties (which, as we see, was no revolution in consciousness at all) swiftly became little more than an excuse for the biggest backlash of all time.

What shall we do with our sexophobia? It manifests itself on all sides of the political spectrum—from Women Against Pornography to the fundamentalist right. Our sexophobia impedes medical research for contraception, impedes needed reforms of women's health care, even impedes our ability to prepare teenagers to enjoy their sexuality safely in an overpopulated world.

When I was thirteen, kids were terrified of sex because abortion was illegal and one might die of a back-street abortion. Now my thirteen-year-old daughter and her friends are terrified of sex because of AIDS. *Plus ça change, plus c'est la même chose.* Must we conclude that we have created a society in which teenagers are compelled to hate their own most powerful urges, their own bodies, their own drives? Must we conclude that the excuses vary but the sexophobia remains constant? Must we conclude that on some deep level we *want* such a world?

Sexophobia is ever present, stronger every day. We are creating a sexually tormented younger generation just as our grandparents and great-grandparents did. We no longer say that masturbation causes blindness. We merely say that sex causes death.

In the years since the AIDS epidemic began, I have been accosted again and again by well-meaning journalists who ask me, regarding my early novels, "What about AIDS?"

"What about it?" I say.

"Well—how can you write sexual books in the age of AIDS?"

The reasoning is clear. Sex still equals death. A writer who writes about sex is somehow promoting death. In other words, nothing has changed in the essential paradigm, except that now we have AIDS to prove that sex equals death. If AIDS did not exist, we would have invented it, so powerful is that paradigm.

I usually answer my well-meaning journalists by saying that I shall stop writing about sex when people stop caring about it. As long as it remains a powerful force in people's lives, it cannot but be a powerful force in novels.

Why is our society so sex-hating, so sex fearing? This is a big question, and one seldom even asked. Why should sex be more despised than hunger, aggression, or any other basic drive? I think we must look to the eighteenth century, to the industrial revolution and the consumerism that even today keeps it humming. There is little doubt that sexophobia became entrenched along with the entrenchment of bourgeois culture. Before that, sex was seen as part of life, rather than as disease. The rich in England and America could have it, the poor could not be stopped from having it, and an amused wink or shrug greeted sexual matters there then as it does in Italy and France today. But in the eighteenth century, the English and American middle class coalesced, finding its basic function as cannon fodder and as consumers of industrial goods. Sex was increasingly seen as a dangerous opiate—a force for revolution. Better drug the masses with gin and cheap entertainments. At least these promote docility.

Miller saw this sexophobia as early as the twenties and related it, even then, to money, consumerism, and war. Money drives out sex, as we all know: the anxiety about getting and spending is anaphrodisiac. The more we focus on money, the less free we are, the less lusty, and the less revolutionary. As Miller himself says regarding *Tropic of Cancer* in *The World of Sex*, "The problem of the author was never one of sex, nor even of religion, but of self-liberation."

And what was he liberating himself from? The bourgeois need to be a getter and spender, a cog in the wheel of life. When Miller left the Cosmodemonic and went to Paris with June, he was declaring himself free of consumerism. When he became a beggar, he was declaring himself no longer in the thrall of the great god Money. Miller's economic and his sexual ideologies are totally related. *Your money or your life force*, says the great god Lucre! *Your money or your balls. You can't have both.*

Miller's detractors understand this better than they let on. If they thought him just a garden-variety pornographer, they would hardly blame him for the death of Western civilization as we know it. It is precisely because they understand, on some deep level, that he is talking about *self*-liberation, that they attack him.

Miller's self-liberation is sexual in the cosmic, not the genital sense. Yes, he writes of genital sexuality in the

*Tropic*s, in *Clichy*, in *Black Spring*, in *The Rosy Crucifix-ion*, but as he explains in *The World of Sex*, the sexual is the first step towards the spiritual:

> In that first year or so in Paris I literally died, was literally annihilated—and resurrected as a new man. The *Tropic of Cancer* is a sort of human document, written in blood, recording the struggle in the womb of death. The strong sexual odor is, if anything, the aroma of birth, disagree-able, repulsive even, when dissociated from its signifi-cance. The *Tropic of Capricorn* represents another death and birth, the transition, if I may say so, from the con-scious artist to the budding spiritual being which is the last phase of evolution. . . .

Henry was wise enough to know that the sexual and the spiritual were twins. He was wise enough to know that by flinging ourselves with utter abandon into the sexual we find that the spiritual beckons. "The road of excess leads to the place of wisdom," as Blake said. Or, as Miller says, on a similar theme, "Like every man, I am my own worst enemy, but unlike most men I know too that I am my own saviour."

What does sex have in common with salvation for Miller? Each is liberating. Miller often said that his only subject was self-emancipation. He was right. The sexuality of his books points the way to self-liberation. So does the spirituality.

What is it about sex that is so freeing? It is an affirma-tion of *I am;* an affirmation of life, and at once an affirma-tion of flux and change.

> We go along thinking the world to be thus and so. We are not thinking, of course, or the picture would be different every moment. When we go along thus we are merely preserving a dead image of a live moment in the past. However . . . let us say we meet a woman. We enter into her. Everything is changed. *What* changed? We do not know precisely. It seems as if *everything* had changed. It

might be that we never see the woman again, or it might be that we never separate. She may lead us to hell or she may open the doors of the world for us. . . .

It is this transforming power of sex that led Miller to focus on it in his books. Above all, transformation interests him, and above all, transformation is what the world of sex offers.

Sex galvanizes the individual spheres of being which clash and conflict. It makes the external world in which we are wrapped shed its death-like folds. It affords us glimpses of that stark durable reality which is neither beneficent or cruel.

Sex, in other words, puts us in touch with the center of existence, makes us see the dance of molecules, makes us feel truly alive.

If men would stop to think about this great activity which animates the earth and all the heavens, would they give themselves to thoughts of death? Would a man withhold himself in any way if he realized that dead or alive this frenzied activity goes on ceaselessly and remorselessly? If death is nothing, what fear then should we have of sex? The gods came down from above to fornicate with human kind and with animals and trees, with the earth itself. Why are we so particular? Why can we not love—and do all the other things which give us pleasure too? Why can we not give ourselves in all directions at once: What is it we fear? We fear to lose ourselves. And yet, until we lose ourselves, there can be no hope of finding ourselves. . . .

This is a message not so different from Dante's, who also found himself lost in a dark wood in the middle of his life, and who also emerged to see the stars, having discovered that love is what moves them.

Miller is more mystic than pornographer. He uses the obscene to shock and to awaken, but once we are awake, he wants to take us to the stars.

"I did a service to people," he said to Mike Wallace during our *60 Minutes* interview. "That was my motive in writing. I was beating down the barriers."

He did not mean linguistic barriers or publishing barriers; he meant barriers to self-liberation. A real sexual revolution—as opposed to the bogus sexual revolution that we had in the sixties—would recognize this liberation as coming from the role of sex in our lives. It would not reduce sex to promiscuity, abandon it to stroke books, porno parlors, and X-rated videos. It would recognize it as one of the great revolutionary forces of our lives, a force that has the power to open eyes and souls.

Is there a place for such sex in "The Age of AIDS"? Of course there is. Sex is more than mere compulsive acting-out, an accumulation of meaningless experiences and deadly viruses. If we are truly open to our own sexuality in the cosmic sense, we are also open to our creativity, our religious awareness, our sense of self-liberation.

In the days when *Fear of Flying* was *the* new sensation, I used to argue in vain that I was not advocating promiscuity, but rather an openness to erotic fantasy. The novel itself concentrated more on the heroine's erotic daydreams than on her escapades, which often proved hopelessly disappointing because her swains proved impotent or clumsy or mechanical. But the idea of an erotically motivated, actively fantasizing woman was, in itself, so shocking at that time that my protests fell on deaf ears. My denigrators were sexophobic, and attacked me for persisting in my belief that sex is a force for life.

How may we be sexual in the Age of AIDS? Let me count the ways. We live in a time when telephone and computer sex ("Hottalk" they call it), costumes, role-playing, and mutual masturbation are apparently proliferating—along with (good grief) monogamy!

HOT MONOGAMY reads the headline on a current magazine. Apparently you can even get off with your own spouse if you have a vivid imagination! Human sexuality is that dazzling in its variety. I know a dominatrix who advertises and sells safe sex—with no exchange of bodily fluids—

because the clients can only look and sniff and whip or be whipped. The sixties equation of sexual revolution with quantitative promiscuity is too innocent. If we are open to the world of fantasy, we can liberate ourselves with one partner or no partner at all. The recent novel *Vox* by Nicholson Baker describes a man and a woman who have sex on the telephone that is, if anything, hotter than sex in the flesh because there is no reality to block the fantasy.

Eventually we will have virtual-reality sets which will enable us to simulate sex with any famous lover of the past. Women will be able to choose anyone from Mark Antony to Shakespeare to Casanova to Byron, and men, like Dr. Faustus, will have their digitally simulated Helens of Troy.

"Was this the face that launched a thousand ships?" they'll ask their computer screens. The mind has an infinite capacity for self-liberation and is, after all, our main erogenous zone. Miller himself would have agreed.

CHAPTER 9

Why Must We Read Miller? Miller as Sage

I am trying to get at the inner pattern of events.

—HENRY MILLER, *THE WORLD OF SEX*

Why must we read Miller? Because he invented a new style of writing, a style as revolutionary in its own way as Joyce's or Hemingway's or Stein's, a style that reveals, as he says, "the inner pattern of events."

Some readers of *Tropic of Cancer, Tropic of Capricorn, Nexus, Sexus,* and *Plexus,* are at first put off by this style. They find it impenetrable, hard to follow, lacking in narrative drive. I confess that I was at first stopped by the density of the long autobiographical narratives and preferred the essays and travel books.

In the narratives, the prose seems to gyrate and meander. One association leads to another. Time sequence is jumbled. The time is the time of the unconscious—which is to say there is no time. The narratives seem like tales told by an idiot (or a brilliant dyslexic), full of sound and fury, signifying nothing. People become furious with Miller for being so hard to follow. They accuse him of having no regard for art or artifice.

The fact is they have not understood his method.

> . . . I am not following a strict chronological sequence but have chosen to adopt a circular or spiral form of time development which enables me to expand freely in any direction at any given moment. The ordinary chronological development seems to me wooden and artificial, a synthetic reconstitution of the facts of life. The facts and events of life are for me only the starting points on the way towards the discovery of truth.

This last sentence is critical. Henry is, above all, a wisdom writer like Hesse or Krishnamurti, and the narrative is far less important to him than the philosophical digressions. He uses his life as a parable; this is not the usual novelist's dance. He seeks to instruct far more than to please. Beyond that, he wants to liberate—both himself and the reader. "I am trying to get at the inner pattern of events," he says,

> trying to follow the potential being who was deflected from his course here and there, who circled around himself, so to speak, who was becalmed for long stretches or who sank to the bottom of the sea or suddenly flew to the loftiest peaks.

Miller is inventing a new rhetoric for inner reality— something akin to what Freud did when he analyzed the dream or what Joyce did when he found verbal notation for the meanderings of the mind during waking fantasy. Miller shares their passion to decode the inner life. Like them, he has been slandered and misinterpreted and his method pronounced no method at all. But, for him, it was the only way to get at the truth that interested him. Normal sequencing would not do.

> There is distortion and deformation, but only for the purpose of capturing the true inner reality. Thus, for no apparent reason, I may often lapse back into a period anterior to the one I am talking about.

Is Miller apologizing here for his lack of artifice, or is he trying to show us that his form followed function? Clearly the latter.

By the time Henry wrote *The World of Sex*, he was aware that many had criticized his ramblings. But Miller is absolutely sincere when he tells us that the style he invented was necessary to the content of his books. Without the spiraling of time he depicts, we would not have the sense that we are inside his mind.

> The reader may find himself puzzled: he may wonder about the relevancy of such lapses. But they are dictated by necessity. A sudden switch, a long parenthetical detour, a monologue, a remembrance which suddenly crops up, all

these, without conscious effort on my part, serve to bind the loose threads together and augment the whole emotional trend. A man does not go forward through life along a straight, horizontal path; often he does not stop at the stations indicated on the time table; sometimes he goes off the track completely; sometimes he dives below and is lost for a time, or he takes to the air and is flung against the side of a steep cliff.

Henry is not only Joyce's contemporary, but Pirandello's and Woolf's. This could be Virginia Woolf describing her "method" in *Orlando:*

Tremendous voyages sometimes occur without the person moving from the spot. In five minutes some men have lived out the span of an ordinary man's life. Some men use up numbers of lives in the course of their stay on earth.

Change the word *man* to *man/woman* and you have Woolf's androgynous hero.

But Miller was also pursuing a method which had much in common with Freud's explorations:

What goes on at every moment in the life of each and every man is something forever unfathomable and inexhaustible to relate. No man can possibly relate the whole story, no matter how limited a fragment of his life he chooses to dwell on.

It was because Henry believed this that he was able to spend most of his life as a writer of narratives (as opposed to essays), focusing on one relationship of nearly seven years' duration: his fateful marriage to June. He found in that marriage enough lives to fill several volumes: *Capricorn, Sexus, Nexus, Plexus*—and he still did not exhaust the mother-lode (pun intended).

Capricorn was, as Henry said in *The World of Sex,* only "a preface, a vestibule to the vast edifice." What he was trying to do in *Sexus, Nexus, Plexus,* or *The Rosy*

Crucifixion, was to offer up a man's life, his meanderings through the labyrinth, "as a sacrifice." He offers himself as a sacrifice in order to show that every man's life is such a sacrifice, and that it is only worthwhile if a new kind of truth is the result.

> He who goes the whole way of course is slain. I have gone the whole way, I have offered myself up as a sacrifice. That is why I can live on now and record it fully with no suffering involved. I can recount the most heart-breaking events almost joyously. I am telling about another man in another life.

Here Henry becomes the man who died. Like Christ or Adonis, he dies for truth. But unlike Christ, he is both the sacrifice and its chronicler. He is reborn as a writer to write his own gospel.

This is an utterly new thing in the history of the art of chronicle. I am careful not to call it "the art of fiction," because, like Henry, I believe fiction is outmoded, and perhaps, if we are honest, was outmoded as early as Richardson's *Pamela* and *Clarissa.* For, of course, even the eighteenth-century English novels pretended to be spilled truth.

But Henry is rare in being both Christ and St. Paul, both Hamlet and Horatio. He goes down into the underworld, is reborn, and his rebirth takes the form of writing. Writing becomes redemption. And redemption is the ultimate form of self-liberation.

There is only one subject, as Henry says often, "the supreme subject"—liberation:

> But the struggle of the human being to emancipate himself, that is, to liberate himself from the prison of his own making, that is for me the supreme subject. That is why I fail, perhaps, to be completely "the writer."

So even Henry himself proclaims what his critics accuse him of! Writerliness is far less important to him than truth.

We live in an age of mannered writing, an age of writers who forget that their purpose is to tell truths, not merely to be clever. Perhaps truth-telling makes us uncomfortable because we no longer have any consensus about what truth is. We look to our writers to help us find a consensus, and, book by book, we hope to grope our way toward it. But we have no cohesive worldview. We do not really believe in the spirit, yet we are unhappy with sheer materialism and uncomfortable with the idea of imperishable realities beyond the self and beyond the flesh.

Henry reminds us that the ancient function of the writer is to be a truth-teller. He also reminds us that the only truth is self-redemption. In this, his message is not so very different from Christ's. It was Thomas Merton, after all, who praised Henry for his "real basic Christian spirit which I wish a few Christians shared!" Merton and Miller were kindred spirits, who exchanged some fascinating letters. They both were intimate with the divine dictation of "the Voice." Merton the poet-monk and Miller the eternal vagabond recognized each other at once as participants in the same quest—the quest for spirit in a materialistic world.

The experience of taking dictation from "the Voice" is riveting and unforgettable. A large part of a writing teacher's task is to convince students that they, too, can listen to this inner voice. We all have it to some extent, but writers cultivate the ability to use it. This may be why they are so apt to believe in the Voice. When your daily work is to be a medium, you must believe in the Voice or it may stop talking to you.

For the most part, the "fictional" novels we read today belong to a dead genre, a genre that somnolizes rather than awakens. People read mysteries, romances, and thrillers to anesthetize themselves, not to alert their souls. Most books are enslaving rather than liberating. They lull the senses; they hypnotize the moral imagination.

That we have a whole publishing industry based on the production of verbal *soma* (as Aldous Huxley called his all-purpose opiate in *Brave New World*) is not surprising.

But Miller is doing something else entirely—and it is necessary to recognize it. He is using words in the service of liberation. He cannot be judged only as an entertainer. Like Auguste in *The Smile at the Foot of the Ladder,* his ecstasy is our entertainment.

When we consider how long it has been since Joyce, Woolf, Stein, and other geniuses of the first part of this century transformed the very nature of prose narrative, it is astounding that the contemporary novel has been influenced so little.

Film transformed the novel far more than modernist literature did. Film absorbed the lessons of surrealism. The novel speeded up its scenes to match the dwindling attention span of the contemporary reader. Fiction writers learned to cut and edit like filmmakers. But, for the most part, they ignored the lessons of Miller, Joyce, Woolf, and Stein, and continued to write nineteenth-century Dickensian or Dostoyevskian novels in the age of visual media. I suspect that it is for this reason that so many of them are being ignored.

Today's younger generation has become totally comfortable with the sort of antichronological sequencing that Miller employed. The most banal MTV promotional video collapses or reverses time, folds reality into fantasy or fantasy into reality, all with dazzling slickness. Why do we refuse to trust readers to accept this in novels? Or, better, why do our novelists refuse to draw inspiration from the innovations of the great modernists? The reason, of course, is commercialism and the lust for bestsellers.

The poor old popular novel plods along in the footsteps of the past, while occasionally Martin Amis or Harold Pinter makes use of reverse chronology (*Time's Arrow, Betrayal*) to jolt his audience. That such a technique is still jolting only proves how very conventional most contemporary writing remains.

Of course there are adventurous souls like Thomas Pynchon, William Gaddis, Cormac McCarthy, T.C. Boyle, John Hawks, and Robert Coover who do bravely experiment. But most of our published fiction is structured along nineteenth-century lines.

Henry himself invented *spiraltime*, structured like the DNA molecule, time that curves back on itself. His "novels" constitute an immense Mobius strip. In the end is their beginning. Is this "the true inner reality" of our lives? Henry thought so. And it is time our contemporary fiction writers trusted his lead. They have followed him into the bedroom, but not into the world of unconscious time. The writers who can pick up the mantle of Miller and reinterpret him for a new generation will tap a young audience that is largely bored with contemporary popular fiction.

Henry also led the way for contemporary writers in the manner in which he took fact and made it into parable. He often predicted that autobiography would be the fiction of the future and I think he has been proven right both by the hunger for "docudrama," and by CNN's instant history, which rivets us far more effectively than television sitcomland. Our most disturbing novels blend fiction and fact. News and novels mingle boundaries everywhere. Even the words mean the same thing.

The birth of the novel in the eighteenth century—the same century that gave us the newspaper and consumer capitalism—owes its impetus to the elevating of the daily life of the average individual to the level of heroism. Instead of kings and queens and mythical heroes and heroines, we have Pamela, Clarissa, and Tom Jones. There is surely a direct line from the serving-maid scribbler of *Pamela* or the orphan Tom Jones to the Paris vagabond Henry Miller. Miller, with his elevation of daily life to myth, with his blurred boundaries between fiction and autobiography is, in fact, squarely in the central tradition of the English novel. If this is so, why has he been seen only as an outcast and renegade?

Part of the problem is sexomania/sexophobia. Henry stirs outrage because of his lust for life. He also stirs outrage because of his happiness at being alive and his truly Christ–like lack of envy. Perlès once called him an amateur writer—in the literal sense: *he loved to write.* Miller also says in *Tropic of Capricorn,* "Envy was the one thing I was not a victim of."

This was surely true when I knew him. He was unstinting in helping me and others. He did not calculate his gifts. He saw the world as having enough gifts for all. He did not hold back as if inspiration were finite.

The rarity of his generosity made others hate Henry. They mocked his openness because they could not emulate it. All his faults were the faults of excess. But it was out of excess that all his virtues also flowed.

Norman Mailer indicted *The Rosy Crucifixion* (in *Genius and Lust,* his meditation on Miller) as "a great cake that fails to rise." And it is true that the trilogy is full of Henry's most uneven writing—great wisdom cheek by jowl with great banality. Reminiscences of childhood in Brooklyn stop the flow of the story, plot gets lost, characters change names, and yet, for all the sloppy writing, one feels one is looking right into the author's skull. There is an unparalleled intimacy, no veil between author and reader. This intimacy was one of Miller's greatest gifts. Try to replicate it and you will see how hard it is to give up literature and have life, how self-consciousness always threatens to intrude and how, even when you do get into the flow, all sorts of flotsam and jetsam come with it.

Miller discovered the automatic-writing technique of never lifting the pen from the page—and so his books have both the feel of life and its dross. They taunt us with nuggets of truth, and disappoint us with flat language from which the clichés have not been pruned. But they give an unmistakable impression of a man who is *alive* and for whom writing is a way of being even more intensely alive. Many writers use writing as an evasion of life. The book becomes a place to rewrite personal history and avoid the pain of confrontation. Miller's works are confrontations, not evasions. For his life force alone, Miller is unique.

The creative life! Ascension. Passing beyond oneself. Rocketing out into the blue, grasping at flying ladders, mounting, soaring, lifting up the world by the scalp, rousing the angels from their ethereal lairs, drowning in stellar depths, clinging to the tails of comets.

This was Miller's gift: to lift up the world by its scalp. I want to send you back to read him—with an open head and heart.

Afterword

The letters that follow were mostly written during the spring and summer of 1974, when I was undergoing a transformation I didn't even recognize from "promising younger writer" to public figure. My first novel, *Fear of Flying*, had been out in hardcover for about six months. Initially, the book received lukewarm reviews but passionate word-of-mouth. By the time John Updike discovered it in *The New Yorker*, the novel was nearly unobtainable and constantly out of stock. It had been underprinted for the success it was to become, and for six months I had gnashed my teeth over the poor distribution of the book, feeling powerless to affect its fate (which I now understand is every author's karma). When Henry's long, enthusiastic welcome came in the spring of 1974, I was grateful.

Looking back, I see how neurotic I was about the publication of *Fear of Flying*—perhaps because it was such a break with the good girl inside me, the part of me that really wanted to write nice things and not embarrass the family. When the novel began to be ferociously talked about, galleys stolen from the publisher's desk, paperback and movie rights sold, I felt guilty: I was winning fame and money for being a bad girl. When critics trashed the book, something inside me felt I deserved to be trashed; when there were raves, I was at once thrilled and guilty. This was because I knew I was breaking old rules of female silence and female submission. I would shout out my rebellion only to become frightened of my own echo.

Henry was in a unique position to understand this fate. And his letters show it. They also reflect his generosity, his taste in reading, his views on sex, literature, anti-Semitism, and women's freedom.

It is especially important that the letters referring to anti-Semitism, Jewishness, and feminism be made available, because Henry has often been accused of anti-Semitism and woman-hating. I have addressed the charge of woman-hating throughout this book, but the anti-Semitism issue deserves some more space here. It followed Miller throughout his life and it has recently been vigorously renewed by Mary Dearborn in her biography of Miller.

Even to my paranoid Jewish mind, Miller was not an anti-Semite. He merely reserved the right, typically claimed by Jews but denied to gentiles, to make fun of us. Most fair-minded Jews will acknowledge that we are the toughest self-critics and the most barbed satirists of all things Jewish, but most of us bristle when a gentile claims the same prerogative. Certainly I do—though I reserve the right of the typical diaspora Jew to direct self-mockery, cynicism, and gallows humor at my own people and their foibles.

Henry saw this hypocrisy and called us on it. If Jews could criticize Jews, why couldn't he? The great fabulist of the Jews, Isaac Bashevis Singer, who was Henry's favorite twentieth-century writer (and mine) and yet another of his correspondents, was allowed to show Jewish thieves, Jewish fools, Jewish knaves, as well as Jewish saints—so why was Miller, a gentile, not allowed? Why should the Jews alone be permitted to tell the truth about Jews?

We know very well why. It is the same reason we alone are allowed to criticize our parents and children, but bristle when others do so. The horrors of twentieth-century Jewish history have given us every reason to be sensitive to the anti-Semitic slur, however subtle.

But let me remind the reader who would like to like Miller, but fears he is an anti-Semite, that for every supposed slur on Jews in Miller, there are startlingly vivid examples of valiant attempts to squelch the banal anti-Semitism of his time. There is the incident related by

Alfred Perlès, in which Henry nearly throttles the saloon-keeper who refers to his place as the "*Judenfrei* café." And there are repeated examples of Miller's wish to be Jewish—if only to justify his differentness, his bookishness, his sense of being an outcast and an eternal vagabond. Note also his admiration for people and things Jewish—from June to Singer to the author of this book.

Miller's feelings toward Jews were complicated. Jews represented New York and home to Miller, and Miller hated New York. Jews represented the admiration of bookishness in men—something Henry yearned for from his mother, and could not have. (Anaïs would give it to him; Louise never would.) No wonder that so many of the pivotal figures in Henry's life—from June to Michael Fraenkel to Abe Rattner—were Jewish. Jews effortlessly had so much Henry coveted: respect for the man who chose to live in a world of books, respect for the man who shunned the practical world for the world of ideas, metaphysics, and religion, respect for the man whose main talents were Torah and procreation. Henry envied Jews. He wanted to be a yeshiva *bucher* himself! That, by the way, was his wistful term for my former husband, Jonathan Fast. "Jonathan, you're a real yeshiva *bucher*," he liked to say. The yeshiva scholar, like the ancient sage, was one of Henry's ideals of manhood.

Inevitably, Henry and I were asked to comment on each other publicly. It was such a promotable combination—dirty old sage and young Wife of Bath—that television producers and print-media editors found us irresistible. So there was a wonderful *60 Minutes* documentary with Mike Wallace, and side-by-side op-ed pieces in *The New York Times* (September 7, 1974). I reprint two of these "boosts" among the letters because they are a continuation of them and share their spirit.

I have kept Henry's spelling idiosyncracies intact and have refrained from editing my own youthful enthusiasm (silly as it often is) out of my letters. You have the exchange just as it occurred.

Letters

The first exchange of letters between Henry Miller and me took place in April 1974 and appears in Chapter 2. Sometime during the early summer of 1974, Henry Miller sent me an essay he had written—"Fear and How It Gets That Way"—which he was planning to submit for publication. I had not asked for this boost and its effusiveness embarrased me. He prefaced it with this letter:

Dear Erica—   *5/6/74*
Please let me or Bradley know as soon as you can if you want any changes or deletions made. He has a copy which he will send to some editor soon as you give the OK.

This in haste.
Henry Miller

TWO WRITERS IN PRAISE OF RABELAIS AND EACH OTHER

Certainly anyone whose book is on the best-seller list (even if at the bottom), needs no review, no boosting. These few words, therefore, are gratuitous, or, if you like, homage from one writer to another. Above all, a warm, heart-felt tribute to a woman writer, the likes of which I have never known.

In some ways, this book—*Fear of Flying*—is the feminine counterpart to my own *Tropic of Cancer*. Fortunately, it is not as bitter and much funnier. The author has quite a gripe about shrinks, which most of us share with her. I say the author, but in my head I cannot separate the author from her chief protagonist, Isadora Zelda. In the case of *Tropic of Cancer,* on the other hand, critics and readers alike were inclined to think I had *invented* Henry Miller. To this day many people refer to it as a novel, despite the fact that I have said again and again that it is not.

Erica Jong, the author, said to me in a letter that she thought it silly to make distinctions regarding the genre or category of a book. A book is a book is a book, to paraphrase Gertrude Stein. However, people do seem to concern themselves unnecessarily over this question of identity. As a rule, the autobiography is not as popular as the novel, unless it is sensational. I think, on the other hand, that publishers are always fearful of autobiographies, because of the threat of libel and slander, or defamation of character suits. But then publishers, in the main, are a timid lot, full of fears of every sort.

The wonderful thing about Erica Jong's book is that she or Isadora is full of fear, all kinds, but makes no bones about it and makes us laugh over her tragic moments.

The book is definitely therapeutic, not only for women but for men too. It should be read for one thing by every shrink, every psychiatrist, every psychologist. It should also be read by Jews. They take quite a drubbing in this book. It's hard to call the book "anti-Semitic", since the author herself is Jewish and knows whereof she speaks. In her biting humor and sarcasm she is merciless toward her own people. Of course she is not unique in this. One has only to think of Swift, O'Casey, Knut Hamsun, Shaw, Céline, and Henry Miller. Yet all of us were writers who loved their country. We merely despised our country's inhabitants.

Yes, I know that of all the peoples in the world the Jews are reputed to be foremost in their ability to make fun of themselves, acknowledge their shortcomings. But if someone other than a Jew does this he is immediately called an anti-Semite.

It's silly to go on pretending that under the skin we are all brothers. The truth is more likely that under the skin we are all cannibals, assassins, traitors, liars, hypocrites, poltroons.

Do not misunderstand. Erica Jong is far from being a misogynist or a misanthropist. I get the impression that she loves life, and people too. But her intelligence does not permit her to overlook their glaring faults. It is this gusto of hers which supplies us with some of the funniest and raciest passages. One is tempted to say—"She writes like a man"—only she doesn't write like a man but like a 100% woman, a female, sometimes a "bitch". In many ways she is more forthright, more honest, more daring than most male authors. That's what I like about her. In short, she is a treat for sore eyes.

Parenthetically, I wonder when or if Germaine Greer is going to give us a book on this order. Germaine Greer is another woman writer who tickles my fancy and elicits my admiration. Certainly, when I read her interview in Playboy, was it, I could scarcely believe my eyes. Men are no match for women of this sort.

The interesting thing is that these two women are endowed with strong intellects, they are cultured, they have read well, and have excellent taste. But above all, they are fearless.

I cannot help but wonder how Women's Lib. regards this book of Erica Jong. Here is a liberated woman who tells of her need for men, or, as she sometimes puts it, her need for a lay. She admits to being horny, and how! We don't hear enough from women on this subject. With all this, and she goes the limit, this book can scarcely be called "pornographic". It is full of obscenity, whatever that means, but underneath it all, there is a most serious purpose. The book is full of meaning and a paean to life. The death-eaters are the shrinks, teachers, parents, and so on.

What is most intriguing of all to me is that she has made a British shrink, who is really a first-class scoundrel, a delightful character. He makes an awful lot of sense, despite his propensity for handing out one-liners, like Henny Youngman.

This lousy bastard turns out to be the saviour of Isadora Zelda, though he may not have meant to be. It's he who, by his unabashed treachery, opens her eyes, makes her face herself, makes her accept reality. He is certainly an "anti-hero." Bastard though he is, he knows how to get along, or, I suppose I should say, "he knows on which side his bread is buttered".

I dwell on this character because too few of us are ready to acknowledge that we can learn (as much or more) from an evil character as from a good one. We *know* that the do-gooders wreak a lot of havoc, but we do not seem to know that the evil-doers can work a lot of good in this fucked-up world. If they accomplish nothing more than to shatter our idealistic dreams, they have done enough.

But I am exaggerating somewhat, as regards Adrian, the British shrink and no. 1 bastard. He is not truly evil, he just doesn't give a fuck if he happens to ruin a few lives in the course of his having his way.

I had a most intense feeling of joy, of liberation, when the bandages finally fell from Isadora's eyes. Thought it was a bit of a let-down to see her return to her husband (another shrink, but an Oriental one), I felt that she would remain on her own two feet. Once the bandages are removed you don't put them on again. Maybe she, author or protagonist, still has a fear of flying—who hasn't?—but she can cope with it.

I feel like predicting that this book will make literary history, that because of it women are gong to find their own voice and give us great sagas of sex, life, joy and adventure.

Henry Miller

When Henry Miller first wrote to me last April to declare himself my loyal and "devoted fan," I was delighted. Feminist critiques of Miller notwithstanding, he is our modern American Rabelais—always as drunk with language as he is with sexuality; as much in love with words as he is with women.

Long before I began hearing from Miller in the morning mail, I loved the sheer energy of his writing, the rollicking, headlong power of his sentences; the way he could make language mimic the inner turmoil of thoughts.

Miller has been the most misunderstood of writers. Because he dared call for "a classic purity where dung is dung and angels are angels"—he managed to incur the hostility of countless critics, post office authorities and censors who had never read Sappho, Catullus, Petronius, Rabelais, Chaucer (or even Shakespeare or Donne, for that matter) and therefore saw the frank sexuality in his work as an instance of modern depravity—when in truth it represented the resurrection of an ancient tradition.

In dealing with contemporary literature, we tend to lose historical perspective. Sexuality in literature is not new. In fact, it could be argued that the last 150 years have been aberrant in this regard. There was greater open sexuality in the arts in Fielding's time, Swift's time, Shakespeare's time, Chaucer's time than there has been in the last century or so. Until very recently, publishing was still governed by the aesthetics of a post-Victorian age which was more comfortable relegating sexuality to pulp fiction (and keeping so-called "high art" free of it) than about realizing that sexuality should be an organic part of literature.

The Victorian, after all, does not give up sex; he only gives up *open* sex. He does not practice abstinence, but only hypocrisy. He will abhor any trace of sexuality in a book of poems, yet drool over a porno novel in private. It was this hypocrisy that Miller set out to challenge. Why relegate sex in the outhouse, the whorehouse, the 42nd street bookstore? Boccaccio, Villon, Rabelais and countless others recognized the awesome power of sexuality in life; why should a modern writer have to write around it?

Yet Miller was banned for years because of his refusal to practice this hypocrisy (and so were Lawrence and Joyce). Quite recently, attempts were made in Vermont to ban *Ms.* magazine on the grounds of having published an allegedly obscene excerpt from my novel, "Fear of Flying." And the British reviews of the same novel have been full of outrage and apoplexy about its frank sexuality. (This from the country of Blake and Lawrence and Fielding and Chaucer!)

Sexual censorship is still with us and is not likely to go away until sexual openness and health become the norm in society. (I expect, never.) Even though it has been proven again and again that censorship accomplishes nothing, that it in fact creates *interest* in a book rather than disinterest, there continue to be outraged parents and school officials who press for censorship. One can only interpret this as their need to censor their own prurience. They are not "sparing their children," for no sooner is a book banned than children become more avid than ever to get their hands on it. Besides, no one has ever proven that sexuality in literature promotes sexuality in life—any more than books about diet promote weight loss. In fact, the analogy holds true to this degree: people seem to read about sex rather than engage in it, just as they tend to buy diet books rather than to diet.

Perhaps Miller was censored, not because he advocated sex, but because he fought hypocrisy. He is one of the relatively few modern authors whom we can speak of as a liberator. His autobiographical novels recount the vicissitudes of a soul in search of itself. The energy of the struggle, the honesty with which the struggle is depicted—lead one to identify deeply with Miller even when one's own experience has not been precisely parallel.

Unfortunately, we do not have a recognized tradition of this kind of novel in America. The first-person mock-memoir is often misunderstood as a *roman à clef* or an autobiography and critics waste their time trying to pry the moustaches off characters to discover their "real" identities. We forget that Proust, Colette and Céline wrote this kind of book before Miller, and that the intermingling of fact and fiction is the stock-in-trade of the novel—that most undefinable of forms. What matters is not what we *call* a book—but whether or not it awakens us, jolts us, makes us see the world through new eyes. Sex can be part of that jolting, but it *need* not be. And that should be for the writer to decide—not the censor.

5/24/74

Dear Erica Jong—

Just a little word to say I am recommending your book to all and sundry and getting hearty "thank you's" for it. I even recommend the book to foreigners . . . Which reminds me—have your publishers submitted it to French, German and Italian publishers? If not, I would recommend their trying Rowohlt in Germany, Editions Stock in Paris, and Longanssi in Milan, Italy. Use my name just as strongly as you wish.

Today I am reading a book about one of my favorite playwrights—Sean O'Casey. Did you ever read or see his "Juno and the Paycock?" or Synge's "Playboy of the Western World?" or, from another angle—"The Dybbuk" (Eye bothers me—excuse spelling.) I'm curious about certain books and authors—if you have read them or not? For instance—"A Glastonbury Romance" by John Cowper Powys—"Mysteries" (and the others) by Knut Hamsun, Isaac Bashevis Singer's books and that epic novel by his brother—wrote something about "Ashkenazi???"

I always see you in my mind reading. A voracious reader. ("Boulimique") How about "She" by Rider Haggard? or "Charles Dickens" by G. K. Chesterton? (a beauty!) or Sean O'Casey's plays? or "The Playboy of the Western World" by Synge?

You must have liked the Dadaists! What a pity that so few of the good, but less well-known French writers have not been translated.

Well, I really have nothing much to tell you. By the way, did you find Bradley Smith a pain in the ass? He's

*not "a great friend" of mine, just another publisher.
Bores me to tears often all ego. And that tone of voice! I
hope it wasn't too painful. I didn't recommend that they
call on you, you know. Despite what Time wrote last
week, I don't like visitors, except unusual ones. And normally not writers. Painters are better. Writers are mostly
like ingrown nails. Do you agree? Worse than shrinks
some times!*

Cheers now!
Love from all your new fans!
Henry Miller

May 28, 1974

Dear Erica Jong—

*The enclosed is from my son Tony's wife. (They are
splitting up after 6 months of marriage. She needed your
book like* poison. *I hope it did the trick!) To tell you the
truth, it did me a world of good too, upon a second
reading. Now Tony, my son, is reading it. Everyone I
have lent it to or bought a copy for has flipped. Mostly
women. They all intend to write you and thank you. It
hits women hard—and it should do the same for men.*

*This time, on rereading, I find Adrian even more
delightful. A lovable bastard. I wonder that you ever got
him out of your hair.*

*I think you have done, for men and women, in this
book, what I did in* Tropic of Cancer. *Those last scenes in
your book—the room in the rue de la Harpe (I think my
"Max" actually lived in that street), the missing Tampax, the toilet in the hall, all are wonderful, like those
vast boisterous reliefs O'Casey gives you after a heart-
rending scene. You really give the illusion of being free
at last. It's quite wonderful. Absolutely therapeutic. And
the way you treat your own people—only you and Isaac
Singer have dared be so honest about the Jews. (He lives
near you, I think. Ever meet him?) I did, once, and what
do you suppose we talked of for an hour or more? Knut
Hamsun. He was Singer's idol, as he was and still is,
mine. I wish I could write like him. I have read "Myster-*

*ies" at least 5 times—and will reread it some more doubt-
less. Must stop.*

my best,
Henry Miller

*P.S. I'm even recommending your book to Europeans
(who read English.) Do let me know which foreign publishers have taken it. Wouldn't you like to see it in Turk-
ish?*

*P.S. No analyst could have thought up a better "cure"
than Adrian by his betrayal. That was a marvelous bit!*

1 June 1974

Dear Henry (if I may),

    *I am up to my ass in Miller! Your absolutely wonder-
ful letters—& now two books sent me by Noel Young
(ON TURNING EIGHTY & THE WATERS REGLIT-
TERIZED)—& Bradley Smith's gift to me: MY LIFE &
TIMES BY HENRY MILLER. I think your great gift is
having learned to write with all the naturalness of
speech—& having learned to put your whole personality
into your writing—to make a generous gift of yourself in
your work. Most writers never learn this. They are nig-
gardly. They try to conceal themselves (which no artist
can ever do), & what comes across is forced & stingy.
What you have—in your books, in your letters, in your
watercolors—is generosity—a greatness of spirit that
cannot be taught; one is born with it. But most people are
born without it. I think I like ON TURNING EIGHTY
as much as any essay of yours I've ever read. I love what
you say about youth being "premature old age." I get
younger too, as I get older. Whenever I feel really lousy,
I look at your example & think—"I can always look
forward to being eighty!" Maybe by then I'll have
learned to stop suffering & to live in the present. ON-
WARD! I also love your line, "One of the big differences
between a genuine sage & a preacher is gaiety." I want
to use that somewhere—maybe as a quote for my next
novel. Literary critics—especially here in America—have*

a real prejudice against humor. They tend to feel that great books are gloomy books. They've never really absorbed the lesson of Rabelais. A few weeks ago a woman I know (a fan of my poetry & a practicing gestalt therapist) called me to tell me about FEAR OF FLYING. "Very amusing," she said, "but now I think you have to drop the humor & write a really SERIOUS book." "But my humor is serious," I said. "Oh," she said.

To answer your questions about foreign publishers, Fear of Flying is due to be published in Denmark & Sweden, in Holland, in England.* So far, no French publisher has taken it—though someone has an option, at present. Don't know who. Laffont in France had it for months. All their "scouts" loved it; but the final decision was "too American." I met the editor who finally turned it down. He said something about how the French weren't interested in psychiatry. I think he had the wrong idea about the book entirely. Maybe you know a French publisher who would understand the book. If so, please tell me where it should be sent. So far—no German publisher either. Maybe they think the book too anti-German: I'd love to have your ideas. There is a British agent working on selling the book in Germany & France, but I'm starting to distrust all agents. My current NY agent is screwing me royally on the movie rights (an enormous mess at the moment). All too absent-minded to keep trace of it. How do you manage????

I don't usually compose at the typewriter (la macchina?); like you, I feel more honest when I spill it all out in ink on the page. But I just bought a new typewriter that lets me change the ribbon colors easily & quickly & I'm having so much fun with my new toy that I wanted to write to you on it. Still, the typewriter constricts me, changes my style. I don't type fast enough. I keep using the same one finger—like masturbating instead of fucking. (Writing in script being like fucking).

Adrian was a bastard—& not that lovable, after a

---

*& In Italy by Bompiani

while. He was really very bourgeois, very much the pater familias, *very un-free. He had a kind of magnetism (what is modishly called) charisma nowadays. There was a post-script to the Adrian story which I never wrote. Shortly after leaving Isadora, he knocked up his girl-friend, & when I visited them both (*en famille*) in London, last year, they had a little girl (with a squint eye like her Daddy) & they called me her "godmother." It was really awful. I ought not to write this. I always deny that any of the characters have any basis in reality—but how can I lie to you? Writer-to-writer, the truth can be understood. You know how characters change when one tries to capture them on the page. Even if you want to tell the truth, the truth escapes.*

Please thank your daughter (& her friend) & your daughter-in-law for their good wishes. I'm delighted to have Diane's letter. I feel a little guilty for being a home-wrecker. . . . Did my book do it? You seemed to imply that. I seem to have become the patron saint of adulteresses. Last week, a young woman told me "I've just read your book & loved it. Spent last night with a beautiful man & now I'm going home to my husband. Thank you!" I stood there with my mouth open. I guess people are so tight-ass about their sexuality that this book (all about IMPOTENCE & unfulfillment) is seen as a ticket to liberation. I do mean to have Isadora survive at the end—& be an inspiration to women who want to survive. There are too damn many books about women who commit suicide, women who go mad, women who destroy themselves over men. . . . I wanted it to be clear (especially in the last chapters of the book—the tampax scene, etc.) that humor was Isadora's survival tool. I myself need to laugh at least 3 times a day or I get sick.

I could go on & on with letter, but I have to get ready to go to a convention of goddamned booksellers in Washington. Thousands of book-salesmen in pinky rings & I am being sent by my paperback publisher (NAL) to sign books & blow kisses & all the rest of it. So I'm off to Washington for three days. If I come to California this summer *(to see about the supposed movie of Fear of Flying)* I want to meet you & the Miller menage. Especially Val & Diane—& friends. I promise not to be boring & literary. I hate visits from writers too. They always *WANT SOMETHING*. Blurb me! *they cry.* Or grant me! Or Guggenheim me! *You must get lots of fans wanting to touch you like the magic man. It must be awful for you at times.*

Lots of hugs & good wishes. . . . .

Erica

6/5/74

Dear Erica—

I wrote a few pages about your book which Connie is typing for me. Will send it late today or tomorrow, so that you may suggest changes or deletions, if necessary. Bradley will place it for me.

I wrote Christian de Bartillat of Editions Stock—6, rue Casimir Delavigne—75006, Paris, France today, urging him to give your book serious consideration. I told him you would send him a copy of the book.

I also write H. M. Ledig-Rowohlt of Rowohlt Verlag—Hamburger str. 17, 2057-Reinbek-bei-Hamburg, West Germany—same thing.

Rowohlt is more than my publisher, he is like a brother to me. Bartillat I only know since a year or so. He is very friendly and has a great regard for me. He listens or pays heed to my suggestions, which is more than my American publishers do.

I'm worry I never saw that review of your book by Updike, or any review for that matter.

About Singer, yes, he is one of the very few Jews I know who is not afraid or ashamed to tell the whole truth about the Jews. Some of the episodes he relates are fabulous. I hope my remarks about your treatment of the Jews won't prove injurious to you. Some people will start calling me an anti-Semite again, but you must know that I am not. I simply can't swallow that stuff about "the Chosen People." *(Unless it is meant—"chosen to suf-*

fer.") *Yes, you are a liberator. But Diane, who loved your book, is not yet liberated. To be honest, she's a pain in the ass. Always a long face, sad, mournful. Always concerned with herself. Can bore the shit out of you. I've given her up, as hopeless. No. Your book had nothing to do with the divorce. . . .*

Can you give me Bompiani's add. in Italy? I want them to send a copy of the Italian version to a woman I correspond with in Sicily. *Must be tough to be a woman there.*

Well, I must stop now. Write me from Washington or anywhere when you have the impulse.

Cheers!

Henry

P.S. Bradley thinks you are coming soon. Finds you very attractive.

Saturday—6/15/74

Dear Erica—

Hugs and kisses to you too. No, I am not Aries, I am Capricorn (Dec. 26, 1891)—really ancient, what! But Aries is my rising sign. I have been in love several times with Aries women—always disastrously. *(Sic) So, don't let me fall in love with* you!

About my review. . . . Bradley took it and thinks to place it with the Saturday Review. (We did think of the others you mentioned.) I have almost no traffic with American mags, nor British. Bradley inserted two sentences, with my permission, which supposedly help clarify my thinking. (Maybe that's what's wrong with par. 2. (?)

Listen, don't waste time on Diane Miller. Not worth it. I know this sounds bad on my part, but I have good reason to talk thus. She is an egotist and worse. She seems to listen, is very grateful and all that, but goes her own sweet way just the same. She's a real (Gentile) neurotic. She thinks highly of me, because I paid attention to her and read her poems. She fucked Tony up good and proper.

His own fault, of course. He doesn't seem to do too well with women. Quite an ego too, very handsome, and outwardly very sure of himself. (Bad combination.) I think he has talent for writing. He just got a job as book reviewer for the Hollywood Reporter—five dollars a review! I read his first two and must say I couldn't have done better myself. By the way, he too loves your writing—has just finished your novel. You think I am loose—but that's precisely what every one says about your writing. I think I'm best when I'm running on endlessly—sort of Dada style. I wish I were crazier! "Madness is all", to paraphrase the bard.

Thank you for the Updike review. It is good, a bit slick here and there, but. . . . Wish there were more like this. By the way, I never read him—I don't read any Americans, it seems, except Isaac B. Singer. But I saw on T.V. "The Ugly American" with Brando. Wasn't that based on his book?

(Detour: Do you know I blushed for Brando when I saw "The Last Tango in Paris". When he gives his first fuck, with overcoat on, all hunched up by the door—he reminded me of The Hunchback of Notre Dame. I thought the film cheap, vulgar. Would you believe that I hate vulgarity?)

I hope you are reading Céline—either "Journey to the end of the Night" or "Death on the Instalment Plan." I don't know if you read French or not. In the case of Cendrars, you should read him only in French. (To translate Céline, by the way, is a feat!)

The truly magnificent writer is John Cowper Powys, now virtually forgotten. If you have the time and the patience for it, "A Glastonbury Romance" will do wonders for you. I paid a visit of homage to him in his old age. He was living in a small town in Wales. Have had only two or three such meetings in my life:—with him, with Cendrars, with Chaplin, for example.

I am getting a lot of fan mail from "cunts", especially in France, where a wonderful documentary on me is now showing. As a result of it, the French government

(M. de Peyrefitte) has written to ask if I would accept the Legion of Honor. He writes—"I know you despise such things. . . ." But I'm accepting it. Why not? It's nice to be despised by the intellectuals and made a Chevalier by the Establishment!

Well, here's a good hug for you. I love to hear from you. Hope you visit me when you get to the Coast, yes?
Henry

June 29, 1974

Dear Henry,

I loved your letter about my "Sexual Guru" piece. I myself had some misgivings after I wrote it. Of course, a writer is seen as a liberator and a giver of truth, and one should not mock that very deep response from people— however nutty they are. I am grateful to have a gift that goes straight to people's hearts and guts—but at the same time I know how impossible it is to deal with all these outpourings of emotion. If I were to get involved in even one-fourth of the people who write to me, my life would consist of nothing but that. Each one seems to think he is unique and that I have received no other letter but his. This week I've been plagued (by telephone and mail) by a young man who is having an adulterous affair in New York (his wife is in Indiana). For some reason he feels that I must meet his beloved and cast blessings upon them both. I told you I was becoming the patron saint of adulterers! I should write this man what Oscar Wilde is purported to have said about homosexuals: "I don't care what people do as long as they don't *do it in the streets and frighten the horses."*

I loved your letter from Lady Jeanne and I am returning it to you for your files after many mirthful readings and rereadings. In general I used to think that it was men *who were preoccupied with penile size. Women know better. It's not the size but the skill and the hardness and the passion and etc. I tend to think the talk about size is myth, too, but up to now I always thought it was a male myth. As for* racial *differences between penises, what can*

I tell you?! The number of Arabs and blacks I have known could be counted on the fingers of one amputated hand! I don't know much about vaginal passages, either. I do think people differ a lot in their love-making, but very little of that comes from anatomy. The movement of the body in some way mirrors the movement of the soul.

Enough of sex! On to money!! Yes, New York *maga-zine pays for articles. Everything from $400 to $700 for a short piece, to $1,000 and up for a longer piece. Do you have something to send them? Or maybe we could some day do an article together? Possibly a discussion of sex?! (Or maybe that would be better for* Playboy.) *I raise this possibility half in jest, but maybe it would appeal to you, and if so, let me know.*

About the nut mail, I value it too, and certainly agree with you that it's more interesting than the academic drivel. I get a little frightened of nuts from time to time, though, because I never know how far they're going to go. Sometimes they actually show up on the doorstep. Once last summer I was dashing into the house with arms full of grocery bags, an umbrella over one arm, a briefcase, a shoulder bag, and a shoe that had a broken heel, and as I stood there struggling with the locks, looking very un-gurulike, hassled and distraught, a young man came forward and said, "Are you the poet?" "I've never felt less like a poet in my life," I said. The question is, do poets shop for groceries? And are you a poet while choos-ing groceries? I leave these great existential questions to you.

I always have a feeling I will disappoint my admir-ers. If they expect me to be serious, I usually wind up making a million wisecracks and acting like a clown. If they expect me to be beautiful, I show up in old bluejeans and my slobbiest clothes. I don't really know why I do this—maybe to emphasize the gap between the writer and the writing. In one way, you know, the writer and the writing are one, but one hates to have a reader make literal *equivalences. I think we are also afraid because when these strangers come to us, they come to us with a very intimate knowledge of our souls and we have no knowledge of theirs. They have read our books, but they have no books we can read. The relationship is unequal from the start. So often I have had the experience of being kind to a person only to discover that I was the only person to tolerate him in so many years that he interpreted my kindness as an invitation to deep, passionate love. At such times I feel like the Pied Piper or a seductress. But what's the alternative? Becoming cold, formal and Edmund Wilson-ish? It's just not in my character to be that way. (Edmund Wilson, as you know, used to have a famous card he sent to correspondents. He would check off one of numerous answers, all of them "no's." Edmund Wilson does not dance, Edmund Wilson does not speak, Edmund Wilson does not read manuscripts, Edmund Wilson does not sing, etc. John Updike told me about a month ago (I met him for the very first time after his review of my book) that he had designed for himself a series of "repellent rubber stamps" to stamp his correspondence—but then he chickened out and didn't have the heart to use them. He gets mostly Jesus freaks, he says. The rubber stamps are interesting to me because in one of Updike's books, a writer named Henry Bech does actually stamp all of his correspondence with things like "It's your Ph.D. thesis, please write it yourself" or "Henry Bech is too old and doubtful to submit to questionnaires." It's the sort of fantasy a writer would have, but it's very hard to go through with it. I myself love writing letters when I have a good correspondent like you, someone who doesn't measure words, but writes straight out of the heart.*

I got a lovely letter from Twinka, who sounds delightful. Haven't answered it yet. If she wants to play the part in Fear of Flying *she ought to get in touch with the producers, Julia and Michael Phillips, who live in Malibu and whose office is at Columbia Pictures in Burbank. Not having met her, I have no idea whether she'd be right for the part, but I suppose she would know the method of making her interest known.*

I loved your description of "Last Tango in Paris."

Yes, Brando did look like "The Hunchback of Notre Dame" in that first fucking scene. I must say that the film was far too anal for my taste. Writing about it in The New York Review of Books, Norman Mailer said the film proved that "love is not flowers, but farts and flowers." Typical Mailer line. The sex seemed terribly violent and crude to me—scarcely tender or erotic at all. One good thing about it was that anonymous room bathed in amber light where the lovers met. But as lovers they seemed very unlikely to me. I didn't like either of them very much.

I congratulate you on the Legion of Honor and I congratulate you on being "despised by intellectuals." There is no surer sign that a writer will live. There are certain super-intellectual writers of puzzles who appeal immediately to academics (I am thinking particularly of Pynchon). They are admired at least in part because they provide such good material for doctoral theses. There are so many puzzles to unpuzzle. A writer like you who defies all categories, who is at once straightforward and passionate yet crafty and clever will always confound the academic critics.

By the way, I have a good friend named David Griffin (he recently married the lady to whom Fear of Flying is dedicated), and many years ago, when he was at Columbia, he wrote a master's essay called the Possibility of Joy: Henry Miller's Role in the American Tradition. I think he sent the essay to you years ago and corresponded with you about it. He's just given me a copy of it, which I have not yet read, but I can tell you that he loves your work and understands it. He has particularly interesting notions about why your work was banned for so long— not because of the four-letter words only, but because of the liberating effect of the work. If everyone were to soar as you do, civilization (Joyce calls it "syphilisation") would crumble. Anyway, David wants to be remembered to you, and is terribly fond of you, though he's never met you. He feels that your books have changed his life and changed all his ideas about writing. I'm sure that many,

many people feel that way. I myself have met dozens who do.

I may be coming to California next week (if not, we'll be there some time this summer) and I will call you. I'd love to take you to dinner and talk. Helen Smith says you are hard to reach by phone, but maybe she will do the phoning for me.

With love,
Erica

P.S. I am enclosing a copy of my newest poem, which is written in the style of Whitman, whom I adore.

July 4, 1974

Dear Erica—

Tell David Griffin to get in touch with me. He's faded out of my memory. And thank you for the dope for Twinka I don't think it's a part for her, but who knows? She's got the makings of a real actress in her.

I've often wanted to ask you, then forget, what is the meaning of that word "menarche", which occurs some-where about middle of your book. Can't find it in the dictionary, English nor French. Did you make it up.

I enjoyed your homage to Walt Whitman, who was truly the greatest, greater, I mean, than Dostoievsky or Tolstoi? On page 2 on top of page, are 4 lines about molars of corpses that baffle me. Am I stupid or did you write it unthinkingly? Forgive me if I put it to you this way, but I have often found on rereading something I wrote the day before a phrase or paragraph which makes no sense to me. I had something in mind but lost it in trying to express it. I know about "poetic license"—but is that what this is?

Your publisher (secretary) wrote me again. They are all out of those blue blurbs, which you wrote and which I like to enclose in my letters. They seem happy that you sold the movie rights (6 figures!) but I am not so sure if it will do the book good or kill it. It may make money, yes. All my movie ventures lose *money!*

This is my 20th letter today. Must stop. Hope to see you later in Summer. I take it you are now adapted to your marriage. Good for you! Cheers & hugs.

Henry Miller

P.S. I have no planets in Aries but three on conjunction in Scorpio, facing Aries. A bit lop-sided. (Mars, Moon, Uranus.)

7/7/74

Dear Erica—

You're right—there is a similarity in our handwriting. Only yours is still more free and open, I feel. Since I lost the sight in my right eye I make mistakes, mis-spell words, leave others out, etc. It's a tribulation.

Your interview was wonderful to read. I would have answered in much the same way. You have a wonderful memory for what other writers have said. Do you keep these phrases in a notebook for ready reference?

I can see from your answers what "teaching" has done for you. I lack all that. I always feel that I am a bit stupid when I talk. (One of the men I greatly admire is _____? can't think of it now! He wrote short books on St. Francis of Assisi, Charles Dickens, Robert Louis Stevenson. Also the "Father Brown" series. He was a converted Catholic and could always make Shaw or any of them look like dummies in a debate. Whom am I thinking of? When he wrote his column for the papers (in a pub or café) he laughed aloud over what he was writing. He could make me swallow the Virgin Mary and all that shit. He was a "believer" and a great wit. Now I remember—Gilbert K. Chesterton! If you never read his little book called "Charles Dickens", please do. I know Dickens is a pain in the ass—but not this book about him. It's a gem.

I am full of thoughts today; could write you a dozen pages but don't want to impose on you. Just gave Val the New York review to read and share with Twinka. . . . I *wrote a savage letter to my New Directions man. Imagine—they have 17 books of mine in circulation and my royalties on them for the last 5 years have not exceeded $6,000.00 a year!!! And they think I should be happy and grateful! I am furious. I am going (at last) to get myself an American agent (probably Sydney Omarr's agents—I know them quite well). Last night I gave Omarr (and his agent's wife, a Frenchwoman) the blurb (blue) you wrote about* Fear of Flying. *I always carry one in my pocket to hand out. (Like Rimbaud carrying that belt around his waist with 40,000 fra. in it—gold francs!)*

Why doesn't your publisher reprint your blurb? Have they stopped their print of you now that you have been sold to the movies? They seemed so proud of that achievement. As I said somewhere—"The publisher, whether good or bad, is the natural enemy of the author." (Like that little critter—Riki—Tike—-Tabi—which always kills the cobra. What's its name again?

Octaroon. Do you know that word? No one in my family seems to know it. I was once in love with an octoroon—she was my secretary and assistant in the Western Union—Camilla Euphrosmia Fedrant. What a name!

When I read your poem on Whitman (who for me is the one and only!) I meant to urge you to look up a chapter in "Books in My Life." It is called "A Letter to Pierre Lesdiam." He was a Belgian poet, who wrote in French. I had a long correspondence with him. He was a wonderful person (almost a saint) and a great reader. He was also my champion in Belgium, a Puritanic country somewhat like Norway.)

I am fond of that chapter because of the comparison or sous I made between Whitman and Dostoievsky. When you find time, do read it. I beg you. It's the nearest I come to you in your critical language. (You have, at least, two languages—one, the poet (whether novelist or poetess), the other the teacher-critic. I love both.

Another book I can't help recommending to you is

Maurice Nadeau's book on "Gustave Flaubert". Flaubert may seem like a dead horse to you but not this book. It's another gem. Should keep you awake nights and pissing in your pants all day. Put out by a small publisher in Long Island. I think it was the Library Press, or something like that. Consult a guide book—or Publishers' Weekly.

The last I have to tell you today is this. You made a "reader" out of Connie, my secretary. That girl hardly ever cracked a book. She hadn't even read my books, even though she was my secretary. Finally she did read two— with much effort. Anyway, I persuaded her to go out and buy your book. She did. She read it. She rejoiced and she suddenly wants to read. Promised me she will now tackle "Mysteries," "The Idiot" and "Tropic of Cancer". Never knew that reading could be such a pleasure. Says you opened her eyes. For which the bard be praised. Hallelujah! Erica Go Bragh! Nam myo ho renge kyo. (Yes, I say the latter every night before falling asleep. I am going to add you to the list tonight).

One last thing. In my last letter I forgot to answer your question about collaborating with you on something for a mag. The truth is, I'm a bit timid. I could do better probably, if we discussed some writer we both liked, as I did with Pierre Losdam.

As for sex, I don't think I have another word to say on that subject. You are only 32 or 33—you can still tackle it. I am 83. Makes a difference.

Once I wrote about—nothing, though I pretended I was writing about a friend's drawings. I consider that a feat. Just words. By the way, Hesse speaks marvelously in a posthumous book—as well as in "Siddhartha" of course—about things like immortality and other words we bandy about as being nothing but words. Yet, "nothing but words" can mean so much, n'est-ce pas?

You and I, we have the itch. We eat words, shit words, and fuck them good and proper too, I suppose.

Enough! Cheerio!

Henry

P.S. I am a little melancholy today. My beloved Lisa Liu, the Chinese actress and opera star, has just left for Hong Kong. She took a copy of your book with her. I won't see her for 3 or 4 months. So, I'll work!!

P.S. I never read or heard of Roethke, whom you mention several times. Twinka is lending me Sylvia Plath's one and only novel.

July 20, 1974

Dear Henry,

I'm delighted to have your letters and delighted to have a new fan in Irene Tzu. I also love the photograph of the watercolor you sent me. Seeing your watercolors has made me want to paint again. I haven't really done it since I was a first-year college student. I painted up a storm the summer I was 18—and that was the last time I really gave myself to it. I was at a writers colony in Massachusetts—had gone there to follow my college poetry teacher, with whom I was in love, of course. He was a pompous little cock-of-the-walk who arranged to have all his infatuated girl students follow him into the mountains where he could seduce them—away from the watchful eyes of the Barnard faculty. He lived (that summer) in a converted chicken coop, which he made a big deal about as a "writing coop." I was in love with him but too scared to sleep with him. When I finally had my big chance, I blew it by getting so incredibly drunk on two bottles of chianti that I puked red puke all over him (and me). He carried me home, put me tenderly into bed, saying, "This is what friends are for." I think he was probably relieved at never having to fuck me. It turned out later that he was all swagger and talk and very little action. Besides, I had a boyfriend at home to whom I was being unbelievably loyal. I still believed in romantic monogamy in those days. (The boyfriend at home turned out to be the Madman in Fear of Flying.*)*

Anyway, during all the imagined sexual upheavals of that summer, I painted. (though I was at the colony as a student of writing). I used to set up my portable easel in a seventeenth-and eighteenth century cemetery and do portraits of people out-doors—in or near the graveyard. I was very melancholy and adolescent and thought myself the most sensitive young woman in the entire world—like everyone else. My paintings were always full of high, brilliant color, but my drawing was never up to my grandfather's Old Master standards. My grandfather draws with all the expert technique of an Ingres, and one of the reasons I suppose I became afraid of a career as an artist was because I knew that my drawing would never measure up to those family standards. Now I begin to realize that the freedom and color sense that I had was very valuable in itself and ought to be reexplored. Your splendid new watercolor reminds me of the fantastic vision of life which is so much more important in painting than sheer draughtsmanship. I have never done watercolors on wet paper, but seeing yours and the joy they embody, I feel I would like to try it. I used to paint in oils on scarcely primed canvas. Sometimes I would make the oil and turpentine into a very thin wash and use it like watercolor, bleeding into the canvas, and sometimes I would use the paint very thickly with a palette knife. (All this is very distant recollection at this point). Also, I seem to have given away nearly all of my paintings. Whenever somebody asked me for a painting, I'd give it, as long as they promised to have it so people would see it. They are scattered now in the homes of friends I never see anymore. Tant pis: Someday I'll do some real painting again.

I thought it would fascinate you to see the shit my paperback publisher is using to promote Fear of Flying. I read with great empathy and shared fury your remarks about being ripped off by your publishers. I agree that the publisher is a natural enemy of the author. It can't be otherwise, really. The kind of openness to experience that one needs to be an author has to be antithetical to the selective blindness of the businessman (or even businesswoman). The woman who is doing the movie of Fear of

Flying *is a case in point. Utterly ruthless, with a kind of foxy brilliance about films, but ready to sacrifice everything and everyone—including her husband, lovers and me—for the project at hand. I used to think that I was one-track minded about writing. I used to think that writing made me "selfish" (my mother always called me "selfish" because I was sitting in a room and writing). But these movie people make me realize that I haven't even begun to understand the meaning of the world "selfish." They make the publishers appear like holy saints.*

Yes, you are absolutely right: we eat words, shit words and fuck words, too. There is nothing more comforting than writing. One of the more intelligent of my shrinks once said, "It makes you feel good to write because in your writing you tell the truth whereas in your life you have to lie to keep people from getting mad at you." It is true that I find it very hard to express anger directly and that I seem to express it through my writing. I feel exhilarated after a morning's work because I have been telling the truth to myself, and what can be better than that?

*I spoke to Helen and Bradley last week and I expect to come to California either at the beginning of August or in the first week of September. I can't wait to see you and talk to you. I don't give a shit whether we write anything together (on sex or writing or anything at all). I just want to talk and share and get to know you. I keep reading your books—*Black Spring *particularly delights me. I am mad about "A Saturday Afternoon" and your cry for "a classic purity, where dung is dung and angels are angels." I promise to get a hold of* Books in My Life, *which I confess I've never read, and your other long reading list, too! I sure as hell have a lot of work to do. Give Connie a hug for me, and tell her I'm glad I turned her on to words, words, words.*

I send you a big hug, too, and hope to see you before too long.

Erica

P.S. Tell Twinka (who sounds like a darling girl) that I will write to her one of these days. I have been working all week at the Sherry Netherland Hotel here with the producer of the movie of F of F. It's where you see famous movie stars talking on telephones plugged in behind the tables while they sip at their gazpacho, eye each other, overhear conversations about deals ("I know I can get him for you, but you better not bother him while he's on location") and watch the roaches crawl over the banquettes. With all that Hollywood opulence, the Sherry Netherland still has roaches!!!

Saturday—7/20/74

Dear Erica—

The Bradleys were here today. Suggested I write and tell you you can stay here in my house while in L.A. Erica, I'd gladly do that, but it all depends on how long my son will be absent. He has just taken on a job which will keep him traveling about the country, but I can't be sure how long the job will last or he will last. In any case, there's a nice place only about 2 miles away—The Santa Yenez Imo—at which you could stay if this is unavailable. I take it you can make your own breakfast, yes?

Did I tell you that I showed or lent your book to my heart doctor—Jewish, very serious and all that—and he liked it immensely. Then he said—"I can tell you what's the matter with her!"

I said—"What's that?"

He replied—"She can't accept romantic love." (sic) Curious observation, no?

I'm going out tonight to appear before about 100 people in an Actor's Laboratory and answer questions—on anything (double sic)

Look for Playboy next month.

Cheers now! Henry

P.S. We have a well-heated pool here—bring your bikini, if you have one. You can also go in in the raw, if you prefer.

July 27, 1974

Dear Erica—

I am in a lousy mood today, so forgive me if I don't respond in kind. The publicity the NAL are giving you is fabulous. Good for you! The bastards won't even reprint my books. Can't get anywhere with them, even thru my astrologer friend Sydney Ommar who is very close to some one at the top. (Incidentally he blames his multiple sclerosis on his women clients. Says they all made him go to bed with him! (Another sic.) "Omarr's complaint." Anyway I took on his literary agents the other day. Maybe they can do something about my fading royalties. Strange about the royalties, because I seem to get more fan letters than ever—from all over the world. (Yesterday I got 6 albums of Stockhausen's music from an unknown fan in Iceland.)

I made a public appearance a week ago at the Actor's and Director's Laboratory here. Apparently it was a huge success! It was a "Question & Answer" evening. No lecture, no reading. I can't do those things. Nor could I teach lit!

Tony is still away, so if you come soon, I can put you up in his room.

Forgive me for suggesting you read all those books—I can't help it—you're a born reader. May I add one more (to read only when you have plenty of time!)—

"A Glastonbury Romance" by John Cowper Powys. That's it for now. Cheers and a good hug. Je t'embrasse.

Henry

P.S. Did you know that the Japanese are not allowed to show the pubic hair? Witness the enclosed. And have you observed the difference between the Chinese and the Japanese erotic pix?

Dear Erica—

Enclose p.c. from my old friend Emil White of Big Sur who I persuaded to buy a copy. Forgive me for answer-

ing you by p.c. yesterday but I am overwhelmed with work.

I think it's too bad you are giving so much time to writing script for your book. You know what those bastards usually do? At first they say—"Bravo, just what we wanted." After a couple of months they write—"Sorry, but we deemed it best to turn over your script to our own script writers in view of their greater experience. They may make a few slight changes." Which means that when you see your script again you won't recognize it. It will be a professional piece of pure Hollywood shit! Think on it! Ask your Julia if I'm not right? Don't listen if she says no. Ask around!

Cheers and a good warm hug.

Henry

September 10, 1974

Dear Henry,

Hope you'll forgive the long delay in answering. To tell you the truth, I'm embarrassed to write you because of all the time I'm spending on the screenplay. I think you're probably right that it's a waste, and it is delaying my new book. It's also delaying my trip out West and my meeting with you. At this point I expect to come more towards the end of September, September 25 or thereabouts. I will bring my rough draft of the screenplay and spend some time out there visiting you and the producers. As I said before, you don't have to put me up.

Allan and I spent two weeks in Italy trying to recover from all the upheavals of this last year. We had been having a lot of problems coping with the book and each other and the demands of millions of new people entering our lives via Fear of Flying. *Ours has been a rocky marriage from the start, but sometimes I think that rocky marriages are the only kind that survive at all. We scream and yell at each other and get all the shit out, and we've been doing a lot of that lately. One thing that seems particularly remarkable about our relationship is that we really do change towards each other—not merely in the*

sense of putting up with stuff silently—but really alter-
ing our expectations of each other. With all the crises, it's
been a good summer.

I was delighted that the Times *ran your* Fear of
Flying *piece and I thought their changes and deletions*
were hilarious. WHAT DID THEY HAVE AGAINST
THE WORD HORNY? *And what's wrong with that*
good old-fashioned word "lay"? The Times *is really an-*
tediluvian. Their little note under your piece made their
exclusions all the more funny. Thank you for approving
of mine. I thought you might not necessarily like my
linking you with ancient tradition, but your link with
Rabelais is clear and indisputable. One of my very favor-
ite of your books is Black Spring *and one of my favorite*
chapters in Black Spring *is "A Saturday Afternoon"*
where you talk about dung and angels and Rabelais
rebuilding the walls of Paris with cunts. From 1964 to
1969 I used to teach English literature to various college
students. I taught a survey course of English lit from
Chaucer to the eighteenth century, and my students al-
ways used to be astonished at how much sex there was in
the poems I made them read! Of course I always chose the
stuff that tickled my fancy. Year after year students used
to say to me things like, "Wow, before I met you I never
realized English literature was so dirty." They were sur-
prised to find out that farting existed in Chaucer's time
and that Shakespeare knew about cunts.

Monseiur Henry, I almost forgot to tell you how
much I loved your "Insomnia" piece from Playboy. *I love*
what you say about belonging to that tribe of human
beings who never learn from experience. Me too. What
you write about the devil rings absolutely true and your
characterization of the entertainer needing that sea of
silly drunken faces is brilliant. The piece starts in light-
ness and ends in profundity. It's very moving—particu-
larly imagining you writing on the walls at 5 A.M. I know
that impulse. You're wrong, though, about women not
liking to hear about the soul. Only some women are bored
by soul. Where the devil comes in is that he always makes

us fall in love with our opposite numbers—those people who will inevitably cause us pain. You could find any number of steadfast, beautiful women who would not keep you awake at night with their antics. But that would bore you because part of the fascination is the unattainability, and part of the intensity comes from pain. What you say about Buddhas and Christs being born complete is probably true, but the very idea of it bores me. They would also get down on their knees and talk to ants and cockroaches, but not about love.

After much thought on the matter, I've decided the strategy of hiding one's love—the "good advice" friends always give—isn't possible. If you're really gaga for someone, they know it, no matter how you hold back and pretend not to call and pretend not to miss them. How do they know? The devil, I guess.

On this subject: I'm enclosing something that was sent to me by a man who has been pursuing me for about four years and has finally decided to give up the ghost. Of course I love him—but I love him like a great big teddy bear, and that isn't exactly what he wants. I find myself doing to him all the cruel things that have been done to me so often. Not that I mean to be cruel, but just that when someone is obsessed by you, everything short of total surrender (as you say) seems cruel. But the trouble is, that the lover would be BORED by total surrender and the whole thing goes around in circles.

I can't wait to read the whole Insomnia book. It's marvelous.

Love,
Cheers,
Hugs,
Erica

Sept. 10, 1974

Dear Erica—

I hope the enclosed doesn't dampen your spirits. It's strange that the only two unfavorable reactions to your work came from women—young women too. I hear your piece and mine appeared the same day (last Saturday) in the N.Y. Times. I haven't seen the paper.

When are you thinking of getting out here—soon? Tony is back home but his sister is still away—for how long I don't know. Twinka is eager to meet you and make dinner for us. Did she tell you that her mother fell hard for your book—bought an extra copy to lend to friends. Is quite crazy about you. So is Midori, the Japanese (American) secretary to my Japanese Dr. Watanabe. I haven't seen or heard from Bradley in several weeks. Have you?

Now I have sciatica, a nasty ailment that hurts like hell. Better see me before I collapse altogether! (Twinka just lent me Sylvia Plath's novel.)

Hope all's well with you and that you're finished with the screenplay.

Cheers now and here's hoping to see you soon.

Henry

Sunday—27th

Dear Erica—

I'm not surprised that you are thinking of returning soon! I remember how I made the same decision on my air-conditioned nightmare trip. After California nothing looked quite the same. And I never regretted the move from N.Y.

Of course, Big Sur is one place out of a million. You have to see it this trip. Too bad I can't show you around, but I'm still a semi-invalid. (Sometimes I wonder if I have a good fuck left in me any more! I am full of erotic dreams and desires, if that counts for anything.

Did Hoki tell you that I wrote the lyrics for that first song in the cassette? She put it into Japanese, altering it somewhat. I forgot the title I gave it now, but it had something to do with the garden door and in Japanese you never refer to the garden door as that is only for servants and tradesmen. What a people, eh! So it became "Love in Osso Buco" or whatever that South American rhythm is.

Erica, I did receive a slew of publicity material from

NAL but not *the books as yet. Before I send those beautiful packets out to my foreign publishers I ought to know
which foreign publishers have already taken the book. If
you can't tell me, please give me the name of your N.Y.
publisher—and address. I have only the British edition
here. If you have a literary agent, I'm curious to know
why they haven't done more work with foreign publishers.
In any case, I am happy to do things, only I don't want
to duplicate any one else's work.*

*Another request—do you mind giving me the names
and addresses of magazines in U.S.A. which pay fairly
well, including the N.Y. mag.? My agents, the Halseys,
sent all my correspondence, problems, wishes and mss. to
their "associate" agent in N.Y.—Scott Meredith. He
wrote them on receiving these things and I read a copy of
his letter. I have the feeling he is not too impressed by the
chapters from my book—"not like the Tropics," etc.
Which to me is* shit *! A writer should evolve, not repeat
himself, no? So I* may *have to place some of my work
myself eventually. I don't have much luck with Americans. (Except the few fans!)*

*And I need to make more money than I have been. My
expenses now just about total my income. The Internal
Revenue gets the bulk of it—am paying $40,000 this
year. Too, too much!*

*But enough of this. . . . I hope to see you soon. Get
out of N.Y. as soon as you can. Get into the sunshine
and—take up tennis or ping pong. You need some sort of
exercise. Of course, if you have a friend who has a warm,
indoor pool, that's the best of all. You'll probably make
a lot of new friends here.*

*Good luck, good cheer, love and continued admira-
tion.*

Henry

*P.S. I still haven't received copies due me of "Insomnia"
nor advances from American or French publisher. Doubleday is the American distributor. The book is out, I under-*

stand, but I haven't seen any publicity of any kind about it anywhere. I hate Doubleday!

10/31/74

Dear Erica—

Enclosed is from American writer I hoped would interest a Japanese publisher in your book. Now it seems unlikely. Strange to me that the Japanese tightening up on sex, eh? Anyway, this fellow wrote an article of 15–20 pages on the Japanese attitude toward pubic hair. Rather scholarly and amusing piece of work. Now, as you see, he asks me for editors' names. This follows on my request the other day for names of good paying mags. (Send both, if and when you find time.) You may like to write Ron Bell (address in margin: Ronald V. Bell

6-8-15 Nakamo

Nakamo-pu

Tokyo 164-Japan)

and see his article on Hair. I feel quite certain he did not send it to Playboy, Oui, Penthouse nor the new one, Gallery. I am going to write one or two good Japanese friends there in Japan for you now.

(Incidentally, P.O. here not accepting any mail for France now. There is a strike there. Japan O.K.)

By the way, Lisa is back for just 3 or 4 days. Phoned from S.F. airport yesterday. She mailed me a big spread in a Hong Kong (British) paper on the film. Seems it's a 12 million dollar production, with 1,000 extras. She received high praise for her role. Was invited to a preview of film based on Hesse's Steppenwolf two nights ago. Afterwards we were all invited to dinner in a new Moroccan restaurant on Sunset & Stanley Ave.—you eat with your fingers. Ellen Burstyn was the hostess—big bill! Anyway, we got talking about your book and to my surprise she said she met you. She first played in Tropic of Cancer. (Paris.)

Just heard from Bradley. Things are moving slowly, especially money. But good things are in the offing.

I had a letter (addressed to the Halsey Lit. Agent, his associates) about my work and problems. Rather cool, I thought. I hope he's O.K.

Best to you, dear Erica. I can hardly see. Must stop now.

Henry

P.S. You should try "The Busy Bee, in Hollywood. I forget—that's my job!

Hm

11/10/74

Dear Erica—

Mike Wallace of "Sixty Minutes" was here a few moments ago with his producer and latter's wife. They want to set a date for me on their program soon. I agreed—Wallace is a hale and hearty man, intelligent and earthy. During the course of our conversation your name came up. Wallace wondered how it would be if he interviewed us (separately) on the same program. I told him that for my part it would be fine and that I thought you would also like the idea. (They would put the same questions to us.)

He said he would get in touch with you, so be prepared. He could also change his mind. Be prepared for that too.

Today in the L.A. Times Book Review Section there was a big review of Doris Lessing's latest novel. After reading the review (which was favorable) I decided never to read her. They also reviewed a new book by Nabokov whom I can't read either.

I am almost finished with The Bell Jar of Sylvia Plath. I must confess I don't like her way of writing at all. I have no sympathy for her either. I fail to see the magic in her words. (Myopia on my part, no doubt.)

Now I have 6 plays of Anouilh to read, 3 of Girondoux and six books on Sufi poetry and philosophy. Too much. I wish some one could help me read all these bloody books.

Hope to see you here soon again. Glad to hear you finished work on your film. The new ending sounds good. O.K. now. Take care.

Cheers!

Henry

Dear Erica—

Hurts me to send you this! I'll fix them yet! I never had a good or intelligent review from them for any *of my books. Fuck them!*

See you soon, I hope.

Henry

[The review in question has been lost. It must have been a negative one of *Fear of Flying*. I include Henry's comments here to encourage the despondent writer. E. J.]

11/24/74

Dear Erica—

This is a feeble reply to your wonderful long breezy letter. First off, yes, the NAL did send the 25 copies. Thank you again. I think I have another letter to enclose from my Japanese friend, Ueno in Ichinoseki. Also a card from Ron _____?, about your book.

I have a hell of a lot of letters to write today and my eye already bothers me. It's great that you still think of coming to California to live. (If you can, try to get some one to drive you up and down the State and around. There are many wonderful living places. (My Negro nurse, Charles, can't understand why you would want to live in a shack. My shack (the original one) at Big Sur was the best home I ever had.

I read that piece by some woman in the L.A. Times today. Sometimes I don't get what these reviewers mean. Yesterday I was interviewed by Joyce Haber, a sort of gossip columnist. Wonder what will come of it?

Too bad you can't be with us for Thanksgiving. Hope to see you very soon. Love and cheers and all that!

Henry

Love from Twinka of course. Val isn't coming until after Thanksgiving. My Lisa Liu won't be back till early February. (But she misses me—that's the thing!)

2/27/74

Dear Erica—

Enclosed are the letters you forgot. The last one, from Kodansko, just arrived today. Sounds very good. I can scarcely believe it. Now it's for Japanese language, not English. I can hardly believe it. It would be a good idea, I think, if you are offered a contract that your agent stipulate they are not to censor, emasculate or bowdlerize your language. This would be, so far as I know, the first book in Japanese to use such language. Any way, good luck!

It was marvelous that you arrived in town in time to come to my birthday party. (Have you seen the photos in People mag.?)

You missed my toast last night. I took it from one of Buddha's sayings. Here it is—"I obtained not the least thing from complete, unexcelled awakening, and for that very reason it is called complete, unexcelled awakening."

Cheers and see you here soon again, I hope.

Henry

End Note

The letters to and from Henry end abruptly at this time because we now lived close enough to visit often and this was a period of much talk, dining, and hanging out. In October of 1974, on the very same day I met Henry, I was entertained by friends from Connecticut, Howard and Bette Fast, and met and fell in love with their son, Jonathan Fast. After many trips back and forth to Los Angeles, I left my marriage and moved to Malibu with Jonathan in February 1975. Henry lived in Pacific Palisades, just twenty minutes away, and it was easy to visit him.

Henry was open and generous about living arrangements. On one occasion when our plumbing broke down in Malibu, Jonathan and I moved in with him in Pacific Palisades. It was a merry house. Henry had a gift for being a mentor to young people and his place was a sort of sanctuary for my contemporaries. Besides Jonathan and me, there were Twinka Thiebaud (who later wrote *Reflections*), Tom Schiller (who made a wonderful film called *Henry Miller Asleep and Awake*), Bill Pickerill, the artist, who cared for Henry at the very end of his life, and many others—including Henry's late-life loves, the actresses Brenda Venus and Lisa Liu.

So the letters ended, but the conversations went on, and the friendship deepened. And then quite suddenly, fleeing the movie business and California, Jonathan and I moved back to New York. Shortly thereafter, we settled in Connecticut. I recovered from the trauma of a lawsuit over *Fear of Flying* by plunging into the eighteenth century, my old love from graduate school, and writing a mock-picaresque novel, *Fanny, Being the True History of the Adventures of Fanny Hackabout-Jones*. During the five-year period of composing that novel, I corresponded with no one—not even Henry. (Writing a book in eighteenth-century English does tend to occupy the mind and I was also pregnant or nursing during the final stages of the book.)

When Henry died in 1980, I was, ensconced in Connecticut, had a new marriage, a two-year-old daughter, and was in the midst of launching my eighteenth-century novel. But I was thrown by the news of Henry's death—he had seemed immortal to me—and I wrote a eulogy called "Good-bye to Henry-San" in which I remarked on the many ironies of Henry's reputation, the fact that he had sent postcards to his literary friends promoting himself for a Nobel prize, the fact that he hated his reputation as a pornographer, and the fact that he was the opposite of what the world presumed him to be: gentle, not rough; a romantic, not a rapist. I knew that I would have to expand that eulogy into a book someday, but I was far from being ready. (Just as I had to wait twenty years after graduate school to write my eighteenth-century novel, I would have to wait ten years after Henry's death to write my Miller book. Books gestate slowly and mysteriously; and the process can't be rushed.)

The memorial service was held at The New School. Arriving late after a long drive from Connecticut, I ran downstairs to the bathroom and was promptly soaked when a geyser of water shot up from the toilet upon flushing.

"Henry!" I cried. Apparently Henry was still hovering, playing tricks with the plumbing.

The event was a typical Miller mishmash. (I have never attended an event in Henry's honor that did not, somehow, go awry.) Norman Mailer was there with his wife and mother. David Amram played music, and various Miller wives and sweethearts had their say. Henry would have found the whole thing ridiculous. That was only fitting.

Chaos was his element. But he understood that chaos was also the precondition for creativity.

Henry left this world still not having been given his due by the self-appointed judges of "culture." And the situation persists to our own day. Perhaps Miller is a hard genius to recognize because he sticks his tongue out at all our sacred cows. Dualism disgusts him. He knows that sexomania and sexophobia are one and the same thing. He has little respect for our so-called freedom of the press—which is more a pious ideal than a reality. He has little hope for modern man unless he is reborn. We need a new race of beings, he says, an explosion of sorts, dynamite to blow up all our false pieties. Women can ignite this dynamite, but both men and women must together remake the world. They can only remake it one way: by first remaking themselves. The question is: will they be honest enough to do it? Honesty has never been more needed. Our very existence as a species is at stake.

After Henry's death, disturbing news began to reach me about his last days. "Henry had little strength, and slept off and on day and night," Noel Young, one of his last publishers (Capra Press) wrote to me. "He spoke much of the richness of his dreams and of the line between sleep and wakefulness not always being clear. Sometimes the dreams were more interesting and comforting than being awake and he'd want to sink back into them." Other friends reported that Henry was not always well served by the crowd of young people who congregated in his house. While he was dying downstairs, some distressing things were happening upstairs, among people who didn't even know who Henry Miller was. Rumors of drug abuse, financial abuse, and neglect haunt the accounts of those final days. Val and Tony were apparently frustrated in their attempts to help their father and eventually the artist Bill Pickerill, Henry's great friend, moved in to be at Henry's side during his last days on earth. He lovingly helped Henry die.

As Noel Young reports: "His faculties were failing—

blind in one eye and poor sight in the other, partially paralyzed in one arm and leg, he moved in a walker with difficulty. Yet he still turned out watercolors using the Ping-Pong table for support, and still enjoyed company at dinner time. Alas, during the last months his memory and ability to recognize friends began to fade, and it tended to embarrass him."

Twinka Thiebaud and Bill Pickerill tried to protect and nurture him. Even in health, Henry was a dreadful judge of character, too open to con men and exploiters. Many times in his life, his generosity had brought him pain (the misadventure with Moricand in "The Devil in Paradise" section of *Big Sur and the Oranges of Hieronymus Bosch* is a good example of this). At the end of his life, Henry was captive to his own excessive generosity and he would hear no evil about those who used him, some of whom were on the payroll.

Yet even this sad end is not inconsistent with Henry's character or his beliefs. Henry was enough of a Buddhist to understand that eternal circles get completed. He had been supported by many during his life, and now it was his turn to support others. If they were not always artists as great as himself, that was inevitable. We are not in control of the cosmic checks and balances, debits and credits.

In *The Red Notebook*, Henry had copied out a quote from the Buddha that reveals his philosophy about all things:

> Believe nothing, no matter where you read it or who has said it, not *even if I have said it*, unless it agrees with your own reason and your own common sense.

Henry knew that even the greatest teacher is not infallible. If this was true of Buddha, it was also true of Henry. Wise as the Buddha in some respects, Henry could also be as naïve as a child in his judgment of people. Sometimes he knew but didn't want to know he knew. He would say to Twinka and Val, "Don't disillusion me, I need my illusions." Some of his late loves also abused his generosity, but if they inspired him to write and made him feel young, wasn't that enough? Henry's friends could not always protect him from himself.

Noel Young reports that he saw Henry "every month or so" in the last days and "was dismayed to see him in ebb tide." Noel "tried to rush the printer to have *The World of Lawrence* in his hands, but he died the *very day* the first copies were shipped from the bindery."

An irony: *The World of Lawrence* was to have been Henry's first published book, and it became his last. At the end, with the help of Noel Young, Evelyn J. Hinz, and John J. Teunissen, this "passionate appreciation" of D.H. Lawrence finally found its form. Like all Henry's books and essays on writers, it is not orthodox literary criticism, and yet it tells us a great deal more about the creative process. The creative process was what Henry knew best, and he had the gift for communicating it to others. He was more than a writer; he was also a muse and a prophet.

Miller's joy and self-liberation threaten people. They claim to be "bored" by his exuberance—a sure sign that something in it frightens the fearful. His cosmic definition of sex is still rejected. It is somehow easier to alternate between the dualities; sexomania one decade, sexophobia the next.

The truth is, we will never fulfill our potential as a species until we properly understand Miller and his cry for wholeness.

Down with sexomania and sexophobia both! Up with the full acceptance of the complexities of our humanity! We have been walking blindfolded through most of history, through our own lives, even, condemning all that we cannot see. Miller is telling us to strip the bandages from our eyes and let the light enter. He is offering us peace in the midst of war and life more abundant on our march toward death.

Only fear makes us fail to hear him—fear of falling,

fear of flying. He wants us to come home to the world and to understand that all true revolution starts inside us. He asks us to recover the divinity of man and woman. We shut out his voice at our peril. He is offering us nothing less than life.

Notes

All titles are by Henry Miller unless otherwise noted. Page numbers listed with sources refer to the currently available edition of Miller's works as listed in the bibliography.

PAGE

Introduction: Why Henry Miller?

6   ". . . has caught the flame he tried to pass on." From an early draft of *The World of Lawrence*, edited out of final text. Ms. is in UCLA Special Collections.

Chapter 1: Born Hungry: Henry & Me

24   ". . . no one lived there." Quoted in Mary Dearborn, *The Happiest Man Alive*, p. 304.

Chapter 2: Henry Hero

43   ". . . but I will sing . . ." *Tropic of Cancer*, p. 2.

45   ". . . and humiliated as in America." *Tropic of Capricorn*, p. 12.

46   "A complete circle." *Order and Chaos chez Hans Reichel*, p. 25.

Chapter 3: Just a Brooklyn Boy

56   ". . . a cussed streak in me . . ." *Tropic of Capricorn*, p. 10.

56   ". . . bringing me out of the womb." *Ibid.*

56   ". . . clutching womb . . ." *Ibid.*, p. 61.

56   ". . . snug and secure it may be." *Book of Friends*, p. 17.

56   ". . . her grip like an octopus." *Tropic of Capricorn*, p. 61.

57   ". . . to fill a hundred books." *Reflections*, p. 20.

58   ". . . one will never be loved . . ." *The Time of the Assassins*, p. 49.

59   ". . . the same with Lawrence and with Rimbaud." *Ibid.*, p. 48.

60   ". . . pillar of society like she wanted me to be." *Reflections*, p. 20.

61   ". . . and can roam the streets at will . . ." *Book of Friends*, p. 15.

61   ". . . except a real pony." *From Your Capricorn Friend*, p. 7.

62   ". . . my mother was stupid and cruel." *Ibid.*, p. 77.

62   ". . . scenes of my childhood." *Book of Friends*, p. 28.

62   ". . . to talk that way to a woman." *Ibid.*, p. 30.

63   ". . . the first artist to appear in my life." *Ibid.*, p. 38.

64   " 'I don't want to set the world on fire.' " *Ibid.*, p. 100.

65   ". . . hates the Jews more than the Jews?" *Tropic of Cancer*, p. 3.

65   ". . . tomorrow never came." *Tropic of Capricorn*, p. 11.

65   ". . . stuff like that, I give up." *Life and Times*, p. 185.

66   ". . . to be my mother." *Ibid.*, from unpaged endpaper.

67   ". . . essay on Nietzche's 'Anti-Christ.' " From an unpublished letter to Huntington Cairns, 1939.

68   ". . . I have regretted ever since." *Ibid.*

69   ". . . to open a man's eyes . . ." *The Black Cat* magazine, quoted in Jay Martin, *Always Merry and Bright*, p. 53.

70–71 "... chancre on a worn-out cock ..." *Tropic of Capricorn*, p. 19.

71 "I couldn't get over it." *Ibid.*, p. 17.

71 "... I gave him an earful." *Ibid.*

72 "... given the company away to the poor buggers." *Ibid.*, p.27.

72 "... to bring all humanity to God ..." *Ibid.*

73 "... spitting, fuming, threatening." *Ibid.*, p.30.

74 "(... more than my wife!)" From an unpublished letter to Huntington Cairns, 1939.

74 "I was scared shitless." *Tropic of Capricorn*, p. 34.

75 "... and sulphur in my blood." *Ibid.*

75–76 "... less than 300 pages, and ruined." From an unpublished letter to Huntington Cairns, 1939.

Chapter 4: Crazy Cock in the Land of Fuck

83–84 "Nobody *dies* here. . . ." *Tropic of Cancer*, p. 29.

85 "hours together, discussing ideas." Author conversation with Georges Belmont.

86 "... *movement*, all the time!" *Ibid.*

86 "That was Montparnasse in those days." *Ibid.*

88–89 "... death of everything sensitive ..." *Letters to Emil*, p. 87.

89 "... direct as a knife-thrust." *Ibid.*, p. 72.

89–90 "... like some evil dream ..." *Ibid.*, pp. 93–95.

90 "... his whole being." Brassaï, *Grandeur Nature*, p. 12.

90 "I am singing." *Tropic of Cancer*, p. 2.

91 "... for deigning to notice him." From the original ms. of *Crazy Cock* in the UCLA Special Collections.

95–96 "He is like me." Anaïs Nin, *Henry and June*, pp. 5–6.

96 "... on his own introspective journey." *Ibid.*, p. 6.

97 "Henry faded." *Ibid.*, p. 14.

97–98   ". . . the same madness, the same stage."
         Ibid., p. 15.
99   ". . . he writes his book." *Ibid.*, p. 37.
99   ". . . in the space of a generation . . ." *Tropic of Cancer*, pp. 11–12.
100   ". . . from my shoulders." *Ibid.*, p. 97.
101–102 ". . . it presented itself." *Ibid.*
101–102 "I go forth to fatten myself." *Ibid.*, pp. 97–99.
103–104 ". . . spit out two franc pieces . . ." *Ibid.*, pp. 5–6.
104–105 ". . . a fraction of my feelings . . ." *Ibid.*
105   ". . . like a dead clam." *Ibid.*
106   ". . . with this kind of enthusiasm." *Ibid.*, p. 171.
106   ". . . to the bottomless pit." *Ibid.*, p. 94.
106   ". . . what is there is the heart." *Ibid.*, p. 163.
107   ". . . hungry seeing mouths." *Ibid.*
107   ". . . two enormous lumps of shit." *Ibid.*, p. 97.
108–109 ". . . a sheer loss of time. . . ." *Ibid.*, pp. 139–49.
109–10   ". . . since it's not my fifteen francs?" *Ibid.*, pp. 142–43.
110–11   ". . . such a degree of perfection." *Ibid.*, pp. 153–54.
113   ". . . with strangled embryos." *Ibid.*, p. 165.
113   ". . . the process of disillusion quickens." *Ibid.*, p. 164.
115–16   ". . . its course is fixed." *Ibid.*, p. 318.

Chapter 5: The Last Man on Earth
123   . . . "entangled and indebted." Author conversation with Betty Ryan, Nov. 14, 1992.
123   "in mufti." *Ibid.*
126   ". . . *always Saturday afternoon.*" *Black Spring*, p. 34.
127   ". . . one of the great human joys." *Ibid.*, pp. 37–38.

128 ". . . shouting *Hallelujah!*" *Ibid.*, pp. 44–45.

129 ". . . all of life in this art." Author conversation with David Black.

129–30 ". . . except a finger bowl." *Black Spring*, pp. 91–92.

131 ". . . break her heart?" *Ibid.*, p. 110.

133 ". . . women don't want to be worshiped." *The Wisdom of the Heart*, p. 141.

135–36 "I smelled it." Alfred Perlès, *My Friend Henry Miller*, p. 132.

136 . . . ordered Ryan to knock on a pipe . . . Author conversation with Betty Ryan, Nov. 14, 1992.

137 ". . . for all the French care." From an unpublished letter to Huntington Cairns, 1939.

138–39 ". . . the Obelisk Press." Alfred Perlès, *My Friend Henry Miller*, p. 178.

140 ". . . a totality which is inexhaustible." *Tropic of Capricorn*, p. 333.

141–42 ". . . whose head has just been lopped off." *Ibid.*, p. 34.

142 ". . . you are Lilith, and I know it." *Ibid.*

142 ". . . enjoying the celestial fireworks!" *Ibid.*

142 ". . . beneath my coat." *Ibid.*, p. 339.

137 ". . .—also Hamlet *Ms.*" *The Durrell–Miller Letters*, pp. 100–101.

145–46 ". . . *to last the rest of my life.*" From an unpublished letter to Huntington Cairns, 1939.

146 ". . . finished canvases by a master." *The Colossus of Maroussi*, p. 3.

147 ". . . painters, legislators, visionaries." *Ibid.*, p. 48.

147 ". . . as well as from the heavens." *Ibid.*

147–48 ". . . scattered far and wide." *Ibid.*, pp. 53–54.

148 ". . . the world of light and beauty." *Ibid.*, p. 55.

Chapter 6: Heart Filled with Light . . .

to censorship in the United States are the following cases: *United States* v. *One Book Called* Ulysses, 5 F. Supp. 182, (SDNY 1933; *aff'd* 72 F.2d 705 (2nd Cir. 1934); *Roth* v. *U.S.* 354 U.S. 476, 77 S.Ct. 1304, L.Ed 2d 1498 (1957); *Jacobellis* v. *Ohio*, 378 U.S. 184, 84 S.Ct. 1676, 12 L.Ed.2d 793 (1964); *Grove Press, Inc.* v. *Gerstein*, 378 U.S. 577, 84 S.Ct. 1909, 12 L.Ed 2d. 1035 (1964); *Miller* v. *California*, 413 U.S. 15, 93 S.Ct. 2607, 37 L.Ed.2d 419 (1973).

183   ". . . combination of sex and intellect." Charles Rembar, *The End of Obscenity*, p. 179.

185   ". . . that ignoble reputation." The case in question is *Grove Press* v. *Gerstein*, 1964.

185   ". . . disgusting book." *Ibid.*, p. 210.

188–89   ". . . duality and elusiveness." Anaïs Nin in *The Booster*, November 1937, p. 27.

Chapter 7: Must We Burn Henry Miller? . . .

193   ". . . this onerous burden of sexuality falls." Kate Millett, *Sexual Politics*, p. 295.

204   ". . . home of a lunatic." *The Cosmological Eye*, p. 290.

204   ". . . that which we are seeking." *Ibid.*, p. 270.

205   ". . . only the hate, the violence." Anaïs Nin, *Henry and June*, p. 86.

207   ". . . makes these conditions sexual." Andrea Dworkin and Catharine MacKinnon, *Pornography and Civil Rights*, p. 36.

Chapter 8: Sexomania/ Sexophobia or, Sex-Libris

215   " '. . . dreaming it up to make money!' " *Big Sur and the Oranges of Hieronymus Bosch*, p. 129.

216   ". . . our way of thinking which makes death." *The World of Sex*, p. 59.

217   ". . . any justification for life." *The World of Lawrence*, p. 17.

217   ". . . usurp the body's proper function." *Ibid.*, pp. 175–76.

218   ". . . in all primitive peoples." *Ibid.*, p. 176.

218   ". . . to behave like the animal he is. . . ." *Ibid.*

218   ". . . refuses to be resolved." *Ibid.*, p. 177.

219   ". . . he is finished, he can croak." *Ibid.*, 185–86.

220   "It is the rape and scorn of the mother." *The Great Cosmic Mother*, p. 193.

221   ". . . the waste of contemporary disintegration." *The World of Lawrence*, p. 187.

222   ". . . the evil seed of the Christian ideal." *Ibid.*, p. 188.

222–23   ". . . he wanted to overthrow." *Ibid.*, p. 191.

227   ". . . did not invent the obscene." Walter Kendrick, *The Secret Museum: Pornography in Modern Culture*, p. 33.

230   ". . . the last phase of evolution. . . ." *The World of Sex*, p. 10.

230   ". . . I am my own saviour." *Ibid.*, p. 11.

230–31   ". . . open the doors of the world for us . . ." *Ibid.*, pp. 57–58.

231   ". . . is neither beneficent or cruel." *Ibid.*

Chapter 9: Why Must We Read Miller? . . .

237   ". . . the discovery of truth." *The World of Sex*, pp. 53–54.

238   ". . . to the loftiest peaks." *Ibid.*, p. 54.

238   ". . . the one I am talking about." *Ibid.*

238–39   ". . . against the side of a steep cliff." *Ibid.*, pp. 54–55.

239   ". . . their stay on earth." *Ibid.*, p. 55.

239   ". . . he chooses to dwell on." *Ibid.*

240   ". . . in another life." *Ibid.*, pp. 56–57.

240   ". . . to be completely 'the writer.' " *The Books in My Life*, as quoted in *Henry Miller on Writing*, p. 126.

241   "... a few Christians shared!" Unpublished letter from Thomas Merton to Henry Miller, June 22, 1964. Private collection of Charles Monk, New York.

245   "... clinging to the tails of comets." *Sexus*, p. 29.

The quotes from Noel Young in the End Note, in which he describes Henry's last days, come from a letter to Erica Jong dated 30 September 1992. Other information in this section comes from conversations with Twinka Thiebaud and Bill Pickerill.

Annotated
Bibliography

A bibliography of Henry Miller's complete oeuvre presents a daunting challenge. Because his works were often published first as pamphlets, small-press, or privately printed editions, many of the titles recur. I have limited this bibliography to the noting of the first appearance of the work and the currently available edition.

Henry's early books were published in France (in English) to take advantage of a loophole in the French obscenity law. Consequently we find first editions appearing in Paris and then the same work reappearing later in America, often after much litigation. In other cases, various anthologies of Miller's work (minus the sexually oriented pieces) were put together as a way of avoiding prosecution for obscenity

FULL-LENGTH WORKS

Tropic of Cancer. Obelisk Press, Paris, 1934; Grove Press, New York, 1961.

Henry Miller's first published book, but not the first he ever wrote. Preceded by *Moloch* and *Crazy Cock* (not published until well after his death), *Tropic of Cancer* is the exuberant sound of a new voice in American literature. A picaresque rant about one man's odyssey through bohemian, depression-era Paris. The sex was what everyone noticed first, but reading it now we notice the directness of description and the almost Zen-like acceptance of the good and bad in life.

Black Spring. Obelisk Press, Paris, 1936; Grove Press, New York, 1963.

Henry's second book-length work, conceived as a self-portrait, contains such short and hallucinatory pieces as "The Angel Is My Watermark!" "A Saturday Afternoon," "Into the Night Life . . . " It also contains the autobiographical gems "The Tailor Shop," and "The Fourteenth Ward." Prefaced with the quote "What is not in the open street is false, derived, that is to say, *literature*," this book is dedicated to Anaïs Nin and remained one of Henry's favorites. Many of the pieces in it first appeared in the U.S. in *The Cosmological Eye* (see below).

Max and the White Phagocytes. Obelisk Press, Paris, 1938.

A miscellany of essays and tales, many of which later appear in *The Cosmological Eye.*

Tropic of Capricorn. Obelisk Press, Paris, 1939; Grove Press, New York, copyright © 1961, released in 1962.

Henry Miller's second novel, dedicated "TO HER." This novel jumps back to Henry's New York life, childhood, mother, Brooklyn, first loves, The Cosmodemonic Telegraph Company, and the pivotal mad love for June. Henry creates a vast tomb in which to bury this agonizing and inspiring muse.

The Cosmological Eye. New Directions, New York, 1939.

The first book of Henry's to be published in his native country, it contains essays, memoirs, pieces which first appeared in *Black Spring* and *Max and the White Phagocytes.* Reprints such treasures as Henry's autobiographical memoir "The Tailor Shop," "Un Etre Etoilique," (Henry's discussion of Anaïs Nin and her journals), and many other wonderful genre-defying shorter works.

The Colossus of Maroussi. Colt Press, California, 1941; New Directions, New York, 1958.

Henry's spiritual travel book about Greece. His central work, and one of his best written. Has none of the unevenness one finds in *Nexus, Sexus, Plexus.* Its "hero," the so-called colossus of Maroussi (George Katsimbalis), is marginal in the book, but he became a "hanger" for Henry's own heroism. *Maroussi* stands squarely in the tradition of *Walden.*

Hamlet, Vol. I and II. With Michael Fraenkel, Carrefour, Puerto Rico, 1939; Mexico, 1941; *Hamlet Letters.* Capra Press, California, 1988.

Letters between Henry and Fraenkel (written 1935–38), which started out with Shakespeare and strayed everywhere else, as usual. Miller's letters are philosophical essays on writing, philosophy, movies, Jews, and the thought-disease of modern man.

The World of Sex. Argus Book Shop, Chicago, 1941.

Henry's explication of the role of the "obscene" in his art and the relationship of sex to literature. A central self-analysis. Though Henry was only known to a coterie at this point, he treats his own contribution as if he knows how major his oeuvre would prove to be.

The Air-Conditioned Nightmare. New Directions, New York, 1945.

Henry's phantasmagoric travel book about America. Deliciously antipatriotic and prophetic of the current decline of America.

A Devil in Paradise. Signet (New American Library), New York, 1946.

A long essay (eventually incorporated into *Big Sur and the Oranges of Hieronymus Bosch*) relating the invasion of

Henry's Big Sur paradise by Conrad Moricand, an old friend from Paris of the thirties, who, hearing of Henry's "success," decided to descend upon him. Typically, Henry cabled him "our home is yours." He was certainly to regret it. One of the most amusing accounts of the troubles Henry's generosity got him into.

Remember to Remember. New Directions, New York, 1941.

Subtitled Volume 2 of *The Air-Conditioned Nightmare*, this book is really a series of essays and portraits. It contains studies of such Miller-friends as Jean Varda, Abe Rattner, and Jasper Deeter. "Obscenity and the Law of Reflection," Miller's major piece on the uses of sex to awaken the reader, appears here, as does "Artist and Public" and "Remember to Remember," a strange and beautiful piece about memory, forgetfulness, and Miller's recollections of his expatriate decade in Europe.

The Wisdom of the Heart. New Directions, New York, 1941.

Another Miller miscellany, dedicated "to Richard Galen Osborn . . . who rescued me from starvation in Paris and set my feet in the right direction. May heaven protect him and guide him safely to port." Contains "Mademoiselle Claude," the first piece in which Miller's direct first-person voice asserted itself clearly; "The Philosopher Who Philosophizes," a curious little riff, written on Corfu, about Keyserling, and "The Enormous Womb," a Henryish essay on birth, death, illusion, and world peace.

The Smile at the Foot of the Ladder. Duell, Sloane & Pearce, New York, 1948; New Directions, New York, 1948.

Henry's story of Auguste, the famous clown who wanted more than to make his audience laugh. He wanted to give them ecstasy and illumination, and in so doing found it for himself. A most atypical Miller text, both for its brevity, and because it is a philosophical parable, written in the third person. Henry says in the epilogue that it was provoked by a request from Fernand Léger that he provide a text to accompany forty illustrations of clowns and circuses. By the time Léger had rejected it as unsuitable, Henry found he had already written something he was very pleased with. The first edition (1948) had reproductions of works by Picasso, Chagall, Rouault, Klee, among others, and a later edition (1958) was illustrated by Henry himself.

Nights of Love and Laughter. Signet (New American Library), New York, 1955.

Anthology containing "The Brooklyn Bridge," "Mademoiselle Claude," an excerpt from *Maroussi,* and an excellent introduction by Kenneth Rexroth that evokes Henry's innocence and naïveté. Rexroth recognizes that Henry is a naïf and a truth-teller like Petronius or Casanova.

The Books in My Life. New Directions, New York, 1952, 1969.

Proof that Henry regarded books as living beings, which influenced him every bit as much as the people in his life. Idiosyncratic Henry-essays on Rider Haggard, Blaise Cendrars, Jean Giono, John Cowper Powys, Krishnamurti, and others. Contains a marvelous essay entitled "Reading in the Toilet," that brings together all Henry's preoccupations, from bookishness to excrement to enlightenment. A wonderful collection. It proves that the impetus to become a writer is the joy of having been a reader.

The Time of the Assassins: A Study of Rimbaud. New Directions, New York, 1946, 1962.

Purportedly a study of Rimbaud, but really a study of Henry. It illuminates his attachment to his mother's womb and his many efforts to struggle free. By analyzing Rimbaud's passion for liberty, he analyzes his own. Contains the amazing sentence: "There are obsessive, repetitive words which a writer uses which are more revealing than all the facts which are amassed by patient biographers." Henry points to Rimbaud's constant repetition of *eternity*, *charity*, *solitude*, *anguish*, *light*, and pronounces them "the warp and woof of his inner pattern." Not proper literary criticism, but criticism lifted to the level of philosophy and self-analysis.

Big Sur and the Oranges of Hieronymus Bosch. New Directions, New York, 1957.

Henry's poetic evocation of the wild, rocky coast of California's Big Sur, its birds, its magic, its mystery: "Nature smiling at herself in the mirror of eternity." For Henry, the West was full of "dreamers, outlaws, forerunners." He became a westerner himself and Big Sur was the catalyst. Unfortunately Henry blasted this earthly paradise by writing the book. From then on fans and curiosity seekers were drawn to Big Sur, and they made it impossible for him to continue writing there. Like *Maroussi*, this book is a strong response to the spirit of a place; it goes beyond nature writing and becomes meditation.

The Intimate Henry Miller. Signet (New American Library), New York, 1959. A paperback original.

Still another assortment—many published elsewhere before. This collection contains an excellent introduction by Lawrence Clark Powell, the U.C.L.A. librarian who became Henry's friend, inspired *The Books In My Life*, and brought Henry Miller's collected papers to their present place of honor in the Special Collections of the U.C.L.A. library.

The Henry Miller Reader, edited by Lawrence Durrell. New Directions, New York, 1959.

A fairly complete Miller reader, containing literary essays, portraits, stories, pieces of *Big Sur and the Oranges of Hieronymus Bosch, Maroussi, Black Spring,* and *Tropic of Cancer,* as well as a chronology of Miller's life, written by Henry especially for this edition. The introduction by Lawrence Durrell calls Henry a "great vagabond of literature." Here, Durrell stresses Miller's uncategorizability: "I suspect that his final place will be among those towering anomalies of authorship like Whitman or Blake, who have left us, not simply works of art, but a corpus of ideas which motivate and influence a whole cultural pattern." Also has an introduction and headnotes to each selection by Henry himself.

SEXUS, The Rosy Crucifixion, Book One. Obelisk Press/ Editions du Chêne, Paris, 1949; Grove Press, New York, 1965.

A vast, chaotic novel of Henry's New York origins and his emancipation into the writing life. *Sexus* begins with Henry's meeting Mara, the taxi dancer (based on June), who turns on him "the full incandescent radiance of her love." It is Mara who proposes: *"Why don't you try to write?"* This book is the story of Henry's response to that provocation. Full of insights into the writer's life, it has a driving energy, but, as a whole, proves V.S. Pritchett's theory that if you remove the weaknesses of a book, you also remove the strengths. Bombast and bad writing abound, but it is nonetheless worth reading for the accuracy with which it captures Henry's desperate need to become a writer.

PLEXUS, The Rosy Crucifixion. Olympia Press, Paris, 1953; Grove Press, New York, 1963.

Another installment of the June/becoming-a-writer story. Here the muse is called Mona and the book begins with our hero's moving in with her in Brooklyn. Covers Henry Miller's Greenwich Village life, the speakeasy, Henry's first attempts to compete with James Joyce by writing for a fee. It seems that each time Henry went back to this old material he discovered new treasures. And yet, it is the ending digression of *Plexus*—an elaborate cadenza about Spengler, Nietzsche, Ibsen, Hesse, and the *Tao Te Ching*, that makes it most interesting. Here Henry says "perhaps in opening the wound, my own wound, I closed other wounds, other people's wounds." In short, Henry discovers the reason for all his suffering: to give something back to the world.

NEXUS: Volume I. Obelisk Press, Paris, 1960; Grove Press, New York, 1965, 1987.

The last installment of Henry's New York life. Again, the setting is Greenwich Village in the twenties and again the heroine/muse is Mona (who is betraying Henry with another woman). The marvels here are the digressions. They cover everything—from America, to philosophy, to writing, to memory. At the end of the book, Henry is launched from America to Europe. He says good-bye to Daniel Boone, the Street of Early Sorrows, Sherlock Holmes, Houdini, Oscar Hammerstein, O. Henry, P.T. Barnum, Jesse James, and Rudolf Friml.

Order and Chaos Chez Hans Reichel. Loujon Press, Alberquerque, New Mexico, 1966.

A strange and beautiful essay about the origins of art. It is here that Henry describes his love affair with chaos, his desire to be as creative as God.

Quiet Days in Clichy. Olympia Press, Paris, 1956; Grove Press, New York, 1987.

Two erotic tales set in Paris in the thirties, written in 1940 for a collector of pornography who rejected them as "too poetic." The price was supposedly "one dollar a page." Even as a pornographer, Henry couldn't hold a job. This book is rawer than *Tropic of Cancer* and doesn't have as many digressions, but it is still not *proper* pornography, i.e., "the copulation of clichés" (Nabokov).

Insomnia or The Devil at Large. Loujon Press, Albuquerque, New Mexico, 1970; Gemini Smith/Doubleday & Co., New York, 1974.

The story of an old man falling in love with a beautiful young woman, who taunts him and causes him to lose sleep. The devil here is love, longing, imagination, sleeplessness. This exquisite account of Henry's infatuation with Hoki, his ultimate wife, is full of wisdom about the eternal riddle of unrequited passion. Illustrated with Henry's "Insomnia" series of watercolors, which are among his best.

My Life and Times. Gemini Smith/Playboy Press, Chicago, 1971.

A large illustrated book containing photographs, watercolors, an autobiographical essay by Henry, an introduction by Bradley Smith, a chronology of Henry's life made by himself. A typical Henry-mélange of wisdom and humbug. The recollections of childhood are valuable, but the pictures of Henry playing Ping-Pong with bosomy naked blondes did his reputation more harm than good.

The Nightmare Notebook. New Directions, New York, 1975.

Facsimile of Henry's notebook during the tour of America with Abe Rattner that was the basis for *The Air-Conditioned Nightmare.* Fascinating descriptions of places, people, moods, as well as watercolors by Henry.

Book of Friends: A Tribute to the Friends of Long Ago. Capra Press, California, 1976.

An octagenarian Henry recalls the Brooklyn of his youth and the friends he made on the street. As Brooklyn recedes, it gets rosier and rosier. There is a wooliness to the writing here; it is not Henry's best work. Useful for autobiographical background.

Sextet. Capra Press, California, 1977.

The short works collected here were first published separately by the Capra Press. They are: "On Turning Eighty," "Reflections on the Death of Mishima," "First Impressions of Greece," "The Waters Reglitterized," "Reflections on the Maurizius Case," and "Mother, China and the World Beyond." Another miscellany of works first published as pamphlets. In "Mother, China and the World Beyond," Henry anticipates reunion with his mother in paradise and allows her a sweetness he has never recorded before. He seems to be preparing for his own death.

The World of Lawrence: A Passionate Appreciation. Capra Press, California, 1980.

Begun after Kahane's acceptance of *Tropic of Cancer* in 1932, and worked on intermittently for the next twenty years at least, this study of D.H. Lawrence never really found a coherent form. It chases its tail—Henry in search of Lawrence, finding Henry—but is full of revealing insights into Miller's patriarchal view of the universe, sex, death, creativity.

Opus Pistorum. Grove Press, New York, 1983.

(Republished in paperback as *Under the Roofs of Paris*, 1984.) Under any title, this pornography-for-hire experiment is horribly written and besmirches Henry's reputation. Some have argued it is a forgery. Forgery or not, it exemplifies the way fame betrays the famous. At his best, Henry Miller understood that sex and spirit were very close. At his worst, he played right into the hands of his critics.

Paint As You Like and Die Happy: The Paintings of Henry Miller, ed. Noel Young. Chronicle Books, San Francisco, n.d. (circa 1990).

Illustrated volume of Henry's watercolors from the thirties to the seventies. Also contains interesting prefaces by Noel Young and Lawrence Durrell. Reprints four Henry Miller essays on painting, including "To Paint Is to Love Again," "The Painting Lesson," and "The Waters Reglitterized."

Crazy Cock. Grove Press, New York, 1991. Introductions by Mary Dearborn and Erica Jong.

An early effort at fiction from the twenties, abandoned after Henry found his voice in *Tropic of Cancer*. It is not very good, but should be extremely encouraging to young writers in that it makes one see how desperately far Miller's early voice was from the voice he eventually found. Henry seemed to know that this book should be burned, but unfortunately he didn't burn it. It was found at U.C.L.A. after his death. He apparently told many friends it had been lost. Wishful thinking.

PAMPHLETS, BROCHURES, SHORT WORKS

What Are You Going To Do About Alf? Privately printed, Paris, 1935; American edition: Bern Porter, California, 1944.

Miller's first "open letter to all and sundry" to raise money for Perlès so that he can go on with his Paris life. Reprinted "not as an appeal for alms but as a good joke." Henry was to make something of a specialty of these open letters—both for his friends and for himself. The first (Paris) edition of this pamphlet is the rarest of all Henry's Paris works.

Aller retour New York. Obelisk Press/Editions du Chêne, Paris, 1935; Scorpion Press, England, 1959.

A very long letter to Alfred Perlès recounting Henry's trip back to New York from Paris in the mid-thirties. Useful in demonstrating what New York meant to Henry, and in contrasting it with the freedom that he found in Paris.

An Open Letter to All and Sundry. Privately printed, Chicago, 1943.

An appeal for support in exchange for watercolors. Portions of this letter were later published in *The New Republic* where they had "a howling success" (in Henry's words), even though the same magazine had just "printed a critical villification of me as a man and artist."

Dear Friends . . .". Privately printed, Big Sur, 1944.

An appeal for money so that Henry can continue his assault on literature. This was also placed in quarterlies. Henry requested $2,500 to enable him to write for a year. He was then at work on *The Air-Conditioned Nightmare* and *The Rosy Crucifixion*.

Murder the Murderer: An Excursus on War from The Air-Conditioned Nightmare. Berkeley/Big Sur; Porter/Miller, 1944

A diatribe against war published in 1944 was guaranteed to bring trouble. And it did. It was in 1944 that Miller was visited by the F.B.I. for having given a supposedly seditious speech at Dartmouth. This pamphlet was not widely distributed for political reasons and "Murder the Murderer" eventually appeared in *Remember to Remember*, 1947.

Semblance of a Devoted Past. Bern Porter, Berkeley, California, 1944.

Letters from Henry to Emil Schnellock, written in Paris and Corfu between 1930 and 1939. Illustrated with Miller watercolors, they are full of insights into the writing of *Tropic of Cancer*. These letters later appear in *Letters to Emil*, edited by George Wickes, New Directions, New York, 1989.

Sunday After the War. New Directions, Norfolk, Virginia, 1944.

A miscellany of earlier work.

The Angel Is My Watermark. Holve-Barrows, Fullerton, California, 1944.

The earliest version in book form of "An Open Letter to All and Sundry," with seven watercolors by Miller. Also contains the essay "The Angel is My Watermark!" a description of the process of making a watercolor, with digressions about writing, Spinoza, Bosch, and Miller's New York family.

The Plight of the Creative Artist in the United States of America. Bern Porter, Maine, 1944.

A collection of open letters including the famous "An Open Letter to All and Sundry." The begging letter raised to an art form. Fund-raisers take note.

Varda, The Master Builder. Circle Editions, Berkeley, California, 1947.

Biographical essay about Jean Varda of Monterey, Henry's artist friend. Later reprinted in *Remember to Remember.*

Echolalia: Reproductions of Water Colors. Bern Porter, Berkeley, California, 1945.

Henry Miller Miscellanea. Bern Porter, Berkeley, California, 1945.

Another anthology of early work.

Obscenity and the Law of Reflection. Alicat Book Shop, Yonkers, New York, 1945.

The use of obscenity to awaken the reader. Henry sees obscenity as a form of revelation.

Why Abstract? With Hilaire Hiler and William Saroyan. New Directions, New York, 1945.*

The Amazing and Invariable Beauford Delaney. Alicat Book Shop, Yonkers, New York, 1945

A biographical essay/story about the African-American artist Beauford Delaney. He was an artist in Africa, long before the white men began raiding that dark continent for slaves. Africa is the home of the artist, the one continent on this planet which is soul-possessed. But in white North America, where even the spirit has become bleached and blanched until it resembles asbestos, a born artist has to produce his credentials, has to prove that he's not a hoax and a fraud, not a leper, not an enemy of society, especially not an enemy of our crazy society in which monuments are erected a hundred years too late. We discover that Henry was a multiculturalist before the term was invented. This essay/story appears also in *Remember to Remember.* It is a paean to blackness, which Henry equates with Buddhahood and enlightenment.

Maurizius Forever. Colt Press, California, 1946.

A review/essay of *The Maurizius Case* by Jacob Wassermann, 1929. The piece begins as a review, but becomes a philosophical essay about war, human civilization, and the possibility of mankind's reaching a new level of consciousness.

Men God Forgot by Albert Cossery. Gotham Book Mart, New York, 1946.

A book review by Henry, which originally appeared in *Circle,* a literary magazine.

Money and How It Gets That Way. Booster Publications, Paris, 1938

Henry's philosophy of money, written in response to Ezra Pound's. Pound wrote Henry after he read *Tropic of Cancer* and asked him to think about the meaning of money.

"The Pointilliste of Big Sur." Raymond & Raymond, California, 1946.

Announcement of Emil White's exhibition of paintings, with short text by Miller.

Of, By & About Henry Miller. Edited by Oscar Baradinsky. Alicat Bookshop, Yonkers, New York, 1947.

Contains the essays "Let Us Be Content With Three Little New-Born Elephants," "The Novels of Albert Cossery, Another Bright Messenger," and "Anderson the Storyteller." Also contains articles on Miller by Herbert Read and others.

"I Defy You." Henry Miller Literary Society, Minneapolis, Minnesota, 1962.

An offprint from *Playboy* magazine in which Henry defies the Boston censors who banned *Tropic of Cancer* in 1962.

Journey to an Antique Land. Ben Ben Press, Big Sur, 1962. Privately printed.*

Just Wild about Harry: A Mel-Melo in Seven Scenes. New Directions, New York, 1963.

Henry's only play, written in two days.

Henry Miller on Writing. Edited by Thomas H. Moore. New Directions, New York, 1964.

A compendium of excerpts from *Tropic of Cancer, Tropic of Capricorn, Black Spring, Sexus, Nexus, Plexus, The Hamlet Letters, The Cosmological Eye, The World of Sexus,* etc., which deal with the writing process and the supreme subject of writing—liberation. A wonderful book, showing the heart of Miller's lifelong struggle to become a writer. Contains his commandments to himself, his daily program (1932–33) as well as his painting and reading agendas. Also contains the charts he made while writing *Plexus*. Fascinating, if you've ever wanted to write.

Face to Face with Henry Miller: Conversations with Georges Belmont. Sidgwick & Jackson, London, England, 1971; published as *Henry Miller in Conversation*, Quadrangle Books, Chicago, 1972.

Interviews by Georges Belmont, originally made for French radio, ranging over such subjects as Henry's life, the writing process, religion, etc.

Four Visions of America. With Kay Boyle, Erica Jong, and Thomas Sanchez. Capra Press, California, 1977.

Originally conceived as a series of essays about America in her bicentennial year. Henry's "A Nation of Lunatics" takes off from a phrase of Whitman's. It is a burning indictment of America in 1976. It shows that even at eighty-five, Henry had lost none of his iconoclastic fire. The present author's essay is a meditation on living on two coasts; Kay Boyle's is about the longing for "Report from Lock-Up," and Thomas Sanchez's is about the liberation of Wounded Knee. A passionate, four-handed critique of America at two hundred.

Gliding into the Everglades, and Other Essays. Lost Pleiade, Lake Oswego, Oregon, 1977.

Six brief essays on Japanese women, Picasso, Cabeza de Vaca, Marie Corelli, and Jack Nicholson, as well as the title piece, which deals with Miller's trip to Florida in 1927–28 with Joe O'Regan and Emil Schnellock.

Love Between the Sexes. Greenwich Books, New York, 1978.

Miller pamphlet in which this stunning line appears: "At the root of all evil . . . is the innate Puritanism of the Americans. Though they boast of sexual freedom, they do not mature as other peoples. . . ."

My Bike & Other Friends. Volume II of *Book of Friends*. Capra Press, California, 1978.

More recollections of Henry's Brooklyn childhood, from the vantage point of his eighties.

Notes on Aaron's Rod *and Other Notes on Lawrence from the Paris Notebooks*. Edited by Seamus Cooney. Black Sparrow Press, California, 1980.

"Lawrence is writing *my* story here," says Henry of *Aaron's Rod*.

O Lake of Light. Capra Press, California, 1981.

Sent as a Christmas card by the Capra Press, this is Miller's only published poem.

Nothing but the Marvelous: The Wisdoms of Henry Miller. Edited by Blair Fielding. Capra Press, California, 1990.

Miscellany of inspiring Miller quotes.

The Paintings: A Centennial Retrospective. Coast Publishing, Carmel, California, 1991.

Catalogue of posthumous watercolor exhibition. The owners of the paintings recall Henry and how and where the watercolors were made. Some of them are of his third wife, Lepska.

LETTERS

The Red Notebook. Jonathan Williams, Highlands, North Carolina, 1958.

A reproduction of one of Henry Miller's notebooks, including random notes and drawings. Shows the play of Miller's mind.

The Story of George Dibbern's Quest. Privately printed, Big Sur, 1958.

A broadside reprint review of *Quest* and an appeal for money to support the aging Dibbern.

Defence of the Freedom to Read. J.W. Cappelens Forlag, Oslo, 1959.

When *Sexus* was banned in Norway and two booksellers were convicted for selling obscenity, Henry wrote two letters to Trygve Hirsh, the defending attorney, explaining how "censorship works like a boomerang," always stimulating rather than discouraging the public from tracking down banned books. Henry declares himself as being opposed to judgment, condemnation, and slaughter. He equates the censor with the murderer, and says that it is the censor who is immoral: "How can one guard against evil, in short, if one does not know what evil is?"

"Reunion in Barcelona; A Letter to Alfred Perlès," from "Aller retour New York." Scorpion Press, England, 1959.

See p. 321.

To Paint Is to Love Again. Cambria Books, CA, 1960.

This material also appears in *Semblance of a Devoted Past.* See p. 322.

Art and Outrage: Lawrence Durrell and Alfred Perlès. Dutton, New York, 1961.

A selection of letters between Miller, Durrell, and Perlès.

Stand Still Like the Hummingbird. New Directions, New York, 1962.

Reprint of earlier pieces, including Miller's essay on Walt Whitman.

Lawrence Durrell and Henry Miller: A Private Correspondence. Edited by George Wickes. Dutton, New York, 1964.

Letters chronicling the friendship of Miller and Durrell, 1935–1959.

Miller, Henry and Nin, Anaïs. *Letters to Anaïs Nin/Henry Miller.* Edited and introduced by Gunther Stuhlmann. Putnam, New York, 1965.

A partial record of the Nin/Miller relationship, published when both were alive. More revelations were to come later.

Collector's Quest: The Correspondence of Henry Miller and J. Rives Childs, 1947–1965. Edited by Richard Clement Wood. University Press of Virginia/Randolf-Macon College, Charlottesville-Ashland, 1968.

Miller, Henry, and Gordon, William A. *Writer & Critic: A Correspondence with Henry Miller.* Louisiana State University Press, Baton Rouge, 1968.

Miller arguing with a critic who is writing a book he hates.

This Is Henry, Henry Miller from Brooklyn. Nash publishing, Los Angeles, 1974.

Dialogues between Henry and Robert Snyder, the filmmaker who created *The Henry Miller Odyssey,* a most revealing and intelligent documentary about Henry. This book is a companion piece to the film, which is available from Master Works Video, 15313 Whitfield Avenue, Pacific Palisades, CA. 90272.

Miller, Henry, and Fowlie, Wallace. *Letters of Henry Miller and Wallace Fowlie, 1943–1972.* Introduction by Wallace Fowlie. Grove Press, New York, 1975.

A fascinating correspondence between Miller and the Yale professor and critic. Sheds light on Miller's life and philosophical preoccupations.

"An Open Letter to Stroker." One Nine Two Seven Press/ Stroker, New York, 1978.

Inspired by the writings and art work of Tommy Trantino, a prisoner in Trenton State Prison, New Jersey, this is a correspondence between Henry and Irving Stettner, a fan who wrote to him late in his life. It later appeared in *From Your Capricorn Friend*. See below.

Henry Miller: Years of Trial and Triumph, 1962–1964: *The correspondence of Henry Miller and Elmer Gertz.* Edited by Elmer Gertz and Felice Flanery Lewis. Southern Illinois University Press, 1978.

Miller's correspondence with one of the attorneys who defended him against charges of obscenity.

The Theatre & Other Pieces. Stroker, New York, 1979.*

Reflections. Edited by Twinka Thiebaud. Borgo Press, California, 1981; Capra Press, California, 1981.

Twinka Thiebaud, who took care of Henry when I knew him, recorded many of Henry's dinner-table pronouncements on women, erotica, feminism, Emma Goldman, spiritualism, death, Nin, Gurdjieff, Mailer, Chaplin, Whitman, etc. If you couldn't be Henry's guest, this is the next best thing.

From Your Capricorn Friend: Henry Miller and the Stroker, *1978–1980*. New Directions, New York, 1984.

An exchange of letters between Irving Stettner (a.k.a. The Stroker) and Henry. Amusing letters from Henry's eighties, with comments on Isaac Bashevis Singer, Warren Beatty, morning erections, and memories of childhood.

Letters from Henry Miller to Hoki Tokuda Miller. Edited by Joyce Howard Miller. Freundlich Books, New York, 1986.

Correspondence between Henry and his last wife.

Miller, Henry, and Nin, Anaïs, *A Literate Passion: Letters of Anaïs Nin and Henry Miller, 1932–1953.* Edited and with an introduction by Gunther Stuhlmann. Harcourt Brace Jovanovich, New York, 1987.

After Anaïs, Henry, and Henry's husband had died, a more complete selection of letters appeared. Essential reading for an understanding of the Miller/Nin relationship.

Dear, Dear Brenda: The Love Letters of Henry Miller to Brenda Venus. Text by Brenda Venus, edited by Gerald Seth Sindell. H. Holt, New York, 1987.

Late in life Henry fell in love with actress Brenda Venus, an affair of the heart that kept him going. The relationship, as usual, took place mostly in Henry's mind—but this was also true when he was young. Reading these letters, one feels that he fell in love with the name "Venus" as much as anything!

"Dear Bernie Wolfe." Privately printed. n.d. (Probably 1948.)

The text of a letter from Miller to Bernard Wolfe concerning *Really the Blues*, a book by Wolfe and Milton Mezzrow.

Miller, Henry, and Schnellock, Emil. *Letters to Emil.* Edited by George Wickes. New Directions, New York, 1989.

Essential letters describing Henry's first years in Paris, when he was abandoning *Crazy Cock* and beginning *Tropic of Cancer.* In these exchanges we hear and see "the raw, living imprint of my Paris life." Shows the transition from the turgid style of *Crazy Cock* to the fearless fuck-every-thingness of *Tropic of Cancer*.

*Fugitive Miller publications.

BACKGROUND READING

Most useful works for understanding Henry's life and times.

Brassaï. *Henry Miller: Grandeur Nature.* Gallimard, Paris, 1975.

————. *The Secret Paris of the Thirties.* Pantheon Books, New York, 1976.

Charney, Maurice. *Sexual Fiction.* Methuen, London and New York, 1981.

de Grazia, Edward. *Girls Lean Back Everywhere.* Random House, New York 1992.

Dearborn, Mary. *The Happiest Man Alive.* Simon and Schuster, New York, 1991.

Dick, Kenneth C. *Henry Miller: Colossus of One.* Alberts-Sittard, 1967.

Dworkin, Andrea. *Woman Hating.* E.P. Dutton & Co., New York, 1974.

————. *Intercourse.* Free Press/Macmillan, New York, 1987.

————. *Letters from a War Zone.* Secker & Warburg, New York, 1987.

————. *Mercy.* Four Walls, Eight Windows, New York, 1991.

————, and MacKinnon, Catharine A. *Pornography and Civil Rights*. Organizing Against Pornography, Minneapolis, Minnesota, 1988.

Ferguson, Robert. *Henry Miller: A Life*. W.W. Norton & Company, New York, 1991.

Girodias, Maurice. *The Frog Prince*. Crown Publishers, New York, 1980.

Goldman, Emma. *Living My Life*. Alfred A. Knopf, New York, 1931.

Gottesman, Ronald, ed. *Critical Essays on Henry Miller*. G.K. Hall & Co., New York, 1992.

Griffin, Susan. *Pornography and Silence*. Harper & Row, New York, 1981.

Hutchinson, E.R. Tropic of Cancer *on Trial*. Grove Press, New York, 1968.

Kluver, Billy and Julie Martin. *Kiki's Paris: Artists and Lovers 1900–1930*. Abrams, New York, 1989.

MacNiven, Ian S., ed. *The Durrell–Miller Letters, 1935–80*. New Directions, New York, 1988.

McAlmon, Robert and Boyle, Kay. *Being Geniuses Together*. North Point Press, Berkeley, California, 1984.

Mailer, Norman. "Henry Miller, Genius and Lust, Narcissism." In *American Review*. No. 24, 1976.

Martin, Jay. *Always Merry and Bright*. Capra Press, Berkeley, California, 1978.

Millett, Kate. *Sexual Politics*. Doubleday & Company, Inc., New York, 1970.

Nabokov, Vladimir. *Lolita*. Vintage Books, New York, 1989.

Nin, Anaïs. *Henry and June*. Harcourt Brace Jovanovich, New York, 1986.

———. *Incest: From "A Journal of Love."* Harcourt Brace Jovanovich, New York, 1992.

Orwell, George. *An Age Like This, 1920–1940*. Vol. 1. Harcourt Brace Jovanovich, New York, 1968.

Paglia, Camille. *Sexual Personae*. Yale University Press, New Haven, Connecticut, 1990.

———. *Sex, Art and American Culture*. Vintage Books, New York, 1991.

Perlès, Alfred. *My Friend Henry Miller*. John Day Company, New York, 1956.

Porter, Bern, ed. *The Happy Rock: A Book About Henry Miller*. Bern Porter, Berkeley, California, 1945.

Stoltenberg, John. *Refusing To Be a Man*. Breitenbush Books, Inc., Portland, Oregon, 1989.

Vidal, Gore. "The Sexus of Henry Miller." *Book Week*, August 1, 1965.

———. "Pen Pals: Henry Miller and Lawrence Durrell." *Times Literary Supplement* (London), Sept. 9–15, 1988.

Wiser, William. *The Crazy Years*. Thames and Hudson, New York, 1985.

Special thanks to Joni Evans, Ed Victor, Ken Burrows, Enid Linn, Valentine Miller, and Tony Miller, without whom this book would not have emerged. Every book is a triumph over silence. You helped.

ABOUT THE AUTHOR

Erica Jong is the author of six novels: *Any Woman's Blues*; *Serenissima*; *Parachutes & Kisses*; *Fanny, Being the True History of the Adventures of Fanny Hackabout-Jones*; *How To Save Your Own Life*; and *Fear of Flying*. She has published seven volumes of poetry, the most recent being *Becoming Light: Poems New and Selected*. Her essays have appeared in, among other places, *The New York Times Book Review*, *The New York Observer*, *Elle*, *Vanity Fair*, *Vogue*, *Ms.*, *The Washington Post*, *The Los Angeles Times*. *The Devil at Large* is her first full-length work of nonfiction. Ms. Jong lives in Manhattan, Connecticut, and Vermont with her husband and daughter.